Praise for *Leap Year*

'It's brilliant stuff'

Steve Wright, BBC Radio 2

'A wonderful and humorous book. I can't remember when I last read a book which made me smile or laugh so often. Highly recommended if you're considering leaping into something new or making a change.'

Meik Wiking, author of *The Little Book of Hygge* and CEO of The Happiness Research Institute

'Makes some pretty big promises – but with practical life lessons, witty first-hand experiences and no-BS advice, it really does what it says on the tin'

Stella

'If a good hoot with a side order of oh-so-subtle self-help is your cup of tea, *Leap Year* should replace *Lean In* in your reading list'

Get the Gloss

What readers are saying about *Leap Year*

'I love this book! Like *Bridget Jones' Diary,* the author's voice running through the narrative is irresistible, and I feel bereft to have finished the book.' ★★★★★

'Highly recommend if you want a whimsical journey of self-devel ╌╌╌╌╌╌╌╌╌╌╌╌ !' ★★★★★

'Absolutely brilliant – funny, insightful, inspiring, and did I mention bloody funny?! Highly recommended, get this book now and, in the words of Michael Jackson, make that change . . .' ★★★★★

'Changing your life, making decisions, and being resilient – a big ask for anyone. But Helen Russell has written a book which you will read and re-read again to assist, entertain and guide you through. Fabulous.' ★★★★★

'*Leap Year* is fantastic. Helen Russell has managed to follow up her hilarious and fascinating account of Danish life (*The Year of Living Danishly*) with a second book that is equally as honest, funny and informative.' ★★★★★

'Very witty and easy to read. Helen's writing style is extremely pleasant, it's like sitting in your kitchen chatting with old friends.' ★★★★★

'My copy of *Leap Year* arrived at my workplace last Wednesday and after receiving it I spent an hour distracted from my computer and giggling my head off.' ★★★★★

'Witty, sharp, and at times laugh out loud funny. This is the perfect combination of research, real life, and storytelling to enable you to make a change in your life and stick to it.' ★★★★★

'I think if you enjoy Elizabeth Gilbert's books you will love this!' ★★★★★

Leap Year

Also by Helen Russell

The Year of Living Danishly

Leap Year

*How small steps can make
a giant difference*

HELEN RUSSELL

www.tworoadsbooks.com

First published in Great Britain in 2016 by Two Roads
An imprint of John Murray Press
An Hachette UK company

First published in paperback in 2017

1

A CIP catalogue record for this title is available from the British Library

Paperback ISBN 978 1 473 63498 5
Ebook ISBN 978 1 473 63499 2
Audio Digital Download ISBN 978 1 473 64650 6

Typeset in Sabon MT by Palimpsest Book Production Limited,
Falkirk, Stirlingshire
Printed and bound by Clays Ltd St Ives plc

Hodder & Stoughton policy is to use papers that are natural,
renewable and recyclable products and made from wood grown in sustainable
forests. The logging and manufacturing processes are expected to conform
to the environmental regulations of the country of origin.

Hodder & Stoughton Ltd
Carmelite House
50 Victoria Embankment
London EC4Y 0DZ

www.hodder.co.uk

For my hectic household and the bride

Contents

Leap Year

PROLOGUE – A VERY GOOD PLACE TO START

When imagining a life-changing moment, it's often set against a sunset on an exotic beach. Or while seeing a baby being born. Or staring into the eye of a tiger. Or a really bad-tempered bear. Something big; awe-inspiring and meaningful. But when it comes down to it, what actually happens is this: it's midnight, it's minus five, and I'm in the street where I live in rural Denmark in my pyjamas. I'm grappling with a wheelie bin lid that has frozen shut, in an attempt to deposit my son's soiled nappy, when I hear a 'ting' that alerts me to a new text message on my phone. My mother is being taken to hospital, one of her friends informs me. She can't call now, but she'll keep me posted. I should '*try not to worry*'.

I should try not to worry.

I should 'try'? Not to 'worry'?

This isn't easy as I'm currently 1,000 kilometres and an ocean away. I search for flights from my corner of Denmark to south-east England, but there's nothing available. Trains and ferries are also ruled out. Another message tells me to sit tight for further updates. So I do.

All night.

By the time the sun starts to flirt with the horizon, sending the world a weird neon pink, I'm exhausted. Morning is broken and so am I.

After what feels like an eternity, my mother gets the all-clear, bar a few check-ups, and normal service can resume. Only it doesn't. Something has shifted, and I can't shift it back. And the one, big, scary thought that keeps circling around my head is: 'You have to move home.'

I suspected this day would come. But in common with the rest of my life to date, I never planned for it.

A few years ago, I agreed to leave London and emigrate when my husband was offered his dream job working for Lego in Denmark. We decided to give it a year and I set myself the challenge of living as Danishly as I could to uncover the secrets of the country that kept getting voted the world's happiest. It worked out well and the year-long experiment slipped into two, with us barely noticing. And then three. But it was never meant to be forever.

I've enjoyed living Danishly. I've learned to have something approximating a work–life balance; I'm healthier; and I'm happier. My husband, AKA Lego Man, is a cross between Bear Grylls and Liberace who has embraced both the Danish design culture and their outdoorsy way of life. He's experienced career fulfilment on a scale he'd never contemplated and built some ludicrously large models of historic landmarks out of plastic bricks. We've also built our very own Viking – a mini flame-haired warrior we affectionately call Little Red, born in 2014 after years of fertility treatment and thanks in part, I'm sure, to a different pace of life in Denmark. I've been working as a Scandinavia correspondent and writing about Nordic living and happiness, which in turn has made me more fulfilled career-wise. We love it here. But our family is in the UK and the idea that my mother, who lives alone, could need help and not have me anywhere nearby has shaken me.

As the only child of a single mum, we've always been close. A team, even. And although neither of us wants to live in each other's pockets, I'd like to be able to reach her in an hour or so, if needed. But right now I can't. She has good friends and a gentleman caller she's been stepping out with for some time, but it's not the same. Lego Man is feeling the distance from his family as well. Our son was wary of his paternal grandparents on their last visit. They only see him every six months due to a spectacularly busy retirement schedule and an aversion to Skype. I'd love my son to have the same close relationship with his grandparents that I had with mine. But that's not going to happen across the North Sea. Everything in Denmark is centred around family life, but there are only so many 'grandparent days' at my son's nursery that I can attend before Ingvild's grandfather starts to think I've developed a crush on him. (I haven't, FYI. It's Otto's I've got my eye on.)

We'd also like a home of our own. We rent at the moment, but because we didn't quite understand the Danish paperwork, we've inherited a landlord who occasionally lets himself into our basement unannounced and claims no responsibility for the perpetually mouldy windows that regularly leak. We have a communal garden, but our mutt of a dog is a nutter and really fond of licking/tail-whipping the neighbours more enthusiastically than I suspect they might like. We still haven't mastered the Danish language (apologies, Vikings), so can't imagine staying for ever. And if it's a case of 'when' rather than 'if', well, then we should probably start thinking about it sooner rather than later.

After my nappy bin epiphany, Lego Man and I talk long and hard about the pros and cons of leaving. Despite the cons list getting longer with each depressing news report from our home country, the one word 'family', in the pros column, makes a big move look like The Right Thing To Do. But, despite this, the decision is far from straightforward.

As well as going 'home', we'd be starting over. Places and people change, so we wouldn't be slotting back into our old life. My husband could carry on working at Lego from their London hub, but I'd need to think about what direction my career should take. I worked in-house on a glossy magazine when I last lived in the UK, only going freelance because I couldn't write for Danish-language publications. My last staffer job was exciting, and occasionally glamorous, but the tempo of city living was relentless and I – along with many of my peers – felt burned out. Moving to Denmark pumped the brakes on my expected career path. I learned to make the best of freelancing but always assumed I'd go back to a big shiny job in the UK. But should I really rejoin that particular race? And would they want me, anyway? There's very little that's glossy about me these days. Now I work from a desk in the corner of the living room, often in clothes that have elasticated waistbands. And with a toddler in tow most of the time, I'm lucky if I leave the house unstained.

We'd need to find a place to live and after years of wholesome rural pursuits in the Danish countryside, Lego Man is adamant that the answer to the question of *where* this should be is 'not in the city any more'. So we might be on course to join the throngs of commuters in suburbia.

Friends have moved on, or moved out of London to their own corners of the country. And we have a child now, so our social life and our priorities have shifted. Drinking until 4 a.m. doesn't hold the same appeal when you're habitually woken at 5 a.m. by an ebullient toddler. Moving back to the UK would be as much of a fresh start as setting sail for Denmark was, and would mean changes in every area of our lives. And I am *terrified* of change. But I realise I'm going to have to get better at coping with it, as well as finding a way to bite the bullet and Decide Things. Because, apparently, assuming the foetal position and hoping 'change' will just go away isn't tenable, long-term. So, as a short-term measure, I opt for my second-favourite coping strategy — eating baked goods and Googling. I kick off with a few vague enquiries, like 'how on earth to make a big decision' and 'can you learn to enjoy change?', then look up to find a whole morning has vanished, along with a packet of Cadbury's Fingers.

Just as there are psychologically accepted phases when experiencing a loss, it turns out that there are seven classic psychological reactions to big changes in our lives. We go from denial to anger, confusion, depression, crisis, acceptance and then finally (hopefully) new confidence. But getting through these phases and out the other side requires some effort — and, in my case, courage. Thankfully, The internet assures me that there are some great things about starting over, too.

Trying new things releases dopamine — the 'happy hormone' — in our brains, and doing something new can even make our lives seem longer. In the same way that the journey home from a new place always feels shorter than the outbound trip, researchers have found that time appears to slow down during new experiences — and accelerate during repetitions.

Turning over a new leaf can also be invigorating. While I

may find the thought of change paralysing, studies show that when *most of us* begin a new relationship – or job, or even a friendship – we are the best version of ourselves. This is because we're motivated, focused and our energy 'bank' is still in credit. There's nothing quite like that sense of the possibilities that lie before us when we're starting out – or starting over. At the beginning of any new life stage, all of us tend to behave well. We make an effort. We pay attention. We try to be thoughtful and we're polite, mostly. We are our best selves. There's a thrill involved in doing something for the first time. Then, as it becomes familiar, this lessens. From the 'hunt' to the 'honeymoon period', we move into habit-forming and then, well, then things can get a bit . . . humdrum.

And so, because I'm a terrible procrastinator and still in the 'denial' stage of change, I take a detour from contemplating the practicalities of leaving Denmark. I start thinking instead about the power of fresh starts and how, actually, there are a lot of areas in my life that might benefit from change, if only I were braver.

Take love, for example.

Having been with my other half for seven years at the time of writing, I've become acutely aware of the 'seven-year itch'. Primarily because people keep reminding me of it. This is the bona fide psychological term to describe the 'decline in relationship satisfaction' that classically occurs after eighty-four months, 364 weeks or 2,555 days of romantic 'bliss'. *Deck the halls* . . . It's often referred to in relation to the 1955 Marilyn Monroe film, but the phrase originated as a descriptor for a variety of irritating and contagious skin complaints. Like scabies.

My husband and I do not have scabies. What we do have is an imperfect, regularly ridiculous, real relationship. We're happy enough, but it's nothing like it was in the early days. Then, he would cook for me, using elaborate recipes, artisanal ingredients and *ramekins*. Now, he occasionally gets out his waffle machine and makes a lot of mess with batter before presenting my son and me with something that looks as though it should be used to pack hi-fi equipment. He'll drizzle liberal quantities of maple syrup over the plate, the table and – often – the dog, then announce with a flourish: 'Ta da! Dinner is served!' During our initial courtship, I would epilate and moisturise every inch of my body like a woman possessed. Since then my lady-grooming standards have slipped rather and my body hair mantra is now: 'More than Barbie, less than Chewbacca = good to go'.

But with the wind of change blowing, I start wondering about whether it's possible to recapture the magic and kick-start a relationship.

Of course, fresh starts aren't all of our own choosing. Not all new beginnings are welcome and one of my oldest friends has just been unceremoniously dumped. A former colleague-turned-comrade has been made redundant, and a third friend is having to find somewhere else to live, fast. Plenty of gin has been consumed to cope with all of these things and it has been unanimously agreed that 'life sucks sometimes'. I've been in each of these scenarios and they aren't pretty. One unseasonably stormy August some years back, I had a break-up that necessitated a complete relocation. I scored the hat-trick of losing my home, job and boyfriend in the space of a month. Careless, I know. I did not cope well and the fallout included a period of incapacitating insomnia, many unsuitable rebound dates, crying during interviews for new jobs (professional), and midnight *M*A*S*H** marathons while basting in my own misery.

Most of us have unwanted change thrust upon us at some point in our lives, with 42 per cent of marriages in the UK ending in divorce and the average person being made redundant three times in a lifetime. Being a grown-up isn't always a hoot. And if a relationship, job, friendship or living arrangement is terminated without our say-so, making a major turnaround work for us takes on a different heft.

But life *is* change, I rationalise. Living is all about uncertainty and venturing into the unknown. As my Danish neighbour likes to almost-quote: 'To try something new causes stress; not to try something new is to give up on yourself'. Denmark's founding father of philosophy Søren Kierkegaard is long gone, so can't set her straight on his original wording, but I find myself agreeing with the sentiment. Everything that stands out as giving my life meaning has involved taking risks, both personally and professionally. There isn't a safe way to make the leap; we just have to jump. And it can feel like a long way down.

I'd like to learn to be more resilient: robust and better placed to deal with the slings and arrows of outrageous adulthood. We've all met people who appear Teflon-coated and remain unfazed in the face of adversity – chameleons who manage change effortlessly while maintaining their dignity and good hair throughout. Like Beyoncé. Or Maverick from *Top Gun*.

I am not one of those people.

Change chameleons inspire a sort of awe and curiosity in

me, because I tend towards the other end of the spectrum, clinging doggedly to the status quo (not the Francis Rossi version) regardless of good sense or circumstances – like a flamingo on a dual carriageway.

Lego Man finds this baffling. He's better at change than I am and after years of living Danishly, I'm now convinced he has Viking DNA, with a wanderlust that would put King Cnut to shame. It's exhausting, but he does offer a much-needed counterbalance.

Discussing a possible move with him one evening and pondering what this would mean for my work, he tells me, breezily: 'You just need a plan.' He says this while loading the dishwasher in a style I can only describe as 'free-form jazz'. I wince as I watch a wine glass get crushed by a pan. 'You know,' he goes on, 'for how you'll reach your goals.'

'What goals?' I frown, opening the fridge to see what might constitute a post-dinner snack.

'What do you mean "what goals"? Goals! For everything! *Life* goals!'

'Er, have you met me?' I pull out some foil-wrapped cheese that could do with 'neatening up': 'I don't set myself *goals*. That way, I can't possibly fail. See?' I offer him a hunk of Cheddar to distract from my failings and lure him away from the dishwasher before more fragile glassware lives are lost. He takes the cheesy bait but shakes his head as though it's a miracle I've made it through life thus far. He's just come back from a management course and I can see by the glint in his eye that I'm in for some 'shared learnings', whether I want them or not.

'You need goals,' he tells me sternly: 'and proper plans!' He stuffs cheese into a cheek and waves a soiled spatula at me to emphasise the point (it's been a waffle-heavy week; the dog is slowly turning into a toffee apple). 'You need to start *happening* to life, otherwise you're just letting life happen to you!'

I'm pretty sure this appears on a motivational mug somewhere and that it's another gem from his work seminar. But it does get me thinking.

When he puts it like that . . .

I have never had a strategy beyond the ingrained work ethic of 'keep busy'. I tick off items on an extensive to-do list each day – but I'm never 'done'. Because to plan and set goals would necessitate choosing. And I'm about as confident at decision-making as a snowflake. I can spend forever trying to decide, considering every option until time is lost and my energy levels are depleted by the sheer effort of it all. My mood declines and my soul shrivels as the world passes me by. I usually end up feeling that I'd have been better off picking an option – any option – right at the start and just going for it, whatever the outcome. I read an article on the BBC about Emotions Anonymous, an AA-inspired organisation where procrastination addicts meet to discuss indecision. I wonder whether I should go to a session but can't make my mind up. So I phone a friend who's great at deciding things and ask her what to do. Once she's finished laughing, she tells me to get in touch with a former colleague of hers ('who can help sort you out!').

Ellen Bard is a psychologist and motivation expert with fifteen years' experience in helping people to get better at making decisions and handling change. She tells me straight away that I'm pretty typical in my fear of change and making decisions – and that the two often go hand in hand.

'As human beings, we're scared of committing to just one future,' she says. 'We think that as soon as we commit, we rule out all the alternatives. As though once we make a decision, that's it. But actually, there are very few decisions you can never go back on.'

I think about this and conclude that, bar parenthood, she's right: *Everything else is reversible, if needed.*

'Once you realise this, it's very freeing. Life isn't a chess game: we don't need to think fifty moves ahead.' I wonder whether I could record Ellen saying this and play it back to myself, several times a day. Or set it to music, Baz Luhrmann style. 'It's normal to be wary of change,' she goes on, 'and fear is a big part of most of us.' Just how much of a part it is apparently depends on our personality and the five factors psychologists use to assess this – known as The Big Five, or the OCEAN test.

I like a test.

This one measures our openness to experiences (the 'O'); conscientiousness ('C'); levels of extroversion as opposed to introversion ('E'); agreeableness and how much we like other people ('A'); and finally, our position on the neuroticism spectrum ('N'). A quick online search brings up the test and I answer a few questions to reveal that, shock horror, I'm 'not at all' open to new experiences. What I am is highly conscientious, extroverted and pretty agreeable, scoring high on 'liking people' and trying to please them wherever possible. But I also rank above average for neuroticism and have a tendency towards anxiety. I'm basically Judy Garland trapped in the talc-scented exterior of a 1950s WI member. It's a heady combination that doesn't sound hugely conducive to a balanced, confident approach to change. So I ask Ellen whether there's any hope for me.

'There are pros and cons to each personality trait – it's just how you are,' she tells me. 'If you're extroverted, you may be great at making friends and speaking in public. If you're not terribly confident, you may be more empathetic. Worriers are often good at putting themselves in other people's shoes. If you're very open to new experiences, you're more likely to take risks and make fast decisions, so you might need to remind yourself to take a little longer to consider the factors.'

I had assumed that there were certain characteristics possessed by the super-confident that meant change came easily (because: Beyoncé). But Ellen tells me: 'Change is something we all have to work at. It's also becoming more and more important for everyone to be able to adapt – because our pace of life is accelerating more quickly than ever. So it's vital to know how to handle it.'

'Right. Yes. And . . . *how is that?*'

'First up? Understand that there is no perfect decision or ideal solution. To any change option. Ever.'

This sounds radical and I want to object: '*Really?*'

'Yes.'

'But what about—'

'No.'

'Or maybe—'

'Nope.'

'Oh.'

'A huge amount of time and energy can be invested in attempting to make the "perfect decision", but no such thing exists,' says Ellen. 'Every possible decision will have pros and cons, and accepting this will speed up your decision-making – and help you relax about choosing an option.'

'Okay. So what *should* we be doing?'

'Well, you need to understand what the critical criteria are. Decide what the deal-breakers are for you and make a decision with these in mind. Then once you've decided, accept that sometimes you'll get it wrong.'

This brings me out in a cold sweat. Having been raised to be a 'good girl' and a terrible people-pleaser, the idea of getting things wrong takes me right back to my schooldays. I don't like being told off and spend much of my time trying to avoid this. I explain my phobia to Ellen and she commiserates: 'It's tough – and the idea that sometimes you *will* make mistakes is hard to swallow. But being comfortable with errors is crucial. You can't waste energy beating yourself up. You need to take action, then move on. It's not easy but it is possible.'

I ponder this. For a week.

I'm encouraged to learn that there are strategies I can use to get better at making decisions and even embracing change. I'm going to need these, whatever happens. But I always seem to find a reason to put off starting something new until a later date.

Making changes doesn't seem like a very Tuesday-ish thing to do, I tell myself. Perhaps I should wait until next week? Monday seems like a much better day to start over. Or I could wait until the first of the month. Maybe, even, the new year. Everyone knows the new year is the best time to make changes. Right?

'Wrong!' chimes Dr Benjamin Gardner, an expert in behaviour change at King's College London, when I call him for confirmation and approval (because: indecision). 'Studies show that there's no point waiting around. If you really want to change, there's no need to wait for January first – you should just do it. And in fact, new year's resolutions tend to fail, because we're pitting our limited willpower stores against our "autopilot" of established behaviours and habits.'

In other words, if I've spent the past thirty-five years eating all the cake in the world, my body's not going to understand why it's only getting kale just because there's a new calendar on the wall.

A recent British YouGov survey found that 63 per cent of us planned to turn over a new leaf along with the new year, with losing weight, getting fit and eating healthily topping our wish lists. But 90 per cent of those polled admitted that they 'always' fail on one of their resolutions and 32 per cent admitted that their resolutions are usually broken by the end of January. That's one-twelfth of the way in. And we've been making and breaking new year's resolutions for millennia. The Babylonians vowed to return objects they'd borrowed and repay debts at the start of each year, while the Romans started January by making pledges to the god Janus (hence 'January' – pub quiz fun fact). *So that's 1,700 years of broken promises . . .*

This shouldn't come as a colossal surprise. My resolutions for this year were: 'drink more water' and 'eat healthily'. What I have actually done is: 'drink more gin' and 'eat pulled pork'.

'New year's resolutions are often unrealistic, too,' says Benjamin. 'If you're not currently doing any exercise and set yourself the goal of going to the gym five times a week, you'll probably feel terrible by the third visit and give up because your body's not used to it.' Sloth one, gym bunny nil. 'Another cause of failed resolutions is that people aren't necessarily ready to change. External pressures have been proven time and again to be less good indicators for success than internal motivation and desires for change.' So setting ourselves a deadline based on the date and other people's expectations is bound to fail. 'We've seen in studies that someone making changes for the sake of their health, for example – an internal factor – is far more likely to lose weight and keep it off long-term than those who are motivated by pressure from, say, friends and family – external factors.'

For behaviour change to occur, Benjamin tells me, we need the capability, opportunity and motivation to make it happen.

'Assuming you're making a resolution for the right reasons, the next question is: "Are you physically and psychologically capable of doing what it takes to succeed in making this change?"' He leaves a pause as though waiting for an answer. I catch sight of my reflection in the window and mouth the word: 'No . . .'

'Because we all have motivation at the start,' Benjamin goes on, 'but studies show that this usually wears off.'

Oh God.

'And then it's just down to willpower?' I'm panicking now. 'What if I haven't got any?' I look at the disgrace of chocolate wrappers and coffee mugs currently adorning my desk like a Tracey Emin exhibit.

'Well, willpower isn't a character trait you're necessarily born with. Studies show that you can train yourself to have more of it, but it also gets depleted if you overuse it – like a muscle.'

So the evidence of light snacking strewn around my desk may not be my fault: it could just be that my willpower has been overused!

Benjamin tells me about a study from Florida State University where a group of volunteers were invited to eat as many biscuits as they fancied from a spread laid out for them. So far, so science-lovely. A second group were told to resist the biscuits and eat radishes instead. Both groups were then given a tricky geometry puzzle to solve and observed to see how long they stuck at it. Those who'd had their fill of baked goods spent far longer on the puzzle than those who had just eaten radishes. Scientists took this to prove that a) radishes are NOT brainfood[1] and b) willpower is a resource that can be 'used up'[2]. Further experiments found that we find it harder to exert self-control after making difficult decisions and when we have low blood sugar. Which explains a great deal about my life to date.

'So what can we do about this?'

'Well, when we exhaust our willpower, we need to let it rest, again, just like a muscle,' he says. 'A good tip is to just engage your willpower when you really need it. So if you want to eat more healthily but always have a sugar-crash at 2 p.m. and crave biscuits, be aware that at 2 p.m. you need to make a plan to do something to avoid temptation. To change ourselves permanently, we need to focus our self-control on precise behavioural targets and overwhelm them.

---

1 This is purely conjecture on my part.

2 This is science-fact.

Then we need to replace the unwanted behaviours with good behaviours and make them habits.'

'Fewer Crunchie Bars, more CrossFit?'

'Something like that.'

'Right.'

'Monitoring your behaviour is a good place to start,' says Benjamin, 'as it helps us to be aware of our habits and what triggers them. So, just for instance, I know that I have a really sweet tooth and if there are biscuits in the house I will eat them. All.' This is the third time he's mentioned biscuits. I believe him. 'By self-monitoring my behaviour, I've learned that I can't just eat one or two and keep a half open packet in the house. So now, I don't buy biscuits. Ever. I avoid the temptation — and so the depletion of my will-power reserves. Knowing yourself is key, then working out what you really want to change. Then, you just need to find the best way to do it depending on the change you want to make.'

I thank him and hang up, with the beginnings of a cunning plan.

And then I get the second Bat-Signal from the mother country in as many weeks.

A family friend I have adored since I was three is dying. I write and tell him how much he's always meant to me and try to make him laugh, because, what else is there? And he writes back and says 'thanks' but that he's pissed off. Understandably. He's angry that he hasn't done more 'living' and that he's spent time being held back by worry. He tells me that if I want to change anything, I should do it now and that being afraid isn't a good enough reason not to. And suddenly biscuits don't seem so important any more. But finding a way to stop fear from holding us back does. So I promise that I'll try.

In common with most non-experts, I don't know the best ways to make changes. But I'd like to. I know that I'm deferring the big decision at hand – whether to leave Denmark or not. *Though perhaps,* I think, *if I could change-proof all the other areas of my life, I'd become such a self-assured, resolute, She-Ra Princess of Power[3] type that the decision might just . . . make itself?*

So I spend some time with my head buried in books that throw up a wealth of conflicting advice about change and how to implement it. *And this is just scratching the surface . . . What if there are distinct theories of change and optimum ways to 'start over' in every area of modern living?*

I wouldn't use a kettle to cook steak, or a wrench to unscrew a jam jar, or a power washer to deal with dirty dishes (though my husband probably would). Just as most tools have a specified use, there must be change theories that are better suited to specific realms of life, from the worlds of science, psychology, academia – even business.

Lego Man regularly goes on residential 'change management' retreats and does strange things with balance beams, whiteboards and beanbags. He comes home, drunk on jargon, saying things like: 'I'm going to be stepping out of the engine room and on to the bridge for a while' or 'I'm going to give you more opportunities to fail and that's okay.'

---

3 As anyone who grew up near the 1980s knows, She-Ra is where it's at. Put your 'Power Sword' away, He-Man, no one's interested . . .

I'll normally respond with an eye roll as our toddler looks bemused and the dog rolls over, displaying his undercarriage in the hope of a tummy rub. Last week he returned from a three-day '*Celebration of Change!*' conference (the exclamation mark was apparently mandatory) and held forth on the 'manifold merits of adaptability'. I tried to nip it in the bud and move the conversation on to more domestic realms, but he just held up a hand and told me:

'Change can be challenging and it's clear you're in the denial stage right now.'

I told him he'd be in the 'spare room' stage shortly and the dog gave me a look as if to say: '*This is the guy you've scrambled your DNA with?*'

After a few hours, Lego Man will usually decompress and revert to an approximation of normal. But the next day our kitchen table will again be the recipient of all manner of shoutily titled business manuals brought home from work. Each promises to make him the next Bill Gates overnight, and yet every morning he wakes up as himself – and we accumulate more books. Occasionally, while conveying these from the kitchen table to the bookcase (destined for the top shelf, above Nigella, Jamie and all the other books featuring recipes with more than ten ingredients), I have a flick through.

In the business world, I glean, there are various 'change processes'. Many of them, to be frank, seem a little wanky (technical term). *But could they work? And would big businesses bother investing in them if they didn't?*

I decide to find out which WMTs (wanky management techniques) can help in the 'real world', as well as gathering together the less-wanky tweaks and adjustments proven by science – and, hopefully, me – to make everyday life better. For all of us.

In a moment of madness and uncharacteristic bravado, I tell Lego Man my plan, announcing that I'm going to set my first ever 'life goal' to get to grips with this change business and attempt to . . . er . . . 'master it'.

'What if,' I say, 'I could take psychologically endorsed theories of change and WMTs, and, you know, *science* and stuff, and put it all to the test? In every area of life, from work to money, family, relationships – even fitness!'

I won't lie: I've had a glass of wine.

'I could look at the evidence, speak to experts and then road-test their recommendations – on *me*!'

'Like a guinea pig?'

'*Yes*, like a guinea pig! And for anything I can't try out myself, I'll rope in—' I stop myself: 'I mean, "*invite*" friends to trial the theories! I could have a whole army of change guinea pigs! And we can all become lean, mean, decision-making machines! Bye-bye flamingos on dual carriageways, hello change chameleons! I'll have a whole menagerie of change animals! This could be my year of making leaps into the unknown!'

'The Great Leap Forward?'

'Yes! Oh no, wait . . . no. Less Chairman Mao, more Beyoncé – and then we'll know exactly what to do with our lives next! And we'll just . . . you know, do it!'

I'm on fire now. Or drunk. You decide. Either way, after years of not making goals, you can't say I'm not trying. I've often thought that enthusiasm is half the battle won, but my husband is less sure.

'Cool,' is his effusive response to my momentous declaration.

He slopes off to read an interior design magazine while whittling a rudimentary survival tool out of wood.

Unperturbed, I stand tall, make my way to the 'stationery cupboard' (a cupboard where we keep some stationery as well as the Hoover) and remove the film from a brand new notebook. I run the heel of my hand down its stiff centre until two blank pages of lined cream paper are fully exposed. Then I get a pen and write today's date. And this feels like a very good place to start.

Take the Quiz:
How Do You Handle Change?

1. Change makes me feel:
  A: Brilliant! Doesn't it for everyone?
  B: Okay . . . but can I have a stiff drink now please?
  C: Exhausted. I'm off for a lie-down.
  D: *'Change'*? What is this *'change'* you speak of?

2. When I think about something I wish were different in my life, I:
  A: Change it. Immediately. If I haven't already. (Yesterday. Before breakfast.)
  B: Form a plan and work out what I need to do to make it happen.
  C: Think about doing something. One day. Maybe. If only I knew what . . .
  D: Tell myself things aren't so bad really, just the way they are.

3. In order for me to make a major life change:
  A: It needs to be a day with a 'y' in it.
  B: There should be more ticks in the 'pros' column than in the 'cons'.
  C: Bribery/blackmail/no viable alternatives are required.
  D: Nope. Uh-uh. Not going to happen. Not on my watch . . .

4. When I decide to change something, the first thing I do is:

A: Get my 'busy' on.

B: Find books, websites and connections to help.

C: Feel overwhelmed but make lists (so many lists . . .) of what I need to do.

D: Hear the failure klaxon going off in my head and think better of it.

5. Thinking about changes I've already been through, I:

A: High-five myself then do twelve burpees. Just because.

B: Feel proud of what I've achieved and grateful to those around me for their support.

C: Recognise how tough these were at the time. Thank God *that's* over . . .

D: Feel physically sick. *retches*.

6. My friends would say that I:

A: Can't keep still and am always looking for the next challenge. Like a Jack Russell interbred with the Duracell Bunny. On Red Bull.

B: Am good at pushing myself out of my comfort zone.

C: Really like watching *The Way We Were* while crocheting 'There's No Place Like Home' on a pair of ruby slippers.

D: Avoid change At. All. Costs.

Mostly As: Embracer

You are Beyoncé/Maverick from *Top Gun*/Lego Man. You don't just handle change, you actively seek it out, hounding it down and bothering it into submission. You were a Viking in a past life and your passport is always on hand, ready for the next adventure. You probably only need this book to help you understand the rest of the population – but welcome! Come on in, the water's lovely (if, occasionally, murky).

Mostly Bs: Adaptor
You're familiar with change and accept the shifts life deals you whenever necessary. You're good at adapting and asking for help when you need it but don't tend to have an over-arching strategy for life's grand journey.

Mostly Cs: Resister
It's not that you're anti-change, you just wouldn't choose it and would much prefer to have a nice sit-down with a cup of tea and a biscuit. And isn't it raining outside? Oh well then, best not start anything new today . . .

Mostly Ds: Denier (a word that looks so much like I'm talking about tights, I have to check several times. I am not talking about tights, just to clarify.)
Although it seems as though putting your fingers in your ears and singing 'la la la la la' will make change go away, what's actually happening is that you're experiencing some-thing called denia— *'LA LA LA LA LA LA LAAAAAA!'*

It's tough out there. I hear you. But we're going to be all right. I promise.

CHAPTER ONE

CAREER

Working It Like A Super Hero(ine)

In which I learn how interrelationship diagrams help overhaul a career; why having an office crush can make a 'meh' job meaningful; that power posing and samba could be the key to success; and how Imposter Syndrome can be turned into an advantage

When deciding where to begin with my Grand Plan, I make a list of things I think I need to do differently in order to become the kind of resilient 'change chameleon' who can decide big important things, like where to live and what on earth to do with the rest of my life. I like a list because a) I get to use stationery, with which I have an unhealthy obsession and b) the thoughts shimmying around my head make a lot more sense on paper. Only I still can't make my mind up. *Quelle surprise.*

So I leave the list lying around for a few days, hoping for inspiration, until Lego Man swipes my notebook from the kitchen table over breakfast and tells me to 'just eat the frog!'

I have no idea what he's talking about ('Wha . . .?' I point at my bowl: 'This is porridge . . .?'), so he explains that in business-land, this refers to tackling your biggest fear first.

'No one wants to eat a frog, right?' he says, swigging orange juice.

'What about the French?'

'Apart from the French,' he concedes: 'so it means you have to work out what your "frog" is – the thing you're most concerned about – and start with that.'

Huh, I think, realising he's given me the answer already: work is my frog. Without it I'm hopeless. And poor. And it's the area I'm most concerned about if we move back to the UK. Or if we don't. So if I want to make any monumental, grown-up life decisions, 'work' is where I have to begin.

Candles flicker on the windowsill as I fire up my laptop and drink tea, resting woollen-socked feet on a snoring dog to start my day. It's not a bad way to pass the nine-to-five (or, in Denmark, eight-to-four). But writing from home as a freelancer only came about for me out of necessity. I left my editor's job in London to wing it in the wilds of rural Denmark without a single word of Danish in my repertoire, so I had no option but to go solo. Miraculously, it's worked out pretty well. I like the quiet potential for contemplation and concentration that working with only a dog for company can offer. It's been a relief to find out that I'm just about disciplined enough to resist the magnetic pull of the sofa and can work, unsupervised, for seven and a half hours straight. The opening hours at my son's nursery mean that overtime is nigh on impossible, and I try not to work weekends or evenings as a rule. Fist-bumps all around, and a big thumbs-up to the Danish work–life balance. But if we move back to the UK, I could work in-house again. I still miss the chat and bustle of office life, plus I'd earn more and have a better chance of career progression in a staffer job (something only marked at present by a move to 'the good biscuits').

A lot has changed since I was last in an office. For one thing, I've had a child, and I'm still unsure how to navigate parenthood alongside freelance work, let alone the demands of the nine-to-five and, in all likelihood, a commute. Most jobs in my field are based in the capital and with Lego Man working in London most of the time, we'd need to be close by. Plenty of friends commute fifty weeks of the year without complaining. But I suspect they're made of tougher stuff than I am.

I've also just spent three years learning how to be happier by recalibrating my work–life balance, enabling me to be productive, solvent *and* sane (the holy trinity). So should I risk chucking it all away to spend hours a day on a train? Or shelling out all I earn to put my son into nursery for sixty hours a week? Working part-time in London might be an option, but these pots of gold only appear at the end of the rarest of rainbows. I know some committed freelancers who wouldn't have it any other way, but they've always struck me as being far braver than I could ever hope to be and in possession of balls/ovaries of steel. So what should the next phase of my career look like? I need professional guidance and some seriously good change theories to help me make the best of what I've got.

Newly Unemployed Friend is dealing with a similar dilemma. He made a Faustian pact to relinquish such fripperies as sleep and a social life in favour of his career a decade ago and is now understandably outraged that the devil hasn't kept up his end of the bargain.

'It's fine!' he repeats to anyone who asks and many who

don't, several times a day, as he tries to work out what to do next, oscillating between flurries of industry where he applies for new roles and mourning for his old life and fancy lunches.

'But you hated your boss,' I remind him when he calls during a break from a busy day of TV-watching and wallowing: 'He called you a "see you next Tuesday" and you had to steal stationery to "get even".'

'True,' I hear him exhaling heavily down the end of the receiver, 'but at least I knew what to do of a Monday morning.' It's currently Wednesday but since being made redundant, he hasn't paid too much attention to the days of the week. It wasn't always this way. He used to take those little round stickers that the stationery cupboard was apparently awash with and put a red one on the calendar every time he had a truly dreadful day. He'd use a yellow sticker for every 'generically soul-crushing day' and a green one for an 'okay' day. By the end of last year, the wall of his office resembled an explosion from a Lichtenstein painting.

I try to say helpful, motivating things like, 'Did you know, the average Brit gets made redundant three times over the course of their career? Really, you're behind schedule . . .' and 'A typical employee moves jobs once every six years, so all of us have between ten and eleven jobs in a lifetime . . .' but my library of facts doesn't seem to do much to salve the pain. So I tell him that he'll definitely find something else soon and that, actually, starting a new job can be a good thing.

'I read recently that people have been proven to put in extra effort, dress the part and even smile more in a new job?' I take his silence as an encouraging, 'How fascinating! I did not know that! Please tell me more!' and press on:

'Smiling makes us happier, even if it's fake, and we're twelve per cent more productive when we're in a positive frame of mind, according to a study from the University of Warwick.' My lucky friends often get the 'benefit' of my three years' worth of happiness research.

'A new job,' I go on, 'means we're more productive, we feel more positive and generally *nail it*.' No studies have been carried out into the specific science of 'nailing it' but I feel sure there must be some in the pipeline. 'So actually, taking a leap in your work life is pretty much the best thing ever!' I've practically convinced myself, but Newly Unemployed Friend isn't buying it. In fact, he's opting for a more nihilistic approach.

'What's the point of any of it?' he says and I hear the sound of crisp-crunching. 'I'll start a new job,' he goes on through a mouthful of McCoy's crinkle-cut, 'and then that'll get rubbish as well, or I'll get fired, or want to quit, or die or something.' Like I say, it's quite the positivity challenge. He references a mutual friend of ours as an example of someone who is gainfully employed but finding it all a bit 'meh'.

'*Worst. Restructure. Ever. Fourth one in four years. Wish someone would start flipping tables to make it more interesting . . .*' is her latest Facebook status update and I suspect that she's currently in the 'humdrum' phase of her current job. She's thirty-three years old, overqualified and underpaid. She doesn't want to leave, but is feeling stuck. And she isn't unique. A recent Gallup survey showed that 63 per cent of the global workforce feel disengaged and a study published in the *Journal of Occupational Psychology* found that people in their thirties were most likely to experience a dip in workplace happiness. This is because when we're first starting out we're bright-eyed, bushy-tailed – and naive. By the time we hit our thirties, we realise that things aren't quite as we imagined. We've come so far down one career path that it can feel too late to change course. A kind of: *I'd better be good at this because I'm never going to be a doctor/lawyer/vet/the Queen now,* type thing. We're also aware that we've still got almost four decades of work ahead of us – and the prospect is making many of us feel drained.

It's not easy for workers in any other decade, either. Twenty-somethings have to contend with a lack of jobs and the struggle to find an occupation they actually like, while those in their forties and fifties may have caring responsibilities and increased financial obligations. For workers aged sixty plus, there's retirement to think about and the loss of daily 'purpose' as well as a pension pot to eke out. Really, it's astonishing that more of us aren't having a career crisis in every decade of our lives.

My wannabe table-flipper friend blames her new boss in part for her ennui and a *Harvard Business Review* study recently confirmed that having a 'bad boss' is the number one reason people are unhappy at work. Table Flipper needs to vent, so I suggest an outing next time I'm in London, in the hope it might cheer her up. Newly Unemployed Friend even manages to put on a clean fleece and shoes when we meet in a bar to get the low-down on Idiot Boss (his official title).

'I just can't respect someone who pronounces "seismic shift" as "size Mc-shift",' says Table Flipper, 'like it's a McDonald's meal deal or something.' She shakes her head and sucks on the straw in her second vodka tonic until her cheeks hollow. 'And the guy's, like, *twelve*. He still has name tapes sewn into his jumpers!' I laugh and even Newly Unemployed Friend manages a smile. But Table Flipper remains straight-faced: 'I'm serious: all of them, V-necks, stitched in. I know his middle name.'

'Oh'.

'He's so full of it we've taken to playing "Bullshit Bingo" in meetings.'

'Is that a thing now?' asks Newly Unemployed Friend, concerned he might have missed some new business jargon in his five weeks out of the workplace.

'I don't think Bullshit Bingo is a thing—' I start to clarify, but Table Flipper cuts me off.

'Yesterday he told me he was "stuck between a rock and a hard rock".'

'Wow, that's a pretty tough place to be—'

'Yeah,' she's on a roll now, 'then today he described the competition as "like a wolf in shark's clothing".'

'What?' Newly Unemployed Friend sounds perplexed: 'That's a terrible disguise!'

'And you definitely don't want to leave?' I ask.

'I mean, a shark is just as scary as a wolf! If not more so.' Newly Unemployed Friend isn't letting this one go.

'I don't see why I should be the one who leaves,' Table Flipper goes on, drawing air through the straw until the ice in her glass rattles.

'I think that one's empty—' but Table Flipper isn't listening.

'It's a good position,' she says. 'There's nothing wrong with it—'

'Apart from Idiot Boss?'

'—Apart from Idiot Boss. And I'm all right at what I do.

31

I like the job. At the old cubicle farm,' she adds fondly. 'I just need to feel . . . motivated again.'

Interesting, I think, wondering whether I can rope Table Flipper in to my research.

'You could pretend you're in South Korea,' Newly Unemployed Friend pipes up, having finally moved on from the shark-wolf.

'*Sorry?*'

'South Korea,' he repeats. 'It has one of the highest suicide rates from unhappiness at work on the planet.' Since being made redundant, Newly Unemployed Friend has become spectacularly well-read. The employed scarcely have time to scratch the surface of world events and I frequently feel inadequate in comparison to the out-of-work. 'To help people appreciate their jobs more, some companies in South Korea are encouraging employees to act out their own funerals. They watch videos of people worse off than them, to get in the mood – like the terminally ill or victims of war – then they get into a casket for a while to contemplate their career and feel grateful for what they've got. Got me to thinking: I may be unemployed but at least I'm not in a coffin in South Korea.' Neither of us knows quite what to say to this. 'If you don't fancy faking your own death,' Newly Unemployed Friend offers, in a tone that seems to imply '*though I don't see why you wouldn't*', 'they also recommend office-wide stretching sessions followed by outbursts of forced laughter. I saw it on YouTube.'

'Right. Thanks. One to try tomorrow . . .'

'No worries.' Newly Unemployed Friend nods, oblivious to the sarcasm in her voice: 'Who's for another drink?'

Those of us who have work in the morning politely decline

and we leave soon after. On the way home, I mention my plan and ask if they're up for trying out a few change theories.

'As long as I don't have to get into a coffin, I'm in,' says Table Flipper.

'I promise there won't be coffins involved.'

Newly Unemployed Friend narrows his eyes as if to say: '*it's your loss . . .*' before agreeing: 'Sure, why not?'

We are on. I have three guinea pigs: me, a freelancing mother trying to work out how best to juggle creative fulfilment, paying the bills and time with her son; Table Flipper, keen to rekindle the flame in her current job; and Newly Unemployed Friend, wondering what direction his career should take next.

Nine hours, three coffees, two Beroccas and one cross-North-Sea flight later, I'm back at my desk collecting ideas for reigniting the career spark, like a workaholic squirrel hoarding nuts for winter. I want to think about Table Flipper's occupational malaise first, since this is probably something we've all had to contend with at some stage. So how can we make a 'meh' job zing again? Studies show that keeping active and prioritising leisure is imperative, since this makes us happier, healthier and even more productive. Every '*Top squillion things non-mental successful types do before breakfast*' inventory I've ever seen includes some way to balance work with home life – and put an end to the glorification of 'busy'. Presenteeism is pretty much the devil's work, it turns out, and there's no need to work for work's sake. In fact, it's bad for us. Working for more than eight hours a day has been shown to increase stress, heighten the risk of heart disease and generally wreak havoc on personal relationships. By contrast, Danes are world leaders at this work–life balance thing with an average working week of thirty-three hours, according to the latest OECD data[4]. They still manage to be the second most productive country in the EU and have one of the happiest workforces in the world.

So I start my search for practical happier-at-work suggestions close to home.

Copenhagen-based work–life balance expert Martin Bjergegaard lectures internationally and advises everyone to 'pretend' they have children, by which he means giving leisure activities the same attention that a family demands and getting out of the office on time. He suggests creating artificial deadlines, seeking out projects with short-term goals and learning new skills to keep things interesting.

A high-flying, happily married mother of three who's been in her job for seventeen years has a different approach and brings a bit of 'leisure' into the working environment, telling me that her secret is fostering workplace crushes to 'keep energy levels up'.

'It means you always want to go to work in the morning and you make an effort to look good and perform well – I even bought my husband my latest crush's aftershave so he'd smell like him,' she tells me matter-of-factly.

A study published in the *Journal of Sex and Marital Therapy* in 2015 found that a work crush can be beneficial for relationships, too, increasing sexual desire and attraction to our actual, real-life partner.

---

4 The official working week is thirty-seven hours but Danes are so good at work–life balance that they're apparently all knocking off early . . .

'There are a lot of parallels between jobs and relationships – and starting a new one of either gets the adrenaline flowing in our bodies,' explains business psychologist Dr Ilona Jerabek when I call her up to find out more about rekindling things at work: 'Our days are packed with possibilities and we're discovering new things all the time. Then the dust settles and disillusionment comes in. Because no job – or relationship – is perfect. At around three to six months, the honeymoon period ends and routine normally settles in.'

And what then?

'Well, then there are things you can do to make it better – like having a buddy who you can talk to and confide in. This can really help.' Workmates make the days go faster and the bad times bearable. But a tough economic climate, the growing demands placed on staff and increasingly heavy workloads mean that many of us now feel that we're 'too busy' to forge office alliances. The proportion of people who say they have a good friend at work has dropped in recent years, according to a study from Relate – and more of us than ever are depriving ourselves of an office-confidant morale boost. How to remedy this? In the words (almost . . .) of the endlessly erudite Justin Timberlake: we need to bring water-cooler chat back.

'Gratitude is also helpful,' says Ilona. 'There may well be issues you have with your current job but chances are there are positive things about it as well. Most people have something they can be grateful for about their work – and being conscious of this is good for us.' Researchers from the University of South Florida and the University of Florida have found that people who wrote down a brief, end-ofworkday positive reflection – on anything from what they had for lunch to the fact that it was nearly the weekend – experienced decreased stress and improved mental and physical health. So I'll be asking Table Flipper to keep a gratitude journal, too.

'Reframing is useful,' adds Ilona, 'because no matter what our situation, we're working for a reason: our work has meaning. Most of us are working to contribute to our well-being and security, or that of others. It may not be fun every day, but there's still a useful purpose in it.' If we're losing sight of this, it's time to think about what motivates us. 'Studies show that the majority of people aren't primarily motivated by money any more,' says Ilona. 'It's recognition, praise, being helpful and working with a good team that drive the majority. So if we seek out employment that fits with our values, we're more likely to be happy at work. To be fulfilled in our careers, we need to identify what we want. We have to *know* ourselves.'

I'm intrigued by this and realise that I've never really sat down and thought about my values, let alone structured a career to ensure I'm adhering to them. I've always taken a rather 'suck it and see' approach, taking opportunities as and when they arise. If someone asks me to do something, I usually say 'yes'. Just because they've asked. Which, now I stop to reflect on it, seems a little like the career equivalent of one of my mother's old favourites: 'If someone told you to jump off a cliff, would you?'

'*Er, sure. When's the deadline?*'

So now, I thank Ilona for her help, hang up and decide to take on my first work-change task: a values inventory. I sit with a sheet of A4 and write the word '*Values*' at the top, underlining it. Twice. Then I stare at the blank page for a long time, pen poised an inch from the paper, until lunchtime comes around. I know this because I start to get hungry and find myself writing 'cake', then crossing it out rapidly before the dog sees and judges me.

'*"Cake" is not a value!*' his canine trufflings seem to imply. '*Can we go throw sticks in the garden now? How about now?*'

I cave and throw sticks. Then I eat cake. Then, realising I'm getting nowhere, I make an appointment to have lunch with a Jedi Master of occupational change and value-based decision-making the very next day.

Stephen Powell and I have been friends for years and I'm only just beginning to understand what his job title of 'Continuous Improvement Business Partner' actually means. Turns out he has fifteen years' worth of experience as a professional guide to the mindset and tools we should all be using to navigate the shifting world and challenges of work. I demand to know why he's never mentioned any of this to me before now, to which he replies: 'You didn't ask! And the first thing you need to know about change at work is that individuals have to want to change.'

This is lesson one. I open my notebook and write this in block capitals. Then I tell him about where I am right now in my career, how I'm not entirely sure where I need to be next, or what to do to get there. He jots down some notes, then taps his pen against the page a few times before prescribing me an 'interrelationship diagram'.

'An inter-what?' I ask, suspicious.

'Interrelationship diagram. It's a commonly used tool in the corporate world and actually makes a lot of sense for "real life" as well – I use them for everything from finances to family life.'

'Okay . . . so what does it do?'

'"It" doesn't do anything, you do the graft yourself . . .'

'Yes, of course. Sorry.'

If I'm honest, I'm still hoping for some kind of career Magic-Eight ball to instruct me through life. '*Would free-lancing work for me back in the UK?*' **vigorous shake** '*Most likely!*' But this isn't to be, it seems.

'So what does the inter-diagra-whatsit *encourage* me to do?'

'Well, it's useful to help you identify what's important to you. So your values, and what your goals should be based on these, as well as how and where you need to take action to reach the goals you set yourself.' I unfurl an A3 sheet of paper (this warrants the stationery big guns) and he guides me through the process: 'So first off, you write a statement defining an issue that you want to explore – so what it is you want.' In my case this is '*A fulfilling career that enables me to have a decent work–life balance*'.

'Now, place this in a box at the top of the paper,' says Stephen, so I do as I'm told. It looks official already. And far more professional than my '*cake*' version.

Look at me! I want to call out to passers-by, *I am career strategising!* Then I spill coleslaw on my diagram and have to wipe it off with a paper towel.

'Sorry,' I mumble. 'I'll concentrate now.'

'Good. Now you brainstorm – writing down all the ideas or suggestions required to make that statement come true.'

I make a start, writing down things like '*interesting assign-ments*', '*opportunities for career progression*', '*continued*

learning', 'time and space to write more books', 'financial
security', 'flexible hours', 'camaraderie with colleagues-other-
than-the-dog', etc.

'Next, you're going to connect the issues. Choose any item
to start with and compare it to any other. Decide if the two
are strongly related. If they are, identify which is a driver
and which is an effect – so which one is more likely to drive
the other. Then, draw an arrow pointing from "driver" to
"effect" to show the relationship.'

'Like "interesting assignments" might drive "career progression", and "financial security" could drive "time and space
to write more books"?'

'Exactly, if that's how these things make sense for you.'
I'm already scribbling as he speaks. 'But none of them can
be double-ended arrows.'

'Oh . . .' I get the Tippex out.

When I've finished, the page looks like a spider diagram
on acid.

'Now, we analyse!' His eyes light up as he says this. *If
everyone liked their job as much as Stephen Powell, we'd all
be in a good place*, I think. (FYI, Stephen Powell is one of
those friends whose names just don't work in abbreviated form.
Even his seven-year-old daughter calls him 'Stephen Powell',
so Stephen Powell he shall remain). 'Any issue with a lot of
outgoing arrows is a key driver, and any with more arrows
pointing towards it is a major effect. For each issue, count the
out-arrows and in-arrows. You want to find the ones with
the highest number of outgoing arrows and the ones with the
highest number of incoming arrows to plot them on a chart.'

Good grief, this is a paper-heavy process, I think, pulling
out another sheet.

'On the vertical axis, you're going to plot the "drivers", so all your issues with arrows going out. On the horizontal axis, you're going to plot the "effects", so the arrows coming in. You plot each one according to the "outs" and "ins". So a statement that has four out-arrows and two in-arrows would be plotted at four up the vertical axis and two along the horizontal one.'

I do this and squint at it for a while.

'Now, you see the clusters to the top left? These are the "drivers" that are your priorities for action. And they'll make the things further to the right – the outcomes – easier to achieve.'

'So, on mine,' I try to get this straight, 'if I pursue *"time and space to write more books"*, *"continued learning"* and *"networking"*, I shouldn't have to worry about *"creating work I'm proud of"* or *"career progression"*? Because these should come as a result?'

'That's the theory. It also filters out things that aren't really big priorities for you – so you *say* you want more than just the dog for company while you work . . .'

Stephen Powell is a huge fan of the dog and so says this with some incredulity, as though he's not sure how anyone could be less than completely content with such an office-mate. '. . . but actually, this is an outlier. It doesn't bother you as much as pursuing *"interesting assignments"* or the alternative of commuting five days a week while you still have a toddler at home.'

Damn, I think, *he's good.*

'Career progression for you right now might not be moving up the ladder in a corporation, it might be about taking on more varied projects. Could you set yourself goals around this? Like "four new clients each year" or pushing yourself to network more?'

'I . . . could. Yes!'

This is an approach that runs counter to my working life to date. I was a journalist. Then I got good/older at journalist-ing and so obviously I was made to stop it and become a manager of other journalists instead[5]. All of this, against my careers-slash-maths-teacher Mrs Perkins' advice, based on a twenty-page questionnaire at the end of Year 10, that I should be 'transport minister'. But the interrelationship diagram indicates that, hallelujah; I'm on the right track with freelancing for now. I write articles and books and a few times a month I get to emerge, bleary-eyed, from the house and interact with the outside world, giving talks and speaking at events. I get to play to my biggest strengths – talking, listening, researching and writing. There are some things I miss – like office chat and a treats table and IT support, especially last night when my laptop froze for no reason and displayed the spinning wheel of doom for half an hour, pre-deadline. But despite the fear and uncertainty of it all, I like having a portfolio career. Stability isn't as important to me as I had thought it was. I care about doing work I enjoy more than I care about the money. And I can live without a whizzy job title at this moment, as long as I'm doing something I love that also enables me to spend time with my son.

I think about all the years when I was driven by things that weren't really me – like money; prestige; the approval of family members – and feel relieved that I'm free of these now. All I needed to do was to ask myself better questions

---

5 The mad way media – along with many professions – operates.

about what really mattered and to have the courage to act on the answers. *So my career will take a curvier path, so what?* I think, resolving to stop mourning the old-fashioned hierarchy and embrace the brave new world of work.

I thank Stephen Powell profusely, clean up the remaining coleslaw I have flung about in my excitement, and promise him a date with the dog soon. Then I relay all I've learned to my work-change guinea pigs and set them the challenge of creating their own interrelationship diagram.

By the following morning, Newly Unemployed Friend has done his, in full-colour A3. And laminated it. The exercise has reminded him how he's always wanted to work with food (and not in the same way as I like to work, *with* food) and so he's thinking about using some of his redundancy pay to set up a stall at the local farmers' market, importing and selling artisan cheese.

'I really like cheese. And I'm good with numbers—' is his pragmatic approach.

'I should hope so, you're an accountant . . .'

'—so what's not to love?'

He tells me he has sufficient savings to 'last a year' and I splutter my tea at this Midas-like admission, telling him I may retrain.

'I'll still keep an eye out for actual jobs,' he goes on, 'only in companies I respect, because according to my diagram, what I care about is working for someone who makes stuff, not money. But for the next twelve months, I'm going to give cheese a chance.'

I wonder whether this could be the name of his new enterprise and he tells me, 'I'm having that!' as I hear the sound of a pen scratching on paper.

I'm delighted for him. But Table Flipper is finding the interrelationship diagram task trickier.

'Can't I just *think* about my values?'

'No,' I tell her, 'research shows that people who write down their goals are thirty-three per cent more successful in achieving them.' I conveniently omit the fact that I've only been walking this particular walk for the past forty-eight hours.

'I'm too busy!' she tells me next, complaining that Idiot Boss has landed her with a huge document to compile before the weekend on top of all her usual work.

'You've got to make time to sharpen the saw!' I try saying with some authority. And fail.

'Has someone been reading *The Seven Habits of Highly Effective People?*' she asks, referring to the seminal management tome of the 1970s. Stephen Covey's best-selling book advised readers to take time out and review their current methods by using the analogy of a blunt saw, ineffective for cutting a tree. Even when time-strapped, we need to 'sharpen the saw', or think about how best to handle things, rather than sawing on regardless with a blunt instrument – or a strategy that isn't working. I admit to her that I might have skim-read this from Lego Man's management-book mountain and hear tutting in response.

'The point is, you'll always be too busy unless you take the time to think about what you really want and how to make work better!'

Oh God, I hope I'm not turning into a WMT-bore . . . I worry. The dog stares at me. Really stares. As if to imply: '*You said it, not me . . .*'

Fortunately I've known Table Flipper for years and one of

the privileges of long service in friendship is that you are occasionally allowed to be a wanker, in a good cause. We joust to and fro for a few more minutes as she makes excuses and I try to get her fired up, suggesting more things she could change about her working life and the demands she should make of Idiot Boss to ensure her career progression, until finally she snaps.

'Stop it! I can't!'

'What do you mean, you can't?'

'What if they fire me?'

'Why would they fire you?'

'What if they realise I don't know everything or that I get things wrong sometimes, or I just *get found out* . . .'

'By whom?'

'I don't know, my boss?'

'I thought you said your boss was an idiot?'

'He is. But he's a confident idiot. It doesn't seem to bother him that he only knows half what's expected of him. Whereas I got the fear.'

'"*Got*"? As in, past tense?' She doesn't respond. 'Is there something you're not telling me?'

There is a long silence before Table Flipper finally admits that she was invited to apply for her boss's job but didn't feel she had all of the qualifications. So when Idiot Boss came along with fewer credentials but the fearlessness to go for it anyway, she was doubly pissed off. 'I didn't get the job because I didn't put myself out there, and now I have to work for him.'

And there it is. With this revelation, I realise that Table Flipper has outed herself as a fellow sufferer of Imposter Syndrome. This is the term coined by US psychologists

Pauline Clance and Suzanne Imes in 1978 to describe the feeling of 'faking it' in people who believe that they aren't capable enough for the task at hand, despite evidence to the contrary. They, or rather we, live in fear of being 'found out' or 'exposed'. More women suffer from this than men and it can prevent us from throwing our hats into the ring when it comes to promotions, pay rise requests and general professional advancement.

'I know, logically, that I'm decent at my job,' says Table Flipper: 'but I don't feel I deserve "success". It makes me uncomfortable.' She tells me about some consulting she did recently with 'a confident girl' and how bizarre she found the whole experience. 'I was getting paid more money than I should be for something easier than my normal job, and when I asked her if this could be right, she said: 'Yes, isn't it great?' And I thought, '*Why can't I think like that? Why do I feel guilty about it?*'

I tell her I know the feeling. I come from a family of Irish Catholics – we get guilt. We excel at playing the underdog. When the awards are eventually given out for self-laceration and martyrdom, we'll be right up there. If my family had a motto it would be something along the lines of:

'*Oh no, you're all right: jammy things like that don't happen to people like us *sigh**'

Blowing your own trumpet is so frowned upon in my family that when asked in a recent job interview why a company should hire her, my mother neglected to mention a forty-year career history and mumbled: 'Erm, because I'm nice . . .?'

Really driven people make me nervous. I admire them but I'm not sure quite what to do with them. Like ornaments. Throughout school, university and the world of work, I've encountered people with an absolute belief that success was theirs for the taking. And it probably was. Because people who think that they're winners often end up doing better than the rest of us, according to research from the University of Cologne.

Psychologists David Dunning and Justin Kruger from Cornell University in the US found that incompetent people also suffer from 'illusory superiority', overestimating their own abilities because they don't have the means to judge their skills (see Idiot Boss). They're more likely to take advantage of opportunities and, crucially, they just show up.

But new research is emerging that suggests Imposter Syndrome may have its uses – as long as the fear doesn't stop us from entering the race in the first place.

A large-scale study conducted by leadership consultancy Zenger Folkman found that managers who underestimated how good they were at their jobs tended to be the best performers. The more they underrated themselves, or felt like 'imposters', the higher their peers rated them and the better their work. And this is because if there's one thing that self-doubt is really good at, it's keeping us on our toes. Whereas people who get complacent are often *whispers it* a bit crap. And annoying.

Playing low-status has been my modus operandi for as long as I can remember. *But maybe*, I think, *this helps me do my job. No one wants to be interviewed by someone who thinks they're superior. That's not an interesting chat: that's an interrogation. By putting myself down, I can set people at ease and make them relax . . . maybe . . .*

'If we didn't worry,' I try to explain this theory to Table

Flipper, 'maybe we wouldn't care enough to do a good job. As long as we don't take ourselves out of the game – or out of the application process for Idiot Boss's job, just for instance – maybe it's all right to feel as though we have lots to learn. As long as we still give things a go.'

'But what about The Fear?' She wails a little now. I'm guessing she's not in the cubicle farm in earshot of Idiot Boss.

'Well . . .' I'm stalling here, wondering what to say to make my friend feel better. Then I remember some surprisingly useful YouTube procrastination earlier this week and the TEDxBerkeley talk I watched by leadership coach Mike Robbins. He talked about the courage it takes to 'just show up' and the importance of enduring the odd 'sweaty-palmed conversation' that might feel scary and enormous but in reality is just temporarily uncomfortable. *Perhaps*, I think, *we just need to get our sweat on once in a while and plough through* . . . I try to convey this to Table Flipper.

'Maybe,' I start, 'and feel free to call me a wanker here—'

'Wan—'

'Not *yet!*'

'Oh.'

'Maybe we have to "feel the fear and do it anyway"?'

There is a snort-guffaw hybrid and then I hear a muttered: 'Wanker . . .'

'You're welcome,' I tell her and hang up, wondering whether I've got what it takes to follow my own advice.

Regardless of where I do it, a career revamp for me means getting out there, networking and negotiating with potential employers to keep learning, pursuing interesting assignments and writing more. It means being brave, something I'm not currently great at. I'm semi-convinced by the idea that Imposter Syndrome has its uses. But I could do without the debilitating anxiety that often accompanies a lack of confidence. I'd also appreciate an extra injection of brio on the days when 'just showing up' feels like too much of an ordeal. I've had times when the fear has stopped me making a phone call or sending that email or going along to an event. It's something I'd like to get better at, for making decisions, committing to changes, and having the self-assurance to call up editors to implement my interrelationship diagram results.

In one of the podcasts I regularly listen to in an attempt to outsource my stream of consciousness during the limbo between head-hitting-pillow and sleep, I hear an interview that gives me an idea. Dr Peter Lovatt of the Dance Psychology Lab at the University of Hertfordshire, or 'Dr Dance', as he is delightfully known, conducts research into the power of dancing to help with decision-making and boost confidence. So the next morning, once I'm sure I haven't just dreamt the whole existence of a 'Dance Lab' with its very own doctor, I call him.

'Er, hi, is that Dr Dance?' is my opener. Lego Man hasn't yet left for work and can be heard sniggering in the background. I attempt to shoo him out of the room as a voice on the other end of the line responds.

'Speaking!' sings out a cheery-sounding man. I Google him, always keen for a visual when speaking to someone new, and am pleased to note that he looks just as much like a kindly professor from a children's book as his voice suggests. *Excellent.*

Peter tells me that he's always loved dancing: 'The whole

family would go to Butlins[6] every year when I was a child and we'd dance together – the slosh, the Gay Gordon, the mashed potato . . . you name it! Today though, a lot of people feel exposed when they dance. The kids are embarrassed. Everyone's embarrassed. But dance is a hugely important part of being human. It's a primary sensor motor coupling, so we see it in five-month-old babies who instinctively want to respond to the stimulus of music.' On a quest to bring dance-for-all back, Peter started looking at the science behind it.

'We had people in the lab dancing and then problem-solving and we found that different sorts of dancing help with different sorts of problems. When people engage in improvised kinds of dance it helps them with divergent thinking – where there are multiple answers to a problem. Whereas when they engage in very structured dance it helps their convergent thinking – trying to find the single answer to a problem, like "what is the capital of France?" This has implications for the world of work. You get desks fitted with hydraulics these days so that people can stand while they work, but our research shows they should try dancing, too.' Peter suggests that while trying to think creatively, we should move our body in a freestyle, improvised way. Then when we're facing a more logical, single-answer problem, we could break out into a waltz or grapevine.

'I always dance while I work,' he tells me. 'I'm dancing now!' He pauses, allowing my imagination to paint a full-

_____

6 For the uninitiated: a chain of holiday camps in the UK, big in the 1970s and 1980s, keen on red-blazered, rictus-grinning employees in tennis shoes.

colour picture of the scene. It's quite something. 'I have a hands-free headset for my phone and I had a dance floor installed in my study because I was wearing out the floor. I dance all the time! Dancing helps me think. It helps everyone think.' As a typically repressed Brit, I don't consider myself a natural dancer unless I've had two gin and tonics (at which point I become an AMAZING dancer). But throwing some shapes, sober, in the privacy of my own home feels doable.

'And what about confidence?' I ask. 'Could I dance myself more confident?'

'Yes! Numerous studies have shown that dancing raises self-esteem. Any style of dancing will do, so long as it's non-competitive, non-judgemental and it gets the heart rate going. And the effects are long-lasting.'

'So I could dance, say, just before I had to do something scary?'

'That would be a good plan, yes – if you can't do it at the same time, that is,' he adds, jiving away to the music in his mind. I presume.

I'm intrigued by this. With a tricky phone call to negotiate a speaking fee pending, I send Lego Man off for the day, whistling, then I lock the front door. Distracting the dog with a bone, I select Absolute 80s on the digital radio and go for it. Really go for it, with power grabs and spins and sashays and limb-flailing the like of which my living room has never seen before – and that no living person will ever be permitted to see again. After one Bonnie Tyler and two Whitesnake hits, I feel charged; invigorated; ready.

My usual fee is, I've been assured by an unusually forthright colleague, too low. But as a sufferer of Imposter Syndrome, I haven't wanted to ask for more as I worried I wasn't really worth it. I've assumed that doing something that comes fairly easily to me must have little value. At least, that was how the pre-Friday-morning shape-throwing 'me' felt. Now, emboldened and feeling fired up for a 'sweaty-palmed conversation', I call the client as instructed and cite a figure precisely double my normal rate.

I don't know what I expect to happen next. Lightning? Thunderclaps? Uproarious laughter in disbelief? Whatever it is, it isn't this:

'That should be doable. I'll confirm later this morning.'

No drama. No chastisement for being so bold. No problem. Ten minutes later, I get an email agreeing to the fee suggested, no questions asked. I have doubled my pay *and* released some pretty banging 80s power-ballad endorphins (the best kind) in the space of ten minutes. Not bad for a morning's work. I email Peter to thank him and tell him, '*It worked!*' and he lets me in on another life-hack for improving self-esteem:

'*Look into power poses, where you stand like Wonder Woman – you might want to try these, too.*'

He had me at 'Wonder Woman'.

Social psychologists at Harvard Business School studying 'non-verbal expressions of power and dominance' noticed that throughout the animal kingdom, creatures make themselves bigger to express authority and signal that they are 'high-status'. This includes human beings – even the congenitally blind do it when they win at a physical competition – we're genetically programmed to expand; stretching out and making ourselves bigger to signify power. When we feel powerless, we do the opposite: curling up and making ourselves small. Researchers also found that featureless mannequins were interpreted as 'female' when positioned in a closed posture, while the same figures were seen as 'male' when manipulated into an open posture. We learn to associate constrictive body language with 'being female' and expansive as 'male'. Which sucks.

But TED talk legend and Harvard professor Amy Cuddy is seeking to change this. Amy explored the impact of 'faking' the powerful poses seen in nature/the boardroom/on public transport and found that, miraculously, simply holding the body in an expansive, 'high-power' pose for two minutes not only makes us look and feel more powerful, it also causes a shift in our hormones. Researchers found that a two-minute 'power pose' stimulated higher levels of testosterone (the hormone linked to power and dominance) and lowered levels of cortisol (the stress hormone) in the body. By assuming a posture of confidence, even when we're not feeling it, we can summon an extra surge of power. Standing tall with our feet a metre apart, chin raised, shoulders broadened and arms away from the body – either stretched up above our heads as though waiting to receive divine inspiration, or on our hips in a 'Wonder Woman' pose – we can feel more confident. In two minutes.

I love this idea. As someone who customarily turns into a human hedgehog when faced with the merest hint of social or professional anxiety, this feels like a game-changer. *And I get to pretend I am my favourite superhero(ine) at the same time? The one with the big glossy mane and Amazonian thighs that I have considerably more chance of emulating than look-at-them-and-they'll-snap comic-book heroines like Catwoman or Supergirl (who sounds like a starter tampon anyway)? This is BRILLIANT news.*

I learn that similar principles apply to sitting. Instead of sinking back into a chair, we feel and look more powerful when we place our elbows on an armrest or move them away from us so that there is space between our body and our forearms. This stops us shrinking into ourselves, forcing us to take up space and be a presence in a room.

I try this out the next time I have to do an interview with someone I'm a little intimidated by. I'm answering the questions this time, in front of other people. So I sit in as expansive a position as I can manage. And it feels absurd. I resist the urge to cross my legs and instead focus on spreading my elbows wide, out as though I'm about to launch into a poorly timed rendition of 'The Birdie Song'. But the interview runs smoothly.

Afterwards, a friend who comes along for moral support says to me: 'It sounds weird but you just . . . *sat* really well.'

'Yeah, you sat like a boss,' his friend chips in.

'Thanks!' I feel disproportionately chuffed.

The real test of my new superheroine powers comes a week later when I'm due to contribute to a radio show. Because I'm nowhere near where the show is being broadcast from, I bowl up at my local radio station in rural Denmark to be patched in so that I can join the magazine-style discussion in London. But my plan to power pose ahead of, or even during, the show is dealt a blow when I realise that the studio I'm in is glass-fronted. Through a six-foot window, I see a packed office of Vikings – and they can all see me. *It'll be all right*, I reason. *It's just talking. I do 'talking' all the time!* Then I experience reflux and worry it will not be all right at all.

The segment I'm supposed to be doing is delayed by a call-in on 'the strangest things you've ever eaten'. Natasha from Shrewsbury is currently describing, in detail, how she once found a dead lizard in a bag of bananas.

'Bear with us, be with you in five,' a producer's voice sounds out in my headphones. I try to remember the points I want to make, laying my notes out on the angled control desk in front of me, but they keep slipping off. It's hot in the studio, so I pull off my jumper and get my hair stuck in the headphones. Scrambling to untangle myself, I realise that the Vikings have now dropped any facade of work and are looking right at me. My palms start to sweat and I decide I am almost certainly going to wee myself. So I do it. Full on Wonder Woman, that is. The Vikings stare, as though their suspicions have been confirmed and the peculiar British woman has officially lost the plot. One of them raises an eyebrow and gives a double thumbs-up, the universal sign for '*Is everything okay?*'

I nod and hold my thumbs up in the universal sign for '*Everything is okay!*'

'We'll be with you as soon as this caller's off the line,' the producer in the UK tells me through the headphones and I nod, to no one.

'. . . I'm not blaming the supermarket itself,' Natasha from Shrewsbury goes on to the presenter, 'I mean they don't package the bananas, do they? Probably done in a factory somewhere!'

'But has it put you off bananas in future, Natasha?'

'I should say!'

'You don't fancy a banana and lizard smoothie then?' the jocular host says with a chortle.

'No,' Natasha from Shrewsbury says without any semblance of mirth: 'I'm a vegetarian.'

'Oh . . .'

I realise I'm quite enjoying myself, listening so intently that I quite forget I'm supposed to be doing something soon. Then the presenter says my name and suddenly, I'm talking. Just as I would be with you, now. And my palms are still sodden and I'm standing like a loon but I'm totally doing it. *Chatting is easy!* I tell myself. So I do more of it. And standing like Wonder Woman, I don't care what the Vikings think. Because I'm Wonder Woman.

When it's all over and I open the studio door to leave, the Vikings snap their focus back to their monitors and pretend to have been working throughout. No one makes eye contact. So I thank them for their support in bad Danish and once I'm round the corner, waiting for the lift, I do a little moonwalk in celebration.

Later that week, I catch up with my work guinea pigs on entrepreneurial cheese ventures, the power of dance and superhero(ine) alter egos – and find that Table Flipper has her own news.

'So I did the interrelationship diagram and it really helped me understand what's important – what I could be pursuing to make the job less . . .'

'"*Meh*"?'

'Sure. So I samba-d in one of the meeting rooms with the blinds down while I came up with this new strategy and worked it up into a proposal for next quarter. I hid in the loos and did the Wonder Woman thing for two minutes, then I took it to Idiot Boss's *boss* and she agreed that it was a great idea.'

'That's wonderful! Well done you!'

'I may have also taken on board some of the other advice you passed on.'

'This is a red-letter day!' I'm thrilled and intrigued. 'What was it? The gratitude journal?' I wonder, conscious that my own hasn't been updated as much as it should have been this week. 'The workplace buddy?'

'Sort of . . .' She looks cagey.

'What have you done?'

'I may have got myself an office crush.'

'Ooh, tell all!'

She says that she will not. So I do some badgering until she changes her mind and reveals that there may have been a tequila-fuelled 'incident' at the office party, the details of which are so shocking that I snort tea out of my nose (surprisingly painful).

'It's only supposed to be a crush! You aren't actually supposed to do stuff! On the stairs!'

'I thought it might be like the power poses or the dancing: the more you do the better?'

'No,' I tell her, firmly.

'Oh. But we're both single . . .'

'I should hope so!'

'Oh well, I'll just focus on doing more Wonder Woman next time—'

'Rather than Stuart from Sales?'

'Sure.' She shrugs and I marvel at how Table Flipper's utter confidence in her powers of attraction have never translated into confidence in her professional life until now.

The techniques and tools I've learned to make changes in my work life have given me a new approach to my career, and I'm no longer filled with dread by the thought of what I'd do back in the UK. By pursuing my values rather than prestige, I should be able to pay the bills *and* enjoy what I do. For which I am insanely grateful. I still get the fear sometimes, and veer between a sort of jazz hands, 'I've totally got this!' and a *Home Alone*-style scream of 'Arrgghhh! I don't know anything! What am I doing?' but on the whole, there are more jazz hands than *Home Alone* moments. I know now what I want for the foreseeable future, how to get there and that I'm good enough – not perfect, but good enough. Which feels significant. It won't be easy, but in the words of Damon Albarn: 'nothing is'.

I get a healthy dose of perspective on my career concerns the following week when I venture out of my Bat-cave to network at an event where I know no one (see 'braver') and encounter a mathematician for the Ministry of Defence. I'm focusing very hard on standing tall and getting air between my torso and my elbows when Maths Whizz notices and asks if I'm all right. The pose clearly still needs work, but it does serve as an excellent ice-breaker and we get talking. Maths Whizz is my age and very chatty. She asks how my day's been and I mention an assignment I'm finding difficult and the heart-flutter I still experience when I hand in a new piece of work, hoping I've done it 'right'.

'Yeah, I get that all the time,' she tells me, explaining that today she had to do some brain-achingly complex equations to 'ensure that two missiles didn't collide'.

'Oh!' I don't quite know what the protocol is on this or whether I've just been let in on a state secret. 'And, um, was it all all right? With the missiles and stuff?'

She nods, knocking back a handful of roasted almonds.

'This time, yeah,' she says through a mouthful of nuts.

I will never complain about my work again, I think, making a note to write about this in today's work-gratitude journal entry: *If I have a bad day, no bombs go off.*

The process has also reminded me of how much I really love working. Unlike the rest of life, work comes with its own rules and standards that have always made sense to me. Whereas relationships can get rather more complicated. As I'm about to discover.

Things I've learned about making changes at work:

---

1. Faking a family and setting artificial deadlines can help with work–life balance.

2. Spider diagrams on acid create practical career plans and show where we need to make changes. Lamination optional.

3. Feeling the fear can be useful, as long as we do the thing we're scared of anyway. Sweaty-palmed conversations just mean we're doing it right . . .

4. Standing like Wonder Woman for two minutes can help (though you may get funny looks unless you do it in private).

5. If in doubt, dance. Freestyle for creative thinking and samba for problem-solving.

6. Office crushes can be good for our careers – but should not be mixed with 'tequila' and 'stairwells' at 2 a.m.

CHAPTER TWO

RELATIONSHIPS

The Importance Of Being A Little More Earnest

In which I learn how cognitive behavioural therapy can rejuvenate
a relationship; why debunking Hollywood endings is crucial for
changing expectations; how a #nofantasyfilter helps curb jealousy; and why Joan Collins can save your marriage

'It's Saturday!' Lego Man looms above me as I sit at my
desk.

'So?'

'So, you're working! Can't we have a work-free weekend,
like normal people?'

'*Again?*' I'm pretty sure we had one of those last week.

I love my family. And I like to think that I have a pretty
good work–life balance nowadays. But I also love writing.
And when immersed in something really interesting, I
could keep going. For ever. Little Red usually naps at
midday and so for me this is perfect desk-time. Lego Man
disapproves.

'Do you know what day it is today?' His arms are now
folded and I wonder if this is a trick question.

'You just told me: Saturday. I thought I could finish this
piece while Little Red is sleeping—'

'Today,' he says, 'is our anniversary.'

I flick through my mental diary at speed and realise, with a knotting stomach, that he's right.

Shit.

'Oh God . . . I'm sorry!' We don't normally mark our relationship milestones with much fanfare but I have at least been aware of them in previous years.

'Do you know what D and B did to celebrate their anniversary this year?'

D and B are the most loved-up, oversexed couple we know, despite having been together for thirteen years. D and B are not normal.

'No,' I lie, sheepish now, 'what did D and B do?'

'They went to Venice and drank cava through striped straws on a gondola –'

I attempt to sound surprised: 'Oh!'

– 'then she rented an owl to fly over and deliver a velvet pouch with a watch he'd wanted for ages inside—'.

'An *owl?*' *For fuck's sake!* I didn't know this part and am now seriously rethinking my friendship with D and B. *Who does that?*

'That's a bit much, isn't it?' I try. 'I mean, dangerous for one thing—'

'She was wearing a falconry glove.'

'All right, but what if something had gone wrong and a giant bird of prey had clawed their faces off?' I'm clutching at striped-cava-straws here.

'That's not the point,' says Lego Man: 'Have you ever thought about renting me an owl?'

'I . . . I looked into borrowing a drone, once . . .?' is all I can come up with.

'Great. And now you're working. On our anniversary. Thanks.'

And there's the rub. Or rather, the itch. Because as part of my 'embracing change' experiment, I realise that the time has come to address the health of my relationship. Seven years in, I want to make changes to stop the 'decline in satisfaction' that classically occurs around this time and stormproof my relationship ahead of a potentially huge and probably highly stressful move. I need to reignite the spark and make an effort. I'm never going to be like D and B. And in truth, Lego Man wouldn't want me to be. I've always had a phobia of 'earnest' and an allergy to slush. But I would like our marriage to be a bit more like it was at the start.

Having a baby changed things for us, as it does for many – even if both parties behave impeccably. One friend's partner stroked her hair dutifully during labour, told her she looked 'like a goddess' as she lost control of her bowels, cooked and cleaned like a man possessed back at home, and did the night feeds for six months. And even *they're* struggling. Many relationships are dealt a body blow by the arrival of children and, while the initial chaotic fug of caring for a newborn undoubtedly takes a toll, it's the 'daily grind and residual resentment' – as one friend describes it – that comes after that can really be a buzz-kill. Couples typically report the lowest levels of relationship satisfaction a year or so after the birth of their first child. The bloom is off the rose and we've had ample opportunity to disappoint each other. On very little sleep. And infuriatingly, no one has yet worked out a foolproof plan to avoid this. Cheers scientists.

Quite apart from the fact that we have the responsibility of raising a Viking-spirited mancub between us, Lego Man and

I now spend a large proportion of each day dealing with poo. My nails have peeled to the quick because I spend the remainder of my 'non-working' hours up to my elbows in laundry/dishwater/spillages or hosing down my son, who is a magnet for mud. I'm hardly Cinderella (a ball? Fat chance. . .) but busy work schedules, domestic life, cohabitation, pet ownership and a child mean that I regularly smell like Dettol and there are very few owl-moments in my marriage.

Many friends with kids have made no-divorce pacts until the youngest is three, because before then the sleep deprivation, knackeredness and general cheesed-off-with-the-world-ness is clouding their judgement. One mother of three seriously considered the possibility that she might be asexual, so indifferent was she to the idea of conjugal rites. Then she went away for work. She had a few nights of undisturbed sleep, watched a Channing Tatum film and realised she'd just been Insanely Tired for five years.

It's not just women who feel this way. Many fathers I know now choose sleep over sex. Mismatched desires are a constant source of strife and all cohabiting couples fall out over the most minor of domestic issues – from the classic thermostat-vs.-jumper debate to dishwasher-loading technique[7]. When our ancestors promised to love each other until death, they meant for forty years, tops. Now we live for *ages*. A third of babies born today could live until they're a hundred. And that's a far longer sentence than marriage proponents ever anticipated.

Relationships, of any kind, are hard. Whether we're in

---

7 . . . with the exception of Weird Owl Couple. The house-elves probably do their washing up and fan/hug them to maintain optimal body temperature at all times . . .

one, surveying the remnants of one, or looking for something new.

One of my oldest friends, the one who has been recently dumped, really wants a family of her own. What she didn't want was a fuckwit serial monogamist to mess her around for four years, then end it over email.

'I thought I'd grow old with him,' she sobbed to me earlier this week. 'I thought we'd go grey together—' she wiped a tear away and backtracked: 'or rather, I'd get some lowlights and he'd go a bit Paul McCartney aubergine . . .' She cried, hard, again at this thought and blew her nose, noisily: 'And now he's going to go aubergine with someone else!'

I didn't know how to respond to this. Firstly, because I haven't been through a break-up recently and second, because my husband and I are both fair-haired and so unlikely to go down the Paul McCartney route. But Recent Dumpee was heart-collapsing sad. And angry. And confused. And I wasn't sure what I could do to help.

She's just out of the 'what's the point of it all?' phase and thinking, tentatively, about whether she can face doing it all again and getting back out there. Starting over feels like scaling a mountain and she is knackered.

'I'll be okay, won't I? I mean, I do *yoga!*'

I don't know how to break it to her that the ability to put your leg behind your head may not be a solid basis for a relationship, no matter what *Sex And The City* has taught her.

'You'll be great,' is all I can say. And she will, I'm sure. Though maybe not quite yet.

'I don't drunk-text him any more,' she tells me.

'That's brilliant news.'

'Thanks. I just make sure I have a drink in each hand so I can't get to my phone on nights out.'

There is a pause as we both contemplate this and drink more wine.

'I Googled "*What if I end up alone*" the other day,' she confesses, once her glass is empty.

'Oh . . . and?'

'The internet told me "*we all end up alone, eventually*". At first I found this comforting, but then I started to worry about getting eaten by urban foxes.'

'That would be a worry, yes . . .' is all I can think of to say. But it isn't much use. As well as worrying about my marriage, I want to know if there's a way to help my friend get over Paul McC; get on with the rest of her life; and get better at choosing prospective partners who aren't, in her words, 'massive cockwombles'[8].

I want to know what tools and techniques we can employ to make existing relationships feel 'like new' and start again successfully if a relationship ends. To do this, I need to understand what I'm dealing with and so decide to find out, in words Haddaway would surely have sung had he had a little more time in the studio: '*What is love . . .or lust, anyway?*'

At 10 a.m. on Monday, once I'm safely allowed to work again without risking separate bedrooms, I sip a too-hot latte in my local cafe and begin reading the reams of academic reports I've printed off on the science of attraction. The door

---

8 I have nothing against Wombles. Or cocks. I am merely a conduit for my friend's colourful vocabulary.

dings open and a young couple waft in: a girl and a boy in their late teens, dressed simply in jeans and T-shirts. Neither is particularly striking: they are not tall, not short, not slim, not plump – not spectacular in any way, in fact. They speak in low voices and order drinks without ceremony before taking up residence in the corner seats by the loos, the ones no one ever wants. They are not famous. Or infamous. But no one in the place can take their eyes off them. Because the couple radiate shimmering, first-time, 'isn't-life-AMAZING?' love. Or rather, lust. They shine with it – ethereally luminous from their mousy brown heads of hair to their average-sized feet. They are all over each other, as though by compulsion rather than choice – incapable of operating without physical contact with the other. When the girl removes a hand from the small of the boy's back, her foot kicks back like a pony being shod and reaches around to caress the back of his calf. When the boy realises he can no longer safely keep his arms round his girlfriend while receiving two mugs of scalding liquid, he takes a tea in each hand and nuzzles the side of her shoulder with his nose. It's as though they're heavily invested in an elaborate improv game where actors must have at least one body part touching at all times. Once they're ensconced, the boy and the girl look into each other's eyes and grin like loons without saying a word. For ten solid minutes. I know this because when I next look at the clock on my phone, it reads 10.10 a.m.

In my defence, I'm still not alone in my rubbernecking. An elderly lady looks on, misty-eyed, in what I romantically assume to be reminiscence. Or it could be cataracts. The barista scowls slightly in what I take to be envy (I know for a fact he is looking for love/lust because he enquired after the relationship status of a handsome friend I was in here with last week. He was keen. I may set them up . . .). A group of younger teens stare, intrigued as to what may or may not be in store for them, and an older couple who haven't spoken to each other since arriving steal furtive glances at the young lovers while chewing joylessly on muffins.

With a real-life example of the 'science of attraction' in front of me, I put down the sheets of A4 theory and try to remember when I last felt that surging, all-encompassing, veering on obsession, love-slash-lust.

10.20 a.m.: I am still thinking.

By 10.35 a.m. I start to worry that it was A Very Long Time Ago Indeed (an under-explored historical period).

Back at home, I have a eureka moment over a Rich Tea biscuit (so often the way) and experience a strange sort of sense-memory. I remember, mostly, a bowel-churning discomfort and light-headed giddiness: a time when I was so unaccustomed to the hormonal assault on my entire being that I couldn't eat, sleep or do much of anything. I call my mother to confirm this particular period in the late 1990s and she reveals she was so concerned about me that she 'even considered homeopathy'. I dimly recall having just two modes at that time: very up or stupidly down. Whenever I was with the object of my affection, I felt brilliantly drunk: confident, vivacious, witty, captivating (I felt sure). But when we were apart, I indulged in what my mother terms 'mooning about'. I would read poetry – or worse, write it – as well as talking solemnly to any grown-ups who'd listen about our 'future' and how we'd survive when the other left for university/moved house/went to Center Parcs for the week. I have a vague recollection of channelling early Morrissey: wafting around, waving gladioli at the world, occasionally swooning: 'This is living! This is love!'

I wonder whether I was particularly wet or whether these experiences are typical. So I look beyond the wisdom of my mother and old copies of *Just Seventeen* (I really hope Kayleigh, sixteen, from Kettering knows how to French kiss by now . . .), and consult some experts instead.

Neuroscientists, normal scientists and psychologists all seem to confirm that people freshly in love are, frankly, mental. In the throes of passion, we are permanently excited and nervous, something that the body interprets as stress and which can trigger a whole slew of physiological changes, including loss of appetite, nausea – and even, apparently, the runs. We're influenced by the basest of biological impulses (note, 'influenced by', not 'controlled by' – that way misogyny and madness lie) and our bodies secrete more than 200 chemical compounds via our sweat, saliva and genitals. Scientists at Stockholm Brain Institute used brain-scanning techniques to show how a chemical in male sweat causes a rush of electrical activity in the brains of straight women and gay men, while lesbians and straight men treat it like any other odour. Researchers also found that lesbians and heterosexual men responded in the same way to the female pheromone EST. No wonder the young couple in the coffee shop were letting their tea go cold, helpless in ardour's electrified headlock. But these feelings don't last.

Studies show that after twelve months, initial sexual attraction starts to wane. Passion ebbs and it's things like friendship, compromise and patience that keep a relationship going strong – though there's considerably less pornography and erotica dedicated to these. Hormones associated with lust are replaced by the so-called 'cuddle hormone' oxytocin. This is the chemical that induces labour and lactation in mothers, as well as making men more empathetic and increasing fidelity and feelings of well-being in both sexes.

But there's something else that's been impacting on women's mate selection over the past five decades. Studies show that women on the birth control pill tend to pick vastly different partners than they would have had they been drug-free. The pill prevents women from ovulating by fooling the body into believing it's pregnant, so users opt for men who appear nurturing rather than overtly masculine. We want a mate we can trust and rely on for support with small children, not necessarily someone we want to dry-hump during the weekly shop. Since many women I know only came off the pill when they married or started a family, this is a worry. It means they've already committed to someone they may never have chosen had their hormones not been tampered with.

As well as unconscious bias, many of us also lie at the start of a new relationship or when attempting to attract a mate. We twist ourselves to fit an idealised version of what we imagine our other half wants. And although this contortionism lessens as we get older, we continue to present the 'best' version of ourselves to someone new.

Lego Man regularly refers to a conversation during one of our earliest dates when I apparently told him I enjoyed camping.

I do not enjoy camping.

It's cold and clammy until morning, when it's hot and clammy. Nothing ever feels clean; and I really like beds. And sheets. But I was seemingly so keen to impress him that I fabricated a love of . . . er . . . sleeping under fabric.

Something that has been a source of contention ever since. Now, whenever he's particularly cross with me he puts on a special cap with a tent motif on it and plays the Lemonheads song (you lied about being) 'The Outdoor Type'. Loudly.

On the flipside, he conned me into believing he liked to cook and was a veritable gym bunny – hobbies that both mysteriously fell by the wayside once we moved in together.

Another friend felt cheated to discover that his girlfriend didn't have silky-smooth skin that smelled permanently like coconuts when they began to cohabit (at least, not without help from Bic and the Body Shop first). In turn, she was pretty hacked off that he 'didn't believe in daily showers'. They broke up. Both met other people and started again, in relationships that were all shiny and new. Until they weren't any more. And she stayed with her next partner while he moved on. In the flow chart of life we typically take one of two paths: we muddle on or we start again.

People with a string of failed relationships are sometimes told by 'friends' that perhaps the problem is them. Recent Dumpee has had this suggested to her by a particularly outspoken mutual acquaintance who I've never had much time for. Predominantly because she's an arse. But each of us is, by definition, the only constant in our own romantic lives. So being single more than we might care to be *may* be down to us, but it could also just be luck – good or bad. Or it could be timing. Or location. Or our taste in annoying friends ('Really,' I tell Recent Dumpee: 'ditch *that* one'). It's traditionally been suggested that each of us has a market value – based on our looks, intelligence, charm, charisma, bank balance, etc. If this is news to you, congratulations on keeping your life free from haters and your mind on higher things. If this sounds all too familiar, you'll know all about 'mate value' and its supposed impact on our 'worth' in the dating pool (not to be confused with a ball pool, which is far more fun). We may be a seven. Or an eight. Or a ten (YOU are a clearly a ten. Fact . . .). If your value is high, the theory goes that you can take your pick from any number of potential suitors, while the rest of us have to settle for whatever we can get. Surprisingly, there is some science behind this wholly depressing worldview: a US study published in the *Journal of Personality and Social Psychology* asked a group of heterosexual students to rate their opposite-sex classmates for attractiveness, warmth and career potential. At the start, they were united in their scoring of the best 'catches' in the group. Lucky old Phil with the hair and Julie with the teeth (I'm guessing). But three months in, researchers found that this consensus had vanished. As the students got to know each other, more and more of them discovered qualities in their peers that they hadn't noticed at first – and they preferred them. Another study from 2014 found that being a nice person makes us more attractive. Researchers have concluded that the importance of the sudden spark on first meeting has been grossly overrated.

I've never been big on fairytales. The Little Mermaid commits suicide and Red Riding Hood gets torn limb from limb by a wolf. I don't aspire to star in my own Disney princess film and I don't buy the big, bombastic, 'Is it still raining? I hadn't noticed . . .' *Four Weddings and a Funeral* style romcom relationship model[9]. In reality, Charles and

---

9 As a side note, my editor has just sagely pointed out that 'nobody with hair that curly would fail to notice rain' #FriendoftheFrizzEase.

Carrie have probably consciously uncoupled by now, and most Disney princesses look like they snort Ritalin.

Scientific research has proven that romantic movies – like *Four Weddings* – effectively ruin our love lives. A study from the University of Michigan found that the romanticised 'pursuit-behaviours' commonly portrayed as part of a normal courtship in film and TV can lead to 'stalker-supporting beliefs.' Bizarre behaviour we'd never normally tolerate gets rebranded as 'love', so that we begin to normalise, say, a stalker who spies on his childhood crush (*There's Something About Mary*), or a man who films the object of his desire obsessively, then turns up on her door-step with flashcards to entice her to ditch his best friend (*Love Actually*). Another problem, according to US psycho-therapist Dr Wendy Walsh, is that a saccharine cinematic version of what love looks like means that the reality often disappoints.

Several perpetually single friends have had their expecta-tions warped by Hollywood depictions. These are intelligent, attractive men and women. But they've been duped into waiting for a man or woman who comes complete with a Tom Hanks voiceover to narrate their happy ending, or someone with perfect skin and caramel limbs who even looks good by harsh daylight. Or a unicorn. On top of this, films typically end at the beginning of a relationship with the implied summary of the next forty-plus years as 'happily ever after' when, in real life, that's when the hard graft starts.

'Films make us believe that it's all about finding The One,' says Wendy, 'but picking a partner is only about ten per cent of having a healthy relationship. The rest is about relationship skills – and these can be developed.'

One of the best ways to do this is apparently with CBT, which stands for cognitive behavioural therapy and not, as one friend who's a member of the BDSM community recently assumed, 'Cock & Ball Torture'. Just so we're clear.

CBT is a form of psychotherapy originally designed to treat depression, but now used for a wide range of issues – from panic attacks to problems with low self-esteem. It aims to change unhelpful thinking and patterns of unhealthy behaviour, replacing these with new habits that can actually help us. It's also a popular form of relationship therapy – and is even used to help build confidence in dating and starting over after a split.

Veronica Walsh is a cognitive behavioural therapist who has specialised in this and she's also the most no-nonsense Irish woman you could ever hope to encounter. So I get in touch for some tips I can pass on to Recent Dumpee and a newly divorced friend who's having a rough time.

'Dating is stressful and change is hard,' she kicks off briskly, 'and many single clients still strive for what they describe as "a normal life", by which they mean a monogamous, long-term relationship, usually marriage. But this isn't the norm any more. We're not our mothers' or our grandmothers' generation. Many of us don't marry – and nearly half of those who do end up getting divorced. The idea of a relationship for life is often not going to happen, so shouldn't be an absolute *demand* on ourselves that we pursue at all costs. Once we get our head around this, it frees us. Because being happy single is always better than being unhappy with someone else.' This is a sentiment I've long agreed with, having grown up with a solo mum and seen various friends split up over the years. Developmental molecular biologist Dr John Medina has studied the impact of stress on the brain and found that being in a bad relationship, long-term, is akin to sleeping in the same bed as a sabre-toothed tiger. For years. This is because our brains are built to deal with stress that lasts about thirty seconds – enough time for the sabre-tooth to eat us or for us to run away. What we're not built for is prolonged stress, which has been proven to make us sick and even shrink our brains.

'Hoping that something will work out won't *make* it better,' says Veronica of 'toxic' relationships, 'and positive thinking doesn't work when it's not true and we don't believe it. We're not robots. Or the Dalai Lama. So while it's normal to get stressed or angry, if you're always stressed or angry, you need to make a change.'

Veronica tells me that the key to success in relationships is the same as the key to success in 'life generally': 'It's knowing how you're wired.'

'CBT is about the awareness and management of how we explain the world to ourselves – because when stress becomes a disorder it distorts thinking. CBT *undistorts* it. So I get people to track their thinking in a journal and examine it for unnecessary negativity and distortions. Then you need to consider how believing those thoughts impacts on your feelings and behaviours,' she explains. 'The real magic happens when people reframe that thinking – when they examine it for evidence and undistort it. You ask yourself questions like, "What drama do I actually create for myself? Do I self-sabotage? Do I try to read minds, imagining that I know what other people are thinking?"'

'*Loads*', '*Yep*', and '*Of course!*' spring to mind when I think of my own answers, so I'm reassured when Veronica adds: 'And if you're guilty of some – or all – of these, that's perfectly normal: we are irrational beings. But we're all irrational in our own ways, so it's important not to predict what someone else is thinking or feeling. I see a lot of people making magnifying statements or restricting the way they think – so they'll say: "Oh, men only want to date twenty-year-olds", or, "I'm not successful enough to find a mate," or whatever. But these statements are never true.'

Never?

'Never,' she insists. 'Something may be twenty per cent true, fifteen per cent of the time – but those kinds of beliefs and statements are never a hundred per cent true. Men and women aren't so different when it comes to dating. I see men who are lonely, who have been cheated on, or who think they have no luck dating – the same as I see women like this. So you can't make statements that are black or white about what men want or what women want. And actually, when you put pen to paper and examine the evidence in a more detached way, people usually come to this conclusion by themselves.'

This is heartening.

'Next you have to ask yourself, "Is there an alternative view? A different way I could approach this?" The answer's usually "yes". So you write that down, too. And once you're thinking differently, you'll feel and behave differently, too.'

Veronica guides me through the advice she'd give Recent Dumpee.

'You need to approach the whole dating thing with a sense of humour – especially online. You're essentially exchanging romantic ideals with someone you don't know and imposing your life-rules and expectations on a stranger, so it's important to allow yourself to be amused – even *be*mused – by the situation.'

Veronica advises clients not to think of a first meeting as a 'date' at all: 'It's not courtship – you don't know them! And there's no use emailing for ages beforehand and falling in love with a fantasy of someone. You need to meet in real life and treat the online part merely as a useful tool to bring about an interesting experience.'

'Okay,' I say, 'so you're meeting someone new, you're not expecting much and you're trying not to judge. What then? What if you start feeling wobbly?'

'Well that's when you use your new skills to become your own coach,' she says: 'I get people to ask themselves, "What would I advise my best friend here?" Because we're always kinder and more generous to our friends than to ourselves. Then you go back to your thought tracking. You can do this during the meeting to stop you mind-reading or negatively predicting, and then afterwards to work through any negative thoughts that might have other explanations. But mostly, you should try to enjoy yourself – remember, it should be fun!'

I thank her and hang up, keen to relay these pearls of wisdom.

Recent Dumpee accepts her assignments to try tracking her thoughts and keeping a journal with far less reluctance than I had feared. A week later she drops into conversation: 'Of course, one of the key self-sabotaging behaviours in my last relationship was picking fights, but really it was all down to my fear of abandonment . . .' I blink several times in wonderment, before she cottons on: 'Yeah, okay, it's been *slightly* helpful. I suppose . . .' She's getting better at coming up with alternative ways of seeing the world, too, and by writing these down, she recognises that she can sometimes be (her words) 'a bit bonkers'.

'It turns out that the guy on reception at work wasn't ignoring me because he'd heard something bad about me—'

'What? How did you come up with that?'

'I just reckon he must know stuff, what people say when they wait for the lift, that sort of thing. Anyway, turns out he just had conjunctivitis. But the good thing is,' she goes on, 'I'd stopped worrying about it *hours* before I found this out because I'd been writing down alternatives for why he wasn't making eye contact.'

'Was conjunctivitis one of them?'

'No. Although "sudden diagnosis of a life-threatening tropical disease" was.'

'Overdramatic, much?'

'Maybe I'll work on that one next . . .'

And so she does. And the next time we speak she sounds dangerously Dalai Lama.

After a couple more months, Not-So-Recent Dumpee tells me she's ready to 'get back out there'. Despite reminders that it's okay to be single, that there is no 'normal' any more, and that being in a relationship means having to share your Netflix with someone (annoying), she wants in. And having reached her mid-thirties without taking a shine to any of her friends or her friends' friends, she's prepared to try her luck online. So I wave her off into cyberspace, like a nervous parent packing off a child on the first day of school.

One in five straight couples and three in five same-sex couples now meet online and there are sites available to cater for every preference – from the conventional Match.com or OK Cupid, to Uniform Dating ('*for singles in uniform & for those who like them*'), Clown Dating ('*everyone loves a clown – let a clown love you . . .*'), and Gluten Free Singles ('*enjoy life with a GF partner*'. I wasn't aware you could imbibe gluten *that* way . . . but still, you live, you learn). Were I to have my time again, there is a wealth of uniformed, gluten-free, clown-based riches I could scarcely have dreamt of when I last dated.

I discover that it's a pretty good time to be taking a leap online, for both women and enlightened menfolk, with biological anthropologist Dr Helen Fisher recently proclaiming that: 'The era of the macho man is over'. Many men are now apparently looking online for women who are intelligent, ambitious, self-sufficient and not too good-looking. Really. Because if you're unambiguously beautiful, most men – or women – will assume that there'll be competition, so are less likely to make contact. Uploading a profile picture that actually looks like you, flaws and all, means you'll appear more accessible and there won't be any 'surprise reveal' when you meet in person.

An encouraging 86 per cent of straight men surveyed from online dating sites said that confidence and self-assurance were what they're looking for in a woman. Single straight women online said they wanted more time with their friends (64 per cent of those surveyed), more personal space (90 per cent), and to pursue their own interests (93 per cent). Essentially, many women seem happy being single. Perhaps they're just online for the craic.

Despite the old clichés about women wanting commitment, the *laydees* surveyed expected to date someone for one or two years before living together, while single men wanted to cohabit after six to twelve months. *Like massive keenos*, I think. Having recently become alerted to the phenomenon of 'wife eyes' – whereby professional men in their late twenties adopt a mad scanning technique in any new social setting as they cast around for marriage material – this comes as no surprise to me.

Of course, not everyone online is a liberated metrosexual. Internet dating famously offers extra opportunities for lying. '*I enjoy kickboxing,* A Question of Sport, *and eating baked beans from the tin while picking my toenails*' said no one, ever, on an online dating profile. A staggering 81 per cent of us lie about our height, age and physique and a third of daters' profile pictures are misleading.

'All a profile really reveals is whether or not someone can spell and master basic grammar,' Recent Dumpee reports. '"Your" vs. "you're" is a classic.' We both agree that it's vital to instantly reject anyone whose stated hobbies include 'banter', since proficiency at human interaction and a decent grasp of conversation should be a given.

'And I'm blocking anyone who sends unwanted photographs of their genitalia,' she tells me.

'Why would someone *do* that?'

'You'd have to ask Craig from High Wycombe,' is all she says, darkly.

Would-be daters whose profile pictures include the arm/torso/cheek of their ex are similarly discarded, because if someone hasn't been single for long enough to have a solo photograph taken, then they haven't been single for long enough.

If a gent meets these basic requirements (i.e. they can spell, look vaguely human, and avoid 'banter' and pictures of their ex and/or penis), Recent Dumpee will progress to phase two:

meeting up. Numerous studies concur with Veronica that it's good to meet sooner rather than later so you don't fall madly in love over email and then realise they look like Shrek in real life. Unless of course, Shrek works for you and you just don't know it yet. Because researchers from Northwestern University in Illinois found that, just like in the real world, online daters don't always know what they want in a mate, despite thinking they do. We have such a strong idea in our head of the 'type' of person we're after that we routinely overlook positive characteristics in people who may actually be good for us.

Resolving to keep an open mind, Recent Dumpee gets Out There to meet potential suitors IRL (in real life).

A week later, she tells me she's had coffee with an opera singer, beer with a banker and carrot juice with an Olympic rower. It's all very exciting.

'So? How did they go?' I am near bursting with vicarious date-curiosity. Date-osity, if you will.

'Not bad,' she says: 'I just thought of each of them as new people I was meeting, then if I got the fear or worried about whether they noticed the huge spot that appeared on my nose midweek, I imagined you telling me that I looked "okay" anyway . . .'

'"*Okay*"? Surely my virtual voiceover of encouragement in your head is more complimentary than that!'

'All right then, "*nice*—"'

'Try again.'

'"*Hot*"?'

'Better.'

'Right, so I imagined you telling me I looked *hot* and that I was funny and interesting and that cockwomble had his own issues and that was probably why he dumped me, and that we're all a bit mad in our own ways, but that it was going to be all right. And then – it was.'

'That's great! And were they nice guys?'

'Mostly,' she says. 'I mean, one had Robin Thicke's "Blurred Lines" as his ringtone, but you can't win them all. Right?'

'Right.'

A fortnight later she tells me she's going on a second date with someone who 'doesn't appear to be a mentalist . . .' This is progress.

Unfortunately, all is not bliss in the Russell household with work deadlines and sleepless nights (teething child + insomnia + jet lag = heady combination), so my week culminates in an almighty row with my other half over domestic arrangements, family and money. It often starts with one of these and gradually expands to include all three, which is a treat ('I hope you step on a Lego brick in bare feet!' 'You take that back!' 'I will not!'). After twenty minutes or so of simmering silence, the special cap goes on and I hear the Lemonheads starting up.

Oh God . . .

'It's time,' I tell the dog, who nods, solemnly. The hour has come to take a closer look at my own relationship to see if I can make some much-needed changes.

Impressed by the impact of CBT on my friend's dating life, I contact William Phillips, psychotherapist and director of Think CBT, an independent organisation specialising in cognitive behavioural therapy in the UK. I explain my predicament ('it's the hat I can't stand . . .') and he suggests I start by filling in the free online 'conflict questionnaire'[10] to help assess the not-so hot spots in my relationship.

This is a twenty-question multiple-choice delight where users rate how often they're guilty of things like using over-generalisations during disagreements, blaming each other when things go wrong, or using sarcasm – asking me to choose between '*Never*', '*Sometimes*', '*More often than not*' and '*Almost always*'.

I scroll right for an option that reads along the lines of '*Wait, what? There's another way?*', then get the feeling that neither my husband nor I are going to come out of this well. So I do some laundry instead, then run the Hoover around, then decide my desk needs a re-org. Finally, I get on with it and answer the questionnaire as honestly as I can bear – quickly, and in the manner of someone pulling off a sticking plaster. The results appear instantly, indicating that I may be experiencing '*moderate levels of interpersonal conflict*' in my relationship, as well as '*regular negative behaviours*' and '*increasing difficulties*' in the way my husband and I relate to each other.

By the time I speak to William, I'm nearing despair. I tell him it's as though I've just taken a quiz that's told me my life's a bit shit. He assures me that this isn't the intention and that the questionnaire just provides a basis for focusing on some of the specific behaviours that may be 'maintaining conflict' in my relationship.

'For a start, the fact you're talking about it is a really good sign. It shows the relationship is valued and worth the effort

---

10 Treat yourself, here: https://www.thinkcbt.com/couples-conflict-relationships?catid=55.

to improve. And seeking help and facilitation is not a sign of weakness in a relationship – it's a sign of commitment and a willingness to change.' He explains that far from being the beginning of the end, couples who get help tend to fare better, long-term: 'This is likely to be because they're a self-selecting group – they invest time and energy in their relationship because they care about it enough to work through problems and adapt to each other's needs.'

Okay, I tell him, I'm sold. So what do I need to do?

'Well, CBT for relationships is about working on and changing the ingrained thinking and behavioural patterns that encourage a negative tone, maintain conflict and under-mine care and affection in our relationships.' To explain further, William references the work of US psychologist and marital therapist John Gottman.

Gottman found that the success or failure of a relationship could be predicted with 90 per cent accuracy based on the presence or absence of four key behaviours, so deadly that he dubs them 'The Four Horsemen of the Apocalypse'.

'The first is criticism,' William explains, 'so attacking our partner's personality or character, often with the intent of being "right" or making the other party 'wrong". Gottman recommends a "compliments ratio" of five to every criticism made by a partner within a relationship.'

His wife must be exhausted trying to think up new ways to tell him his hair looks nice, I think.

Gottman's second horseman of the relationship apocalypse is contempt, with the third being defensiveness and the fourth stonewalling – withdrawing from a situation or discussion to avoid conflict.

Lego Man and I are guilty of at least two of these.

'Most couples fall out, often over little things,' William assures me, 'but the key to success is exercising your capacity to let go of or tolerate things that aren't relationship-defining.'

'Such as?'

'Well, let's take something simple like laundry management,' he says as a distress signal goes off in my head (*THE SOCKS GO *IN* THE BASKET! NOT *AROUND* THE BASKET – *IN* IT*). 'So if your partner annoys you by leaving dirty clothes lying around, just think of the degree to which it irritates you. Right now.'

I seethe for several seconds.

'Okay, now ask yourself: "Is this an issue I can let go of or tolerate without letting it define the tone of my relationship?" If the answer's "yes" then how is it helpful to focus on this and think about all of the negative inferences that this implies?'

'It's not,' I acquiesce, 'but why should I pick up soiled socks?'

'You shouldn't.'

'Well then . . .?'

'When you think about picking up socks, are you automatically inferring wider negative interpretations? So for example, are you presuming that leaving laundry around indicates a lack of respect?'

I haven't considered it in these terms, but when I think about it now, the answer's a resounding 'yes'.

'All right. But is there a more helpful way of seeing a situation? Can you think, "If I thought about this differently, how would I feel about it emotionally?" This isn't easy – it's a martial art of the mind that requires overlearning ingrained patterns of thinking. But it can be done. So for example, if you think, "Oh, maybe my partner did this thing because they were stressed or in a hurry, rather than because they were deliberately trying to annoy me", you can reframe the way you approach situations. If you assume realistic intent and try to understand how your partner is feeling, you're more likely to talk to them about a behaviour in an assertive yet constructive way. The trick is to catch, check and change negative ways of thinking – before they become negative thinking habits and relationship-defining behaviours.'

William explains that there are five steps in the CBT for couples process:

1. Identifying and acknowledging individual values, expectations and perceptions about the relationship.

2. Exploring triggers, negative beliefs and unhelpful behaviours.

3. Agreeing individual differences and acceptable tolerance ranges.

4. Identifying and practising new behaviours based on shared values, mutual respect, empathy, trust and tolerance.

5. Agreeing a new 'emotional contract'.

'This "contract" expresses the changes each partner commits to and forms the basis of the future relationship,' he says, 'so you're building a shared vision of your future together – overriding conflict with a willingness to respect and tolerate each other's differences.'

I tell him this sounds a bit earnest.

'It's not a binding contract with legally enforceable clauses,' he assures me. 'That would be absurd!' (*Sorry, your honour, I just got really cross about the socks . . .*') 'It's more like a verbal or written summary of your commitments towards each other and a practical basis for concluding the process of therapy.'

'Still sounds earnest . . .'

'It's okay to be serious sometimes when your relationship is at stake.'

'Um, well . . .' I have no comeback for this.

'What are you afraid of?'

'I . . .' I falter. *I don't want to turn into Weird Owl Couple!* is what I really want to say, but only manage: 'I just don't want to be someone who can't laugh at themselves and the world around them. Or a character in a US soap opera . . .'

'And I'm certainly not saying that you have to take yourself too seriously to show you care.'

'So, I'd just have to be *a little bit* earnest? Not using sarcasm all the time?'

'No. Not all the time, Helen.'

'Oh.' That's me told.

William explains that kindness is an important predictor of satisfaction and stability in a marriage, 'because this makes each partner feel cared for, understood, validated and loved.' Gratitude helps, too. Researchers at the University of Georgia found that feeling grateful and expressing gratitude is another major factor in couples who go the distance.

'Strong and enduring relationships are also defined by a shared sense of the future, a mutual understanding of each other's needs, compatible goals, and a willingness to act interdependently as well as dependently,' says William, 'and, most importantly, the willingness to flex, negotiate, adapt, tolerate and accept individual differences. Ask any long-term loving couple why they stayed together. It's always because their mutual connection was stronger than their inevitable differences.'

'This sounds like hard work,' I hear myself muttering.

'It's not about whether it is hard, it's about whether it's worth it,' he tells me, 'and it gets easier the more you do it.'

Love, it transpires, is a verb – and it's going to require some 'doing'.

In an ideal world, I'd adopt William as my live-in counsellor/wise uncle figure, but apparently this isn't how he works. Since I can't make it to his London office for weekly sessions either, I'm going to have to put his theories to the test remotely. So I search for practical exercises I can use to tackle each of William's five steps in turn.

To help with the first two: 1) identifying and acknowledging individual values, expectations and perceptions; and 2) exploring triggers, negative beliefs and unhelpful behaviours, I get in touch with Scott Symington. Scott is a square-jawed all-American jock of a psychologist, couples counsellor and CBT expert who I first got to know via Twitter (how very meta . . .). He tells me that 'faking a start-over' in an existing relationship is all about reincorporating rituals and behaviours that existed in the first flush of courtship. I don't like to mention that these rituals and behaviours consisted mainly of drinking wine and speaking in Australian/West Country accents, in our case. But fortunately, Scott has a caveat: 'The difference is, this time you'll be doing these with a real person instead of an idealised love object.'

'So not the tent-loving, permanently epilated girl and the cheerful-in-the-mornings, gymbo, *Masterchef* contestant?'

'Precisely! There are principles and helpful tools we can use to help reshape the relational dynamics and recapture the three key behaviours that quickly dissipate in the relationship after the honeymoon phase.'

'And these are?'

'Curiosity, gratitude –' *Again? Sheesh* . . . – 'and certain types of physical intimacy, like prolonged kissing, etc. We often prescribe exercises that rekindle these.'

I resist the urge to titter like a ten-year-old at the phrase 'prolonged kissing' and pull myself together.

'One exercise in particular that's simple but highly effective in jump-starting a relationship is the Loving-Action List,' Scott goes on. 'Each partner writes down the things that make him/her feel loved, respected and appreciated in the relationship. At least thirty is a good start—'

'Thirty?' This seems like an awful lot. 'That's like, an A4 side.'

'Thirty,' he repeats, firmly: 'The key is to write down concrete behaviours, like, "when he brings me a cup of coffee in the morning" or something, so there's no mystery or guesswork to the action that makes you feel loved. After the list is complete, you switch lists. Equipped with the other's list, you have in your possession concrete behaviours that make the other feel loved and these act as positive injections into the relationship.' This helps with the first step of the CBT for relationships plan: identifying and acknowledging our individual values, expectations and perceptions.

'The other thing that needs to be addressed – and a

primary reason why existing relationships aren't the way they are in the beginning – is learning how to express pain,' he adds.

I tell him I've been through childbirth and I did it loudly: 'I'm pretty good at expressing pain—'

'Not that kind,' he says, 'I'm talking emotional pain and negative emotion more generally. We all need to relearn how to express this in a vulnerable and relational way.'

'?'

'Okay, think of it this way – in the early phase of a relationship all is good with the world and any emotional pain is masked by a "fantasy filter" and the powerful feelings of love. This dynamic changes with time as we return to baseline. AKA "reality".'

'So, basically, we're so busy being in love that everything's shiny and fabulous at the start but to be in a big, grown-up relationship we need to lose the fantasy filter? Like an update of the Instagram #nofilter – a #nofantasyfilter?'

'Yes!' Scott likes this idea. 'What you both need to do, along with your love list, is be conscious of this and be honest about your emotions with a #nofantasyfilter.'

This will also help Lego Man and me explore our 'triggers', negative beliefs and unhelpful behaviours – like assuming everyone else's relationship is perfect. I think of the endless soppy sentiments and too-perfect pictures posted on social media – flooding my feeds with tsunamis of sentimentality and 'performances' of relationships that can't possibly be as amazing as they're making out. It's something that led Recent Dumpee to abandon Facebook altogether for a while, with another friend embarking on a 'cull', unfriending anyone who posts about how wonderful their other half is ('Why can't they just say it in person over breakfast?'). It seems as though a #nofantasyfilter should be applied not just to all social media, but to all social relations. I make a mental note to start using the #nofantasyfilter hashtag and thank Scott for his advice.

'Thirty things and #nofantasyfilter. We have a plan!'

Now I just need to persuade my husband.

'What's *hash tag*? Is that legal?' is how the conversation starts. I'm wiping the toddler's scrambled egg off the wall and Lego Man is raiding the fridge for a pre-dinner snack. He doesn't do any social media that originated post-2007 and once suggested sending an Instagram for a friend's wedding. He is baffled by my obsession with Twitter notifications and still thinks trending is a reference to the proliferation of skinny jeans round our way.

'The hashtag part's not important right now,' I tell him, 'it's more about being realistic and honest in the way we tell each other how we're feeling – not pretending that things are perfect when they're not. And not looking back with ugly, John Lennon-style rose-tinted spectacles or whatever.'

I realise that I also have egg down my front and what may or may not be yoghurt on the underside of my sock. I take this off and sniff it, tentatively. The toddler liberates my husband's iPhone from the kitchen table and runs away with it, cackling. Lego Man attempts to give chase with a slice of leftover quiche clamped between his teeth. I look at the clock and wonder whether it's time for wine yet (in our house, this is officially 18.00 on a weekday, in case you're wondering. I'm not a total lush . . .).

I decide that a great way to activate Scott's #nofantasyfilter might be to capture daily life on camera in all its imperfection – so that when we look back at photographs we won't assume everything was sunshine and Cadbury's Roses.

'If we only ever take pictures where we're smiling, we won't remember the bad times or know how to handle them when they come around again – we won't have proof that things are never perfect but that we always survive,' I explain to Lego Man.

'So we take pictures of the shit stuff?' is how he puts it.

'Essentially . . . *yes*.'

Wresting the iPhone from our son's vice-like grip, I flick on the camera function and record, for all time, the moment when quiche is smashed into my husband's face by an angry redhead, puce with rage, teeth bared in outrage at having 'his toy' confiscated.

'There, look.' I show my husband the photograph, once he's cleared enough congealed egg from his glasses to see again: '*That's* family life.'

'Great . . .'

After supper and over ice cream, to soften him up for the next challenge, I bring up Scott's idea of the 'thirty things' list.

'Thirty?' My husband temporarily stops ladling super-market own-brand strawberry (we save the good stuff for visitors) into his mouth. 'As in three zero?'

'I know—'

He drops his spoon into the bowl with a clatter: 'That's an A4 side!'

'That's what I said!'

Perhaps, I think, *we're perfectly compatible after all. Maybe we don't need to bother with any of this . . .*

'Then do we do a list of thirty things we *don't* like about each other?'

. . . Or perhaps not.

'No!'

He looks deflated.

'Come on, it won't take long,' I say, optimistically, putting the lid on the ice cream tub and wondering what position '*saving the good ice cream for visitors*' would be on his list of '*Things I Don't Like About My Wife*'.

The kitchen table is still groaning with toddler detritus – wet wipes, kitchen roll, bibs and discarded spoons, mostly – so we decamp to the 'office', AKA 'the corner of the living room with the least kid crap in it where we've crammed in two desks'.

I begin retrieving paper and pens and lay out a single sheet and a 0.7 Staedtler pigment liner on his desk. This, to me, is love: we both know that the 0.7 Staedtler pigment liner is the best pen in the house. I am, selflessly, letting him use the 0.7 Staedtler pigment liner while I resort to an inferior unbranded ballpoint.

'Off we go!' I say, as cheerfully as I can manage.

We sit with our backs to each other (Tetris style; the only way we could fit two desks in), and there is total silence. Or at least, there would be but for the dog panting heavily, adding a horror-film-esque tension to the already strained proceedings.

The next ten minutes is like an elaborate game of Grandmother's Footsteps on IKEA swivel chairs, as each of us tries to have a nose at what the other has written.

'*How specific should we be?*' I tap out an email to Scott surreptitiously.

'*Very,*' is his response. So I kick off with:

1. *The time you rolled socks on to my feet in bed because you said they felt cold* (I suspect that this was because he didn't want my icy size fours tucked under his calves, keeping him awake. But at the time, in that fog of pre-sleep lethargy, I was immeasurably grateful.)

2. *When you make me a frothy coffee from the machine with all the fiddly bits and then sprinkle cocoa on top like a proper barista*

3. *How you try to keep me in those miniature bottles of wine that you get on aeroplanes* (This delights me more than you might imagine because I a) am a lightweight and b) like to pretend I'm a giant/bigger than 5'3" or having a dolls' tea party with tiny wine.)

4. *When you save me the chocolate they leave on your pillow in the fancy hotels you stay at for work* (I used to stay in fancy hotels for work before I started slumming it as a freelancer and miss the experience terribly.)

I continue in a similar vein but by number nine it occurs to me that the majority of mine are food and drink related. *Perhaps I should have eaten more before starting this*, I think. *Perhaps writing a 'what I like about my partner' list after a relatively light supper is the relationship equivalent of going to the supermarket on an empty stomach . . .*

'Is your hand hurting?' Lego Man asks after fifteen minutes. 'My hand's really hurting . . .' He shakes the hand holding the 0.7 Staedtler pigment liner. I tell him that mine hurts too. Both of us are so unused to writing cursively that we're experiencing something akin to the 'exam-hand cramps' I remember from school. Then, I could write half a dozen pages on four-crop rotation, oxbow lakes, or *Othello* before the tingly/achy/spasm feeling kicked in. Now, half a side of A4 has broken me.

Extending the lists to thirty takes us an age. The dog gives up and goes to bed and we break out snacks. But by 10.30 p.m., each of us is holding aloft a sheet of white paper in our hands, Neville Chamberlain style.

We exchange lists and spend some time frowning in concentration as we try to decipher each other's barely legible scrawl. At the top of his list is:

1. *I like it when you're happy and in a good mood in the morning*

'Aren't I always in a good mood in the mornings?' I have spent thirty-five years believing that I am a morning person. A lark. A Pollyanna-in-the-a.m. Have I been living a lie all this time?

'Well . . .' He hesitates, 'it's just that if you haven't slept well you get grumpy.'

Bugger. This is true. If I'm not getting seven hours a night, I'm hopeless. And I'm often not getting seven hours a night. *I need to do something about that.* His list goes on:

2. *I like it when you come running with me*

3. *I like it when you exercise just generally . . .*

I look up from the list and ask, suspiciously: 'Are you calling me fat?'

'No! But you're . . . nicer when you've done exercise. You go all hyper. Even if you don't like doing it at the time. And I like the way you look when you've been exercising . . .'

This is generous: I am not an attractive sweater. I tend to go deathly pale and clammy rather than taking on anything resembling a healthy glow. In addition to this, my running style has been described as 'flailing' (twice, by independent reviewers), and I have zero hand–eye coordination. I do not look hot working out. I've also never thought I was much cop as a running partner as I can't talk – or, often, *breathe* – while doing it.

Since parenthood, my exercise regime has been restricted to 'darting around after a small child' and as long as I fit into my clothes, I've been resigned to this. I know all about the mental and physical benefits of exercise – I've written about them often enough. But at some stage I appear to have stopped putting them into practice.

4. *I like it when we talk through work problems*

I'm touched by this one since we work in very different industries and I'm not hugely knowledgeable about his area of expertise, nor he mine. So the idea that I can be of use and that he values my input – as well as the fact that he doesn't mind helping me out with various quandaries – is comforting.

As the list progresses, I notice that all of the things he likes about me tend to be behaviours, whereas mine are often more tangible. I seem to feel the greatest love for him when

94

there are refreshments involved or he does something considerate to keep me warm in some way.

But there are more useful ones, too – I like it when he's spent time with his friends, because it makes him jollier and so better to be around. Ditto spending time outdoors (hello, Lemonheads!).

Mini-bottles of wine and pillow chocolates may not be a sustainable blueprint for a relationship, but Scott's homework has been helpful in terms of giving us both a written template for ways we can express affection. And being conscious of how my sleep quality or failure to exercise impacts on our relationship has been a wake-up call. When we first met, I made an effort to conceal any irritability and was certainly exercising more. Hiding my tiredness or less-than-upbeat feelings is a perfect example of Scott's fantasy filter. The gloss of a new relationship made everything seem okay, on the surface. But now, seven years in, it's time to go #nofilter – and tackle the grumps.

We each pin our thirty-things lists up above our desks, underneath various life-admin flotsam so that visitors don't get an eyeful of the innermost machinations of our marriage. And we try to take photographs documenting the lows as well as the highs of family life.

Next it's time to tackle points three and four on my CBT-for-relationships gameplan: 3) agreeing individual differences and acceptable tolerance ranges; and 4) practising new behaviours based on shared values, mutual respect, empathy, trust and tolerance.

Clinical psychologist Dr Harriet Lerner has an interesting exercise to help Lego Man and me behave better and practise more mutual respect and tolerance. In her book, *Marriage*

Rules: A Manual for the Married and Coupled Up, Harriet outlines 100 'rules' for improving the state of a relationship and it's #43 that catches my eye – advising couples to pretend they have a houseguest in the spare room. Harriet explains how she once counselled a couple who were constantly at each other's throats until a colleague, an esteemed professor, came to live with them for a few weeks. He stayed in the room next to theirs and the couple were so mindful of being overheard that they didn't row for the duration of his stay – and were the nicest they'd ever been to each other. *'I'm not actually suggesting the reader move someone in,'* Harriet clarifies over email when I get in touch to find out more: *'I'm saying people have a lot more control over their bad behaviour than they think they do.'* Which sounds promising. So could pretending we have a respected guest staying work for us?

That night, I explain the idea to Lego Man – who turns out to be surprisingly game.

'Great!' I say. 'So who should we have?'

'Do we have to agree on one?' he asks.

I'm not sure about this.

'Because,' he goes on, 'I just think we might have different ideas about the kind of person we want to be on our best behaviour for.'

'Ri-ght . . .'

'I think we should each choose.'

'Okay—'

'Me first: Jimmy Stewart.'

'What?'

'Off of *Harvey*!'

I'm about to tell him it should be 'from' rather than 'off of' but then remember the point about the criticisms and the fact that I've already spent mine for the day. At breakfast. After which I hastily reeled off five compliments to balance this out, John Gottman style: 'Erm, I like your green jumper and these waffles you're making smell delicious and have you been working out?' etc. He told me I'd used the green jumper one already and was going to have to try harder. So now, I try to point out, just gently, that the special houseguest doesn't have to be anyone famous: 'just someone we'd want to be polite in front of.'

But Lego Man is resolute: 'I want James Stewart circa *Harvey*. I'd definitely be on my best behaviour if we had him next door.'

'So you want our imaginary guest to be an imaginary character who had an imaginary friend?'

'Or was he just *invisible*?' Lego Man challenges. I fix him with a steady gaze. 'James Stewart was in *It's a Wonderful Life*!' he adds, as though I must surely now appreciate the appropriateness of his choice. I can't argue with logic like this.

'In that case, I choose Joan Collins.' Always. No matter what the question.

'Okay, so Joan and Jimmy are next door,' he says, 'or should I have James Bond—'

'Sorry?'

'Instead of JS . . .'

I do some 'patient breathing'.

'Which iteration of Bond would you be opting for?' I'm hoping he'll go with Daniel Craig. I could handle having Daniel Craig in the bedroom, so to speak. But no.

'Timothy Dalton, *Licence to Kill*.'

'Right . . .'

'When he dresses up as a manta ray.'

There are no words.

'You know! He disguises himself as a manta ray to infiltrate Krest's ship!'

'So you would like us to pretend that we have Joan Collins and Manta Ray Bond in our spare bedroom?'

'Yes. Or Jimmy Stewart.'

'Which one?'

'Umm . . .' He looks genuinely torn.

'Come on *Sophie's Choice*.'

'Both. Sorry, I need both: they're like the yin and yang of modern masculinity!'

I've never heard such nonsense but unless I get an IOU for the rest of the week's worth of criticism, I'm going to have to button it.

We go to bed soon after this, so the first opportunity to employ our relationship Charlie's Angels doesn't come until the following morning when there is a dispute over whose turn it was to give the dog his tick medicine (because nothing says 'I love you' like Lyme disease).

'I did the last one!' he says through a mouthful of Grape Nuts.

'No, that was the month before!'

We go on in this bent, slowly taking in other regular chores that we're never sure which of us is doing when, like car tax or paying the nursery bill. The dog's eyes swivel from one of us to the other like a spectator at a tennis match as we debate his medicinal fate. The toddler cackles and smears Weetabix in his hair.

Imaginary Joan Collins stands with her arms folded over a white silk pussy-bow blouse and observes the whole scene with disdain. Imaginary Manta Ray Bond checks out imaginary Joan's shapely calves and flaps his imitation-pectoral fins in a manner implying appreciation. I worry that we have chosen our imaginary houseguests poorly. But then imaginary Jimmy Stewart puts his trilby on, crouches down between us until he's at eye level and says in his distinctive drawl: 'Well now you two, what are we fighting for? We're all on the same side here, aren't we? We all want the dog –' here he pops the mutt a salute – 'the boy –' he winks at the toddler – 'and each other to be happy and healthy! Right?'

'Right.' My husband nods, humbled.

'Yes, Jimmy,' I mumble.

'So how should we go about fixing this? Who'd like to get us started with an idea?'

'Um, I suppose . . .' I start, keen to prove to Jimmy that we are, in fact, civilised human beings. 'We could write it on the calendar, so that we know who's doing what each month?'

Jimmy places an arm round me. *Bit familiar, Jim,* I think, but keep quiet.

'Well now, doesn't that sound like a great idea?' He's addressing Lego Man, who's now smiling at his pin-up, beatifically. Joan adjusts her shoulder pads and Manta Ray Bond does a celebratory lap of the kitchen. And suddenly, all is well with the world.

The next time our peacekeeping triumvirate come to the fore is the following day. It's Saturday and we have a lunch date that we're already running late for. I am tired. My husband is hungover. The toddler has molars coming through and is mad as hell about it. The car keys are nowhere to be found[11]

---

11 Lego Man had them last, just FYI. I always know where everything is. It's one of my superpowers.

and we're not sure of the postcode of where we're headed, so the satnav is denying all knowledge of its existence. One of us is going to have to map-read. It's a perfect storm.

And yet . . .

No one has raised their voice, flared their nostrils or sighed too loudly in a passive-aggressive manner for at least fifteen minutes. Joan is filing her nails.

'So you'll be fashionably late.' She waves an emery board dismissively. 'Take champagne and no one will mind.' I tell her we have prosecco in the fridge. Joan raises an arched eyebrow and says it will have to do. Manta Ray Bond is helping my husband track down the keys by pretending it's some sort of spy game, which, in turn, is keeping my husband from losing his cool. James Stewart is expressing wonderment at the invention of satellite navigation, turning the black plastic rectangle over and over in his hands and murmuring to himself: 'Well this is just . . . *fantastic*!'

Joan and I roll our eyes in unison and I think this might be the start of a beautiful relationship.

We arrive at lunch, late, a raggle-taggle crew of two tired parents, one sticky toddler and a scruffy dog. But we are smiling. And holding hands, like we used to, when we started out. And we've made it to a social occasion within an hour of the stated time and without a single threat of divorce.

The fifth step of the CBT for couples plan involves agreeing a new 'emotional contract' for our relationship. *This*, I steel myself, *is where shit gets earnest*. So what should our agreement entail?

Moving will be a fresh start for us, and I want to be with Lego Man for a very long time, so I'm committed to making this work. I want to try being less critical and more tolerant (even in the face of sock-gate). I will also keep making an effort, because even though we're unlikely to be like coffee-shop couple again, we can still try.

I share these thoughts with Lego Man and am moved to discover he's been working on his own idea of our future together.

'So basically,' he starts, 'I want to climb mountains with you and go on adventures and go to concerts and try to understand opera and drink wine and argue over dinner when we're seventy.'

I'm blown away.

He and I don't talk like this usually (see 'slush-allergy') – but there's more, too: 'And I want a nice home together where I can build you a special office shed, where you can escape and read for as long as you want and no one will bother you.'

I feel a lump rising in my throat. 'That's the *nicest thing* you've ever said to me!'

'You're welcome.' He nods, a little shy at this outpouring, and flicks the kettle on.

'Even nicer than when you sent me an iTunes gift card for Adele's "Hello"!'

'Good,' he says, pulling out a couple of mugs. I want to offer him something in return, to show my appreciation and reciprocate in kind. *But how to repay the promise of a limit-less-reading shed?* I wonder. Then it hits me.

'I promise I'll try camping again.'

Cups clatter to the kitchen surface as kettle steam fills the kitchen, like we're in an atmospheric railway farewell scene from an old film.

'Camping? Really?'

I can just about make out Lego Man's expression of joy through the localised fog.

'Really.'

'That's amazing! And will this work for your contract thing?' he asks.

'It's perfect,' I tell him. 'Where do I sign?'

Things I've learned about making a leap in your love life:

---

1. Romcoms are officially bad for our health/love life/sanity.

2. We all need to apply a #nofantasyfilter to our romantic lives.

3. Forget about finding 'The One': it's about choosing 'A One' and working at it.

4. Compliments trump criticisms; no one's deliberately out to 'get' anyone else; being kind goes a long way; and walking off is never the answer.

5. A Neville Chamberlain-style list can tell us a lot about ourselves and our other halves.

6. An imaginary James Stewart (or Bond) is a professionally sanctioned relationship tool.

7. It's important to be a little more earnest when it comes to making a relationship last.

CHAPTER THREE

BODY

Keep On Rucking

In which I eat to reduce telomere shortening; get a DNA diet prescription; learn how HIT can counter sarcopenia; try US military rucking; submit to 1950s style callipers; and discover that Prochaska's transtheoretical addiction programme might help me make changes – for good

'The problem with your face –' The doctor prods at me with the non-business end of a Biro – 'is that it's too . . .' He frowns, or at least attempts what I presume once resembled a frown: '. . . *expressive*'. He says the word with something approaching contempt as I stare miserably into one of those magnifying mirrors that make your pores look like the surface of the moon. There are lines around my eyes and mouth that weren't there a few years ago and they're only getting more pronounced. It seems that a lifetime of lip-synching to Tina Turner, hard, is finally catching up with me.

I'm also tired, hungover and – more significantly, perhaps – about to turn thirty-six. I feel old and tired and I want to see if there's anything I can do to make the 'new' me any more youthful. I've become increasingly alert to the ageing process over the past few years and I'm interested in whether there's anything we can do to reverse this – to start again in our existing bodies, or at least look and feel younger. Because my face and body are no longer those of a nineteen-year-old, worse luck.

On a good day, I don't frighten small children and can coerce my features into something resembling 'a human lady face' with the aid of make-up and steely determination. But on a normal day I can feel myself starting to become invisible. Last night I was out with a younger, thinner, prettier friend and realised that, for the majority of the male population, I was in the way – an inconvenient obstacle in the eyeline of all those who wanted to gaze upon her. And on a bad day? I occasionally resemble a hard-boiled egg.

My hair doesn't 'bounce' any more without the aid of some serious product, and while I used to rock the unbrushed boho look a lot of the time, this now makes me look like Medusa. This morning, my 'do' is 50 per cent dry shampoo thanks to a late night and an inability to locate any of the wet variety. Oh, and I currently have an eye twitch like the baddie from the Pink Panther films. It wasn't the best day to interview a plastic surgeon for work.

I'm sitting in the consulting room of a Harley Street clinic for an assignment I took on before my policy of saying 'no' to things that don't 'align with my values' kicked in. No sooner had I unfurled a spiral-bound notebook than Dr Franken-mean, as he shall henceforth be known, started suggesting 'procedures' I might like to consider. So I take this as my cue to begin tackling the next thing on my 'new beginnings checklist': my physical form in all its flawed glory.

I already know a little about surgery and 'procedures' from

being a journalist and a Real Life Woman in the twenty-first century. Colleagues and friends have had 'work'. Many swear by Botox or fillers and two have had nose jobs, only to discover that all the life-angst they had hitherto attributed to their less-than-perfect bridges still existed post-rhinoplasty. Years of therapy ensued in both cases.

Last week I visited a shiny-faced friend who'd recently Botoxed and when she opened the door, I had to check: 'You did say *three* o'clock . . . didn't you?' because she looked so astonished to see me. While we were drinking coffee, her two children started fighting and New Face Friend told them off. They laughed at first, then looked confused:

'Are you . . . angry with us, Mummy?'

'Yes! Of course I'm angry with you!'

'Oh, okay . . .'

They hadn't been able to tell from the subtle change in her expression.

We live in an age where beauty is line-free and a 'good' body for women is that of a twelve-year-old boy with boobs. For men, it's a hard-muscled Adonis/Hemsworth brother with a chiselled jaw, killer cheekbones and a winning smile. But even Victoria's Secret models and Hemsworths don't look that good without serious work (and, often, 'work').

I'm aware that I'm currently getting a hard sell from a private plastic surgeon who was only supposed to give me a few quotes for a feature. I know that I shouldn't let it get to me. But it turns out I'm as susceptible to a facial-critique-slash-body-shaming-combo as the next girl. And it doesn't feel good.

'First we need to address the lines.' Dr Franken-mean circles my head to indicate that these are 'all over' before bringing the Biro back to bear on more specific failings. 'So these laughter lines –' he prods at the sides of my mouth – 'are fairly pronounced . . .' *That's because I've found much of life pretty funny – until now*, I want to shout. 'And I can tell you sleep on your left side because of the lines around your eyes and mouth there.' Maddeningly, he's right: I slept on my back until pregnancy, when I was advised to try the left side, and now it's a habit I can't kick. I've been using silk pillowcases, which I'd hoped were helping (Lego Man sleeps on seersucker and wakes up looking like a teabag most mornings) but clearly there's room for improvement. 'Then I'd go for some filler around your lips and of course Botox around the brow creases and frown lines.' *Of course . . .* 'There's also this . . .' He mimes on himself a big Santa-style beard. I do not have a big Santa beard. 'As we age our skin cells die and they can become dry and, well, yellow.'

'*Yellow?*'

'Uh-huh.' He nods and scribbles something with his Biro. Probably '*Fix big yellow Santa beard*'. 'A series of chemical peels should sort this out,' he informs me, before adding: 'Now, have you thought about your neck?'

I have not thought about my neck, but apparently I've only got ten good years left in it.

'If you wanted, I could refer you to someone for dental work, too.'

My jaw, I learn, is narrower than most and reconstructing it would give me a fuller, younger-looking face.

'With surgery and braces, it would only take about two years in total.'

'*Two years?*'

He nods.

'I don't think I can spare two years,' I bleat, feebly.

'Okay then –' he continues to scan me for flaws – 'implants?'

My hands move involuntarily to my breasts, 'No! Thanks . . .'

'Shall we look at your thighs?' he offers as I begin to gather my coat around me.

Liposuction is the second most common surgical body modification[12] and as the possessor of a pair of sizeable thighs, this has always been the 'procedure' I've been most conscious of. The one that might appeal in a parallel, pain-free and more gender-equal society where women weren't so valued for their looks, in which case I probably wouldn't care about the size of my legs anyway. But I've recently been further put off the idea by research from the University of Colorado Anschutz Medical Campus proving that fat removed by liposuction typically returns, to a different part of the body, *within a year*. What's more, there's no knowing where this will be. Can you imagine how stressful that must be? Just waiting to see where all your fat has chosen to have a reunion? It could be anywhere (*'Oh Helen, your thighs look marvellously slim – but you appear to be morphing into a camel . . .'*).

I politely decline the offer of liposuction.

'How about your knees? We can do great things for knee fat these days . . .'

I've got fat knees? I can honestly say I have never worried about the appearance of my knees, but now Dr Franken-mean is telling me in forensic detail about a fat-digesting enzyme that will set me back £900 and leave me with swelling and bruising 'for about a week'.

---

12 The first is breasts. Still. In 2016 . . . *facepalm*.

'Maybe another time . . .'

'All right,' he says, as though I'm a fool not to take up his offer: 'So when should we book you in for the peel?'

'Well . . .' I stall, 'isn't there, I don't know, some sort of cream that might help?'

He laughs.

I leave. Painful and expensive 'modifications' may be increasingly normalised, but surgery and Botox are not for me.

On my way home I read up on the physical and psychological impact of surgery. A 2013 study found that most people who opted for facial surgery hoped it would make them look at least a decade younger, but the average number of virtual years shaved off is in fact just three. Going under the knife can't make us look significantly younger. Numerous studies have shown a high prevalence of body dysmorphic disorder and other mental health problems among people who have undergone cosmetic surgery, and there's even a heightened risk of suicide among women following breast augmentation. So going under the knife doesn't make us happy, either.

But is there another way that I can make changes to look and feel better? I wonder, as I settle down back at my desk on Monday morning. *Is there ever a healthy, happy way we can start over when it comes to our bodies?*

'Doubt it,' Lego Man sniffs as he reads the sentence I've just typed, over my shoulder. I hate it when he does this.

'You're hovering!'

'Sorry!' He backs away from the laptop. 'Actually, there is something. What about those things . . . "Tia-something" . . . like Tia Maria . . .' He whips out his phone and starts

Googling. Lego Man went out with a doctor for years and so, in his words, 'knows stuff' – exuding a bullish confidence that belies his lack of formal training. 'I'll find it and send it to you,' he says before continuing his daily pre-work game of 'hunt the matching sock'.

'Telomeres!!!' an email subject line pops up moments later, sent from the next room via cyberspace. I read, intrigued, and learn that telomeres (*'pronounced "tea-lo-mears" – like they rhyme with Ray Mears,'* Lego Man has added) are tiny structures that safeguard the ends of our chromosomes (*'a bit like the cap on a felt tip pen that stops it drying out,'* Lego Man helpfully notes). These protective lids prevent the loss of genetic information during cell division but as we age, our telomeres get shorter. This tells cells to stop dividing and die, leading to illness and degeneration. But – and here's the science part – the rate of telomere shortening can be decreased by lifestyle factors, like not smoking or drinking too much and, significantly, diet.

'This is great!' I call out, 'I can *eat* myself younger!' In a burst of enthusiasm I make the mistake of asking The Internet about 'anti-ageing foods' and within seconds I'm overwhelmed by a wealth of woo, bad science and conflicting advice about what might turn back the clock and make me healthier.

I read that coffee will simultaneously reduce my risk of diabetes and cardiovascular diseases and *give* me heart disease; that bacon is as bad for me as plutonium; how chocolate cake for breakfast can help me maintain a healthy weight; and that cheese may improve gut heath but is also essentially morphine (dairy crack: the new MDMA). That's just for starters. Yoghurt can fend off social anxiety ('I'll be at the party soon, I just need to mainline a *Müller Light* first . . .'); champagne prevents dementia (but only if I'm a rat); and red wine is as good for me as exercise. On reading this, I drink as much of it as I can before they change their minds (which they do – by Friday, when 'wine face' becomes a thing and I learn that a glass-a-night habit will age me as much as smoking). Given the inclination to keep going, I could read that every conceivable household item was both the cure for cancer and its root cause in the space of a week. This is because headlines like *Drinking ten cups of coffee may make you feel peculiar, but then again, it might not* or *Bread: better for you than lard* don't make great clickbait or sell newspapers[13].

As well as contradictory reports about what's 'good' for us, we're currently in the grip of 'clean eating' fever. There are 31 million Instagram posts hashtagged *#eatclean* and books on ditching dairy or gluten top the bestseller lists. If I see one more stock photograph of a girl laughing at salad, I may open a vein. Romaine lettuce has never made me ROFL, but I've eaten my fair share of so-called 'dirty' food, in secret, to the drumbeat of guilt. I'm not immune to the lure of a fad, either, as Lego Man can testify from The Week I Gave Up Dairy (And Was Miserable).

'Here's your rank coffee,' he'd announced, handing me a cup that looked as though it contained the scum from a polluted river: 'Almond milk doesn't froth well in a latte, as it turns out.'

---

13 Anyone curious to know more about whether the latest study they're reading is true can look at Behind the Headlines on NHS Choices – where *actual* medical folks dissect the news for *actual* proof.

'Mmm.' I tried to make vaguely positive noises.

'How do you milk an almond, anyway?' Lego Man looked concerned, unable to take his eyes off the pond scum.

'I think you do something messy with a muslin.'

'Oh.'

Neither of us had any intention of finding out. To paraphrase Shirley Conran: 'Life's too short to milk an almond.' Unfortunately, the river-scum latte tasted worse than it looked. I tried black coffee instead, but discovered that I don't really like coffee enough to drink it in its naked state.

'It just feels as though I'm carrying it for someone else – a *grown-up*,' I told Lego Man, looking at the sad mug of black water in my hand.

'Before you go denying yourself anything, don't you think it's worth checking first? You know, with an actual medical professional?'

'Other than you, you mean?'

'Other than me.' He nodded, as though gratified to have his years of medical-training-by-ex-girlfriend-osmosis properly recognised. I promised to consult a professional before attempting any more diet alterations and Lego Man shared his delicious cow-latte with me.

The British Dietetic Association warns against cutting out food groups without medical advice because increasing numbers of us are risking nutrient deficiency. Which is insane. Orthorexia, the obsession with healthy eating, now accounts for 50 per cent of eating disorders in the UK, according to the charity Beat. More and more friends have become exasperating to cater for as they follow the latest restrictive diet – sorry, '*wellness plan*', and meals out now involve a forensic analysis of the menu for 'forbidden foods' as well as lengthy interrogations of beleaguered waiting staff.

So to guide me through the crazy, I sidestep legions of unqualified nutritionists telling us what *not* to eat and seek out registered dietitian Leo Pemberton. We arrange to meet in his London office when I'm next in town and I ask him first off for his take on the 'clean eating' movement. There is eye-rolling and I decide I like him already.

'Don't get me started!' he says. 'Just because a beautiful blogger says she felt better after cutting out dairy and gluten, it doesn't mean that dairy and gluten are "bad". She was pretty and rich before she stopped eating bread: she's the same now. Other people can eat all the veg they like and they still won't have her life or look like her.' I love a good rant of a morning and Leo has plenty more where this came from: 'A lot of these bloggers are obsessed with coconut oil as this new miracle food – people even add a tablespoon or two to their coffee. Retch!'

Leo is way more fun than Dr Franken-mean, I think.

'But coconut oil is a saturated fat – up to ninety-two per cent – and it pushes up your bad cholesterol as well as your good cholesterol. I have a gripe with the phrase "clean eating" because it makes everything else seem dirty. And food shouldn't be about shame: it's just food, and it's mostly fine. Telling people to adopt a really stripped-back diet that may not be right for them and then telling them to spend money on supplements to make up for all the missing nutrients just doesn't make sense. And besides, we're all busy – who has time to sprinkle twelve different superfood powders and bee pollen on their breakfast? With any new wonder food – chia, goji berries, unicorn balls . . . I won't jump on the bandwagon if the claims simply don't add up. I need to see the evidence.'

Leo tells me he spends a lot of time mythbusting and reassuring the worried well that a healthy body isn't necessarily going to look like the kind you see on the catwalks. 'Many women carry weight on their hips, bums and thighs,' he says, 'and if you're a classic pear, you're not going to change your body shape. That's how you're made.' *Oh.* 'There are good things about being a pear-shape – you're more likely to be at a lower risk of both type-2 diabetes and heart disease if you carry weight away from your middle. Apple-shaped people need to be more aware of the risks associated as more fat can accumulate around the vital organs.' So great for me, not so good for my thin-thighed comrades. This health malarkey is very much swings and roundabouts.

'It's also harder to lose weight as we get older because our metabolism changes – we need fewer calories, but most of us carry on eating as we always have,' says Leo. This may explain why a fifth of the UK population are on some form of diet at any one time, yet our waistlines continue to expand an inch every decade. Dieting is big business and the average dieter will have a bookshelf or Kindle crammed with different regimes that they've tried and given up on – because most don't work, long-term. Oprah Winfrey, God love her, has been yo-yo dieting since 1988. If it were possible to *pay* to get thin and stay that way, she'd have done it. But she hasn't, because she can't. And if Oprah can't do it, what hope do the rest of us have? As with the food intolerance industry and clean-eating buzz, we're being sold things to make other people money – not to make ourselves feel any better or get healthier.

So what should we be eating?

'In a word? Mediterranean,' says Leo. I tell him I was hoping for something snazzier. He apologises: 'It's not new or exciting but a diet rich in fruits, vegetables, low-fat dairy, fish, nuts and pulses with only small quantities of processed foods and added sugar has been shown time and again to help reduce the risk factors for chronic disease.' It's also, apparently, the best diet for our telomeres, according to a study in the *British Medical Journal*. Leo shows me a few examples of 'food plate' models from around the globe and enthuses about the US version – a circular plate divided into four, with the largest segment set aside for vegetables, a slightly smaller section for grains, a smaller one still for protein and the remainder dedicated to fruit, with a side order of dairy (*cow-latte-loving air punch!*). 'This is intended to illustrate the five food groups that are the building blocks for a healthy diet,' he says. But judging by the latest OECD obesity figures, everyone in the US ignores this – just as we do in the UK[14].

I study the rudimentary non-pie chart and tell Leo that I eat all these things anyway, just with a fair wedge of chocolate and several baked goods on the side. He asks what time I first reach for chocolate in the morning and I plan to lie until I open my mouth and somehow admit the truth: 8 a.m.

Leo makes an admirable attempt not to look surprised before suggesting that an increase in wholegrain carbs at breakfast might stop sugar cravings later and that I might

---

14 The latest OECD stats on obesity worldwide show that Americans are still 'winning' this race, but Brits are catching up in eighth place.

like to think about upping my lean protein intake. This sounds simpler than I'd feared and feels achievable.

'What about youth-boosting supplements?' I ask, 'are they all nonsense too?'

'A lot of them, yes – some people benefit from vitamin D in the UK as we don't get the right UV spectrum October through March and only ten per cent is obtained by diet. Zinc has been shown to help shorten the duration of colds. A fish oil supplement can help for those who don't like eating oily fish. But that's about it for most people.'

And anything we should never touch, ever?

'The only things I try to avoid are fizzy drinks – there's nothing of nutritional value in there so I just have them occasionally as a mixer.' I'm relieved to hear gin and tonic isn't off the cards. 'And juices and smoothies, because you're breaking down the fibre so although the vitamins and minerals remain, you're drinking a large amount of sugar.'

'That's it?'

'That's it. Most other things have at least some nutritional value – even cake: there's eggs and flour and fat in that. I bake regularly. You just need to view cakes or pastries as an occasional treat rather than something to be consumed multiple times a day.'

I worry about whether my willpower will be up to the 'occasional' part and explain how my son is currently a sleep refusenik.

'Sugar and coffee are my major food groups . . .'

'That's tough,' he commiserates. 'If you're only getting four or five hours' sleep a night, you will be drawn to higher-calorie foods, caffeine and fat. Hunger is often confused with thirst or tiredness or emotion.'

'Yes! Half the time I don't know if I need a cuddle, a catnap or a KitKat.'

Leo recommends wholegrain carbohydrates instead.

'Right. Yes. Good.'

I thank him and leave, feeling slightly better. My current diet is *okay*. I may have thighs that resemble seal pups in skinny jeans, but maybe that's just me. How I'm made. And if I can up my wholegrains and protein and lay off the sugar, I might have more energy, too.

Scientists at Princeton University in the US found that the chemicals released by sugar consumption induce the same brain activity as heroin. It's officially an addictive substance and I am currently caught in its glucosey grip. The World Health Organization recommends that we reduce our daily intake of sugar to less than 10 per cent of our total energy intake. A further reduction to below 5 per cent – roughly 25 grams (six teaspoons) a day – may offer additional health benefits, such as fewer dental caries[15]. So if I want a quantum leap, nutritionally speaking, the daily pastry habit along with a near obscene daily intake of chocolate should perhaps be reined in.

Researchers from Tel Aviv University found that attempting to avoid sweets entirely can create a psychological addiction to them in the long term, and Tim Spector, Professor of

---

15 Experts can't be sure what benefits there might be to reducing our sugar intake to six teaspoons a day, since nobody's curbed their enthusiasm for the sweet stuff this degree since just after WWII, when there was a shortage and Starbucks venti white chocolate mocha with whipped cream (eighteen teaspoons of sugar per serving, in case you're curious) hadn't been invented yet.

Genetic Epidemiology at King's College, discovered that our 'good' gut microbes enjoy eating the polyphenols in dark chocolate, which may keep us slim. Luckily, I love the stuff so dark it makes you flinch and so I valiantly resolve *not* to give up chocolate (because of SCIENCE . . .). But I will try to eat less sugar.

I have a sneaking suspicion that I should probably do some exercise, too, if I want to revamp my body. My relationship love list taught me that exercise may have a positive effect on my mood – and my marriage. I just need to find a way to incorporate it into my life. Right now, things wobble that shouldn't and just yesterday my son performed his customary run-and-fling-arms-around-Mama's-legs routine before finishing it off with a chubby-fingered poke at the soft, fleshy part of my stomach and a 'Poop! Poop!' noise.

Muscle strength starts to decline from the age of twenty and post-thirty-five, we lose between 0.5–1.5 per cent muscle mass and gain half a kilogram of fat every year. After sixty, muscle mass loss is accelerated and we lose between two and three per cent annually. This is known as sarcopenia, which, despite sounding a lot like a baddie from *Harry Potter*, refers to loss of skeletal muscle mass with ageing. It means we need to work harder to stay in shape as we get older, as well as consuming fewer calories. Yes, life is THIS unfair. A study from Toronto's York University even found that a forty-year-old could do more exercise than a twenty-year-old and still wouldn't achieve the same results.

But there is hope. Actual Science shows that working out with weights in high-intensity training – or HIT – can counter sarcopenia (Roth, Ferrel & Hurley, 2000), help prevent type-2 diabetes (according to the American Heart Association), improve aerobic fitness and boost overall health and so healthy life expectancy (according to McMaster University in Ontario, Canada, and the University of Bath, UK). Average *life* expectancy in the UK is eighty, but healthy life expectancy is just sixty-four years old. So that's sixteen years that most of us will be knocking around with 'hurty bits' or suffering from chronic illness – unless we work on our muscles, now.

Stronger muscles also improve posture, helping us stand tall and counteracting the other not-so-cheery side-effect of ageing: shrinkage. My family are small anyway. If we factor in sarcopenia we'll be Borrowers in ten years' time – so I need to do something. There are various forms of HIT that can be done either at home or in a gym, and completing eight to ten exercises in fifteen repetitions twice a week can apparently yield results in a fortnight. I learn that repetitions of squats, press-ups, lunges, side push-ups, tricep dips, bridges, leg raises and The Superman (lying face down with arms and legs extended and raised) to failure – i.e. until I can't do any more – could just sort me out.

I'm interested in whether I can soup up my everyday activity as well and so get in touch with Adam Campbell, fitness director for *Men's Health* magazine in the US. Adam has a master's degree in exercise physiology and is an NSCA-certified strength and conditioning coach. He's also, helpfully, the friend of a friend, and when he hears that I'm researching his specialist subject, informs me that the number-one fitness trend in 2015 was something called 'rucking'. This is an exercise inspired by the US military and simply means marching or walking briskly while wearing a loaded rucksack. While soldiers 'ruck' up to forty kilometres with a pack that weighs ninety kilos, the rest of us can triple the calorie burn of a thirty-minute walk by adding the equivalent of ten per cent of our bodyweight to a backpack. It's good for the spine, too, according to the *US Compendium of Physical Activities*, as a weighted rucksack pulls shoulders back and down, helping to hold the torso up, so that back muscles don't have to work as hard. Bringing the kitchen scales into play, I discover that my ancient laptop weighs 2.2 kilograms. I carry this in a backpack to a coffee shop most days, along with a one-litre bottle of water. *I just need to throw in that dumb-bell that I 'liberated' from an ex in 2007 and I'm there*, I think. *Easy!*

There's an increasing trend for personalised fitness and diet plans, with claims that understanding our medical history, lifestyle and even our DNA can help us look and feel more youthful. This approach sounds logical. A tailored, couture approach to my body is bound to be better than an off-the-peg version . . . So I send off for a DNA swab kit to find out more about the murky world of nutrigenetics – the way our individual genetic variations respond to our diet, lifestyle and exercise. The idea is to come up with an exercise plan and diet designed to match the most distinctive thing about each of us: our genetic code.

My kit arrives and I run an elongated cotton bud around the inside of my cheek to take a sample of saliva (lovely) before sending it back in the post. The company promises to analyse my DNA, assessing my genetic sensitivity to carbo-hydrates and fats; identifying any intolerances; revealing how much salt, alcohol and caffeine my body can handle; uncovering any vitamin deficiencies; and looking at how my body responds to exercise.

After two weeks, my results come back and tell me . . . very little. I discover that I'm alarmingly pedestrian: a little unfit, able to do more endurance exercise if inclined, happily tolerant to wheat, lactose, carbs, cake of all kinds in fact. The only thing I should be watching is my salt and caffeine intake and I could do with eating a few more vegetables. Stop the press. And my optimal 'eating plan'? In common with the majority of the population, it is revealed to be . . . drum roll . . . The Mediterranean Diet.

The standard guidelines on healthy eating and exercise are based on years of accumulated scientific evidence and have been developed to help the majority of us maintain as healthy a lifestyle as we can – for as long as possible. We want to believe there's something 'bespoke', just for us, because it appeals to our ego and we invest in it, financially and emotionally. But wanting something to be true can't *make* it so.

I try to find an independent geneticist who can make me feel better about falling for the hype. But everyone I speak to tells me that there isn't any solid research into genetic predictions of diet and training responses – and that the field as a whole is widely considered disreputable.

The best way to look and feel more youthful really is to go back to basics: eat well and exercise more. I know *what* I need to do. I just need to know *how* to do it. Every attempt I've made in the past at eating more healthily and exercising has failed. So what can I do differently this time?

With a collective fifty years of clinical and research experience behind them, Professors James Prochaska and Carlo Diclemente came up with a model for 'self-change' in 1977 that has now been taken up by the National Cancer Institute and the National Institute of Drug Abuse in the US, as well as the NHS in the UK. The model is renowned for success in tackling unhelpful behaviours and even treating addictions;

I rationalise that a small (okay, large) sugar habit, mild gymtimidation and an unholy fear of Lycra should be a breeze.

The Transtheoretical Model of Behaviour Change, as it's known, takes into account various psychotherapeutic practices to construct a six-stage process that – unlike other theories – allows for relapse. Because let's be honest, when it comes to making changes in diet and exercise, we all slip up once in a while.

The first stage is precontemplation – when you're not ready for change or are procrastinating (hello! *waves*). This is followed by contemplation, or getting ready for change by looking at the pros and cons; then preparation – being ready and taking the first small steps; before action (the off!). The next step is maintenance, sticking with the change for at least six months, and finally, termination – the point where you're no longer tempted and are sure you won't go back to your old ways. Relapse isn't a stage in itself as it can happen at any time, most commonly during the action or maintenance stage. If you slip off a rung, you start again at the bottom – and skipping a step is not an option.

James Prochaska (or, as I'm invited to call him, Jim) speaks to me one Friday morning from his home in Rhode Island, USA. 'We faced a lot of resistance to the programme at first,' he tells me, 'and still do. Psychology likes to think in terms of "straight ahead" progress, but actually change doesn't work like this for most people.' He talks about the emotion that's often behind ingrained behaviours: 'We've learned to act a certain way over a lifetime, so we shouldn't just expect to be able to stop these behaviours suddenly. Like food – it's used as a comforter from when we're babies, so it's hard to unlearn emotional eating.' This is something that rings true. I explain to Jim that food isn't just food to me, and sugar isn't just sugar, either: it's an expression of love.

My first ever memory is of eating biscuits, aged two. There had been a family bereavement and my parents, understandably, didn't know what to do with a toddler while the house heaved with doctors and grief. Biscuits were used as comfort by proxy: a distraction and an entertainment that would set the course for an adult life dedicated to instant gratification and the pursuit of sugar in times of distress. I have stuffed handfuls of chocolate cake and whole packets of bourbon biscuits into my mouth while sobbing through break-ups, losses and other moments of despair ever since. It's only thanks to some decent genes and a fidgety nature that I'm not the size of a house. My sugar habit can't be doing me much good; I've just never found a successful way to stop it before. Jim tells me that this is why the six-stage plan is different: 'Studies have proven that people respond to rewards more than punishment, so anything involving competition or a gamification approach won't work as well for most people.'

Jim even tells me that the process is better than psychotherapy for most people: 'All too often in talking cures, there's an element of trial and error – because everyone is different. But a guided learning programme of self-change has been proven to be more effective and efficient.' *Big talk, Jim. Big talk.*

I tell him my plan to cut down on sugar and exercise more and Jim assures me that his model should help. 'Some behaviour changes are positively linked – so diet and exercise improvements complement each other in a way that, say, diet and smoking might not. I'd advise anyone trying to give up smoking to tackle that one first before dieting.'

I ask if he has any top tips to get me started and surprisingly, he suggests a duvet day: 'There's something called emotional arousal that helps us to get fired up for change,' explains Jim, 'and one of the easiest ways to achieve this is to watch a movie that makes you feel emotionally charged. A good three-hankies film is the best.' I tell him this is my new favourite cinematic classification. Jim's other suggestions include going public with my goal to ensure I stick at it, and enlisting at least one 'buddy' to support me through it. 'I know people can feel uncomfortable about this, but it really helps. It means there's someone you feel accountable to and someone who's there to support you. It stops being something you're just doing on your own and starts being a goal you're trying to reach with the support of friends and family. They've bought into it, so they're more likely to help and make it possible for you to take the steps needed to change.'

I have a friend with ongoing back problems who was recently told to try daily swims to build up her strength. We live in Denmark, where it is cold and wet most of the time, and the idea of getting colder and wetter in a public swimming pool does not appeal, so she will need my help with this just as much as I'll need hers. Swim Buddy = sorted. Another friend is trying to lose weight and is seeing a personal trainer. So PT Friend is also enlisted. I meet them both for brunch to let them in on their mission, should they choose to accept it, and offer them an A4 summary of Jim's transtheoretical change plan.

'Who doesn't love a handout with their eggs in the morning?' PT Friend mutters, conveying it to her handbag without a glance. Swim Buddy shows slightly more interest: 'So this is why I haven't been able to keep up any of the other exercise regimes I've tried before now?'

'Exactly!' I'm glad someone gets it.

They're both a step ahead of me, already taking action, so I have some catching up to do. But my pre-contemplation stage of telling myself I'm too busy and tired to change has come to an end: I will always be busy and I may feel less tired if I eat differently and exercise more. My contemplation stage, of weighing up the pros and cons of change (pros: increased energy, better sleep, a toned body, clearer skin, versus cons: effort) has see-sawed clearly towards taking action. And so I prepare.

I meet with the personal trainer my friend swears by, a smiley Viking named Natascha Nielsen, who measures my vital statistics with 1950s-style callipers to see where I'm storing the most fat (spoiler alert: it's my arse) and then tweaks the basic HIT exercises to give me a plan that will target my hamstrings and stomach. As part of Jim's method, I have had to think long and hard about where my likely pitfalls are and how best to stay motivated. I know myself well enough to realise that I'm never going to do the HIT exercises on my own, at home, with just the dog to hold me to account. I hate gyms, but Natascha points out that I can turn this to my advantage. The whole point of high-intensity training is that it's fast – so if I go to a gym, I'll be more inclined to work hard and get it over with as soon as possible.

I spend an afternoon watching *Truly Madly Deeply* until I feel ready to take action. I have 'cleared' (eaten) all of the biscuits and cakes from the house. I have stocked up on 85 per cent dark chocolate (legal crack), rye bread, vegetables and eggs to see me through the predicted dips. And I've bought a new pair of trainers and some leggings. With Lycra in them!

The next morning I have a protein- and wholegrain-heavy breakfast of scrambled eggs on rye and feel ready to take on the world. For about an hour.

Scientists have discovered that when a body is used to consuming high levels of sugar, it can respond to sugar deprivation with the same kinds of withdrawal symptoms experienced by a drug addict: these can be painful, disorientating and debilitating. Essentially, it all goes a bit *Trainspotting*.

By 9 a.m. I am jittery and irritable.

By 10 a.m. I have a headache, despite two squares of dark chocolate.

By noon I feel distracted and foggy, as though I'm coming down with flu.

At 3 p.m. I quite fancy a little cry and so mainline two bananas, then read that there are fourteen grams of sugar in a medium-sized banana. *But at least it's natural, with vitamins and fibre and things*, I tell myself.

By 6 p.m. I feel sick and by 7 p.m. I'm opening a bottle of red wine and running a bath to drink it in, rationalising that this is the only thing that will keep me away from the fridge. I make the water as close to scalding as I can bear in an attempt to sweat out the toxins, but then get hot and bothered and spill wine in the bath. Now it looks like something out of *Carrie*.

At 9 p.m. I take two paracetamol and get ready for bed to 'make the day be over sooner'. I notice that my toothpaste tastes abnormally sweet and delicious. Lego Man walks in and catches me applying a second stripe to my brush.

'Are you eating toothpaste?'

'Absolutely not,' I tell him guiltily through a mouthful of minty goodness.

On day two, I am still irritable but make it to the gym. Stepping through the sliding doors, I inhale the aroma of stale sweat and convince myself I'm catching legionnaires' disease. I'm further put off by the fact that everyone in there already seems to know each other ('Oh, hey Kirsty!' 'Oh, hi Nick!' *Oh, bollocks* . . .). I'm so clearly a fish out of water that before I'm allowed to join, even on a tempo-rary membership, I'm forced to have an 'induction'. The last time I had one of these, there was a baby twenty-four hours later, so I'm hoping this one's marginally less painful.

Axel is my allocated guide – a 6'7" demigod wearing short shorts and a T-shirt that rides up as he gesticulates, revealing a washboard stomach. I'm led into a large room filled with grey machines and misery. No one is smiling, despite Axel's slow-mo demonstration of 'optimum lunge technique' before he lies on the floor to show me some sort of groin exercise that I'm pretty sure isn't on Natascha's list.

'Look at what my hips are doing.' Axel gestures enthusi-astically as he thrusts a 50kg barbell into the air. 'Do you see?'

'Mmm,' I mumble.

'Watch how I clench my butt while I push . . .'

'Uh-huh,' is all I can say in response, while frowning reso-lutely at my feet and feeling fourteen again.

At the end of my 'induction', Axel offers me a high-five but he's so tall, I can't reach.

'So that was fun, right?' he asks.

'Ha! Yeah right!' I joke, light-headed from lack of oxygen after trying not to breathe in other people's BO for the past half-hour, and traumatised from being in a confined space with so many people making sex noises. And faces.

'You didn't find that fun?' He looks hurt.

'Well, it's just that going to the gym is something I feel I *should* be doing rather than something I want to do. I mean no one really likes it, do they?'

People like cake. They like lie-ins. They don't like spending time doing something that's boring and hurts. That's not fun for anyone. Is it?

Axel says nothing but raises his arm slowly, extends his forefinger and points – much like Donald Sutherland in *Invasion of the Body Snatchers* – at a sign behind my head that reads:

'WE LOVE TO WORK OUT!'

I walk home despondent and do some wailing to the dog along the lines of: *This is impossible!*

But I eat as many florets of broccoli as I can stomach with my healthy salmon supper, and sleep well that night. The next day I go back to the gym with a power-ballad playlist and a will of iron. I do a round of HIT exercises as recommended by Natascha: squats with weights; lying down (always a good start) and pressing my arms to the ceiling with a weight in each hand; 'lateral pull-downs' (which, despite sounding like a satirical roasting on *The Daily Show*, are apparently a type of exercise) and leg presses (nothing to do with sexual harassment; everything to do with pushing a large metal plate away from you with your feet, I discover). Then I 'plank' for a while and do some scissor motions with my legs while lying on my back. And I'm out again, in the fresh air, in twenty-five minutes.

I can put up with anything for twenty-five minutes, I think: *And I only need to do this three times a week? I've totally got this!* I tell myself while walking home – or rather, 'rucking', as I now like to do. Instead of taking the most direct route, which leads me past the bakery, I make a detour – damned if I'm going to undo all my hard work with a cinnamon swirl the size of my head. An exercise-plus-sugar-avoidance win-win.

By day three, I don't feel sick or panicky any more but I also don't want cake any less. I pull on exercise clothes first thing, because once I'm in them I'm more inclined to actually do something. And I do. After my third visit to the gym, the woman on the front desk gives me a wave, as though I'm a regular. At home, I open recipe books that have lain dormant for decades in an attempt to fill the biscuit-shaped holes in my diet, and feel a sense of achievement when I make my very first cassoulet. I get on intimate terms with that funny 'crisper' drawer at the bottom of the fridge and even make 'courgette spaghetti' – feeling a lot like Rumpelstiltskin, having spun vegetables into durum wheat gold.

At the end of week one I check in with Natascha, sending her a training update and a selfie of my still-not-quite-gym-honed body, as she asks of all her clients. Natascha tells me to keep up the good work, which feels like a gold star, and I am more motivated than ever.

I catch up with Swim Buddy and PT Friend at the end of week two to see how they're doing and both look offensively well.

'Being in the pool is like enforced meditation for me,' says

Swim Buddy. 'There's nothing else I can do but breathe and do these repetitive motions. I'm immersed. *Literally*.'

'Doesn't it stink of chlorine? Aren't there people in verruca socks and funny condom hats?' PT Friend asks, echoing my thoughts exactly.

'Yes, but I've grown quite fond of a condom hat – it means I don't have to wash my hair afterwards and makes me feel like I'm an Olympian or something.'

'Good for you . . .' PT Friend's been on her new regime for a month now and exudes a confidence I haven't seen before. 'I just feel like me again, or rather, younger me instead of forty-year-old me,' she says.

'And don't you mind sending the pictures every week?' I ask, still mortified by the experience of taking mine, again, that morning, phone balanced precariously atop a loo roll in the bathroom to get a full-body shot.

'Yeah, that bit's still not great,' PT Friend agrees. 'No one needs to see me in short shorts and a tank top without some serious fake tan first—'

'What?' I nearly choke on my avocado toast.

'"Fake tan"?'

'No . . .' I cough to clear the rye bread crumbs that have now become lodged in my airway.

'"Tank top"?'

'Yes . . . And the bit before that?'

'"Shorts"? What? What's wrong with that?'

'No, nothing,' I protest, 'it's just I thought we had to be wearing . . . less . . .'

'*What?* Why?'

'I thought she needed to see muscle definition and stuff . . .'

I feel a blush rising in my cheeks.

'Yes, but "summery workout gear" is fine.'

'Oh.'

'Why?' asks Swim Buddy, 'What have you been doing?' She sets down her coffee and rests a hand on my arm. 'Is there something you need to tell us?'

'I wanted to look nice,' I start, 'so I made sure it was matching . . .'

'You wore *lingerie?*' PT Friend sounds horrified.

'Just a black bra and pants. In lace . . .'

'You've been sexting our personal trainer!' PT Friend hoots, as Swim Buddy vibrates with the effort of trying not to laugh.

'It's . . . starting to look that way, yes.'

'And now those pictures are out there! You'd better do what she tells you, or you could end up on a specialist website somewhere.'

'Yes, thanks for that. You could have told me!' PT Friend is now wiping away tears of laughter.

We part company soon after, with promises to check in the following week and more jokes about who I might like to sext next.

When I update Natascha at the end of week three, I make sure I am wearing shorts and a very substantial sports bra. Then I delete the pictures from my phone immediately lest Little Red/Lego Man/the dog find them and accidentally upload them to Facebook. Or worse.

A month passes and I'm feeling good about my new body plan. Then we go 'home' for a weekend to see family in the UK. And things go awry.

Back at my mum's house, there is apple crumble on offer. And there is no finer food than my mother's apple crumble. So I have two helpings. Rationalising that I've already pulled the sugary ripcord, I say 'yes' to biscuits afterwards. And half a selection box.

An hour later, I have a headache. It feels as though someone has made the V-for-victory sign just above my eyebrows and then pulled down on my skin.

The next day I wake with puffy eyes and several mouth ulcers. I feel awful. Horrible. It's like the worst hangover I can remember. I take painkillers all day and am uncharacteristically quiet.

'Are you okay?' Lego Man finds me nursing my head in my hands and I explain to him that I'm sad because I really want to eat one of the chocolate brownies a friend has brought round, but am scared they'll 'make me hurt'.

'But I really want one . . .' I near-sob, looking longingly at the glistening, gooey, still-melted-chocolate-chip-laden goodness.

'Why don't you just have one, then?' says Lego Man, exasperated. 'With some ice cream, to neutralise it?'

'Sorry?'

'Doesn't dairy do that?'

His grasp of nutrition is baffling.

'I'm not quite sure that's how it works.'

He suggests a garibaldi instead, but even the thought of this makes me feel sick.

'I've destroyed the thing I love most!' I wail, then, seeing his eyebrows raise in hurt I add swiftly, 'or at least, one of the things in my top five – after my *family*, of course . . .' He is mollified but I secretly wonder whether my first statement was the most accurate. Genuinely, sitting down to a good cake has long been one of my favourite things in life. What if I can't do it any more?

For two days I feel dreadful. Worse, even, than coming off the sugar. I can't believe – or won't believe – that my old friend could make me feel this bad, and so I try to power through. I speak to a friend who is allergic to chocolate but perseveres (*these* are my people) and she reassures me that I will be able to eat cake again: 'But you might feel rough as a dog the first couple of times. There are two options: you can wean yourself back on and work through the pain, or you can just stay healthy.' I know that the right option is 'healthy' and so, when we get home, I resolve to get back on the horse.

Only I don't.

Instead, I wear unattractive Lycra-based clothing every day for a week and make excuses to avoid exercise that range from the mildly credible ('snowstorm'; 'son with gastric flu') to the pathetic ('chance of rain'; 'just washed my hair'; 'it's a Thursday . . .'). After a tough day at work and a rough evening solo-parenting a sick child, I eat a litre of chocolate brownie ice cream. It is, obviously, delicious at the time and I seem to have sufficiently retoxed that I don't have a headache afterwards. But that night I wake up drenched in sweat as my body attempts to process the excess sugar. The next morning my throat feels like bracken.

'I don't feel well,' I croak to PT Friend.

'Probably because you've just eaten your own bodyweight in crap,' PT Friend tells me without a trace of sympathy.

'What can I do to feel better?' I beg.

'Stop being a baby and get back on track,' she tells me, smartly. So I try. But the experience reminds me of something that behavioural change expert Dr Benjamin Gardner told me at the start of my quest – that willpower resources can be depleted. By deadlines, hardcore parenting and gastric flu, in this case. *So what I need to do is make sure I have alternative tactics in place for next time I hit a low*, I think.

Natascha can tell from my latest check-in that I've fallen off the wagon and tries to encourage me back on it: 'This shows how well you were doing,' she tells me, 'that your body reacted in this way! You'd done such a great job of clearing the sugar from your diet, it was a shock to the system. But the good news is you can do it again!' I'm hoping she's right. And I want to try. And so, according to the Transtheoretical Change Model, I have to go back to the start. It's a laborious business, this change lark. But I do it.

If I fill up on wholegrains, veg and lean protein, I am physically capable of getting through a day without cake. Which means I am physically capable of getting through two days. And then three. And then a week has passed. There has been some unattractive sweating and a mood swing or two, but I have done it.

I'm pleased to discover that I have more willpower than I gave myself credit for (which, to be fair, wasn't much). All the squats and the planks have made me feel irritatingly energised – as though I have Actual Muscles, dynamic and ready to dart into action at any time. I still really like cake, but I feel more in charge of this urge now, rather than the other way round.

Six weeks in and I can feel myself getting stronger. With the help of Cher and Europe's 'The Final Countdown' (my workout iPod mix), I can now leg-press 29kg and pull down 30kg. What's more, my knees don't hurt any more and my arms and stomach have stopped wobbling. Little Red tries to 'poop poop' me and hurts his finger.

'Oof!' He frowns and nurses his hand.

'Ha!' I exclaim, thrilled to be in possession of what I believe the kids call 'abs'.

'Are you laughing at our son's pain?' Lego Man stands in the doorway, arms folded.

'Er . . . no?' *Busted.*

I cuddle Little Red and assure him that there are many other parts of Mummy that are still squishy.

I am pincered again by Natascha and she compares my photos from week one with the way I look now. My arms and legs are more toned, I am less doughy and, excitingly, my bottom is higher. I have muscles in there now, which, to my delight, have lifted my behind and make my legs look longer. Natascha's special scales show that I have reduced my body fat percentage by three per cent and taken three centimetres off my hips and thighs. *And all this with minimal effort three times a week?* I think: *Just imagine what I could achieve if I became a total exercise bore?!*

I have another wagon-fall in week seven, mostly because I'm a bit cocky about my progress so far and Natascha has asked me to try a new training plan (did I mention I hate change?). I protest and she emails:

'Everything that's new is always more demanding in the begin-ning, but it's really important to change as the body adapts – you won't be getting much out of your old program any more.'

I complain. A lot. So she gives me another plan that feels a bit better – until I'm three quarters of the way through and realise she's just started each new section with an exercise I already know.

And I fell for it! I think with a mixture of annoyance and admiration, *like a small child conned into eating carrots!*

I go home and bake biscotti as an act of defiance. *That'll show them,* I think, unsure as to who 'they' are, but feeling a need for revolt nonetheless. The rest of the family don't like my biscotti much, so I eat the lot, feel sick, then call my change buddies. PT Friend tells me to 'grow a pair' and Swim Buddy frogmarches me to buy Medjool dates that she assures me are 'as nice as a Snickers bar'. This is a lie, but they're not bad. And between these and the 85 per cent dark chocolate, I just about keep the sugary wolf from the door.

Both of my change buddies are looking lean and healthy and reporting the best sleep they've had in years.

'Most importantly, my back hasn't hurt in months,' Swim Buddy tells me.

'It's the compliments I can't get used to,' PT Friend confides in hushed tones as yet another acquaintance stops by to tell her how great she's looking. 'It's lovely – but weird! Don't you think?'

I tell her I wouldn't know because no one has told me that I look amazing. I wear the same clothes I always have and my skin and hair aren't suddenly radiant – probably because I'm still suffering from 'wine face' or 'coffee face' or 'having a life' face. But that's okay. I have make-up. And I *feel* good. Which, really, is all that matters.

'You just seem happier,' Lego Man tells me, trying very hard not to sing an operatic-style *'I . . . TOLD YOU SOOOOOOO!'* at full volume. Instead, he references points two and three on his relationship 'love list' and tells me he's pleased that exercise is working for me. As an added bonus, my regime has spurred him to get back in the gym, too.

'Nice guns,' I nod appreciatively as I pass him on the stairs carrying armfuls of dirty laundry.

'Thanks, nice buns,' he tells me as I stoop to pick up a pair of pants that have made a bid for freedom. We're still nothing like Weird Owl Couple, but we are trying to give and receive compliments more liberally.

By month three, I'm still only in Jim's action stage but the maintenance phase, starting from the six-month mark, feels achievable. I'm not ashamed to say that I have worked through the pain barrier so that I can now enjoy cake again. I won't deny myself the odd pastry, either, because enforced deprivation only makes me want something more and I don't want to become one of those people whose idea of 'fun' is a fat-free Greek yoghurt. Plus I love everything about the ceremony, presentation and delicious *mouth-hug-followed-by-happy-sated-feeling* that baked goods can offer. Without cake in the world there would be darkness and chaos.

But I don't need it every day now.

Exercising still isn't enjoyable for me, but I do like the results. And with a decent podcast or playlist on the go, I don't mind it. Working out three times a week while trying not to breathe through my nose has become part of my routine. And with my new rucking habit, I've turned daily dog walks into further body-improving endeavours.

My body is in better shape than it has been for a long time. Possibly ever. Only I'm still not hugely confident

about it. It remains, predominantly, a pillar for m
and I wonder what it would be like to rejoice in
corporeal form. And then I meet an American. Who does.
And in the spirit of self-improvement, she inspires my next
experiment.

Things I've learned about changing our bodies:

---

1. The exercise we'll actually do is always better than the exercise we won't.

2. We all have a body shape we need to learn to accept (yawn but true).

3. We need fewer calories as we age – and we need to move more. Rucking and resistance training may be the answer.

4. Watching a weepy is a psychologically sanctioned pre-change technique.

5. Having a buddy to support us and coach us through is essential, and telling everyone about our goals helps us stick to them.

6. Failure *is* an option: we just need to start again at the beginning.

7. It is possible to give up sugar. And get back on it. Both hurt.

8. Eating more healthy fats, protein and wholegrains can help with cravings and keep us full so that we don't feel the need to eat spoonfuls of neat sugar (I have definitely never done this . . .).

9. The Mediterranean Diet works for most of us – no woo or DNA testing required.

10. Almond milk lattes taste like crap.

CHAPTER FOUR

HOBBIES

Reinventing The (Potter's) Wheel

In which I learn how pastimes are spark plugs for change; why 'Optimal Anxiety' improves performance; how neuro-linguistic programming can ease The Fear; and why upping an OCEAN score via hobbies boosts creativity

It's raining, it's cold and everyone else rummaging through misshapen turnips or suggestive-looking celeriac at the weekly vegetable stall[16] is muffled up in technical outerwear that's predominantly grey, black or – for the really racy – navy blue.

And that's when I see her – a woman wearing a fluorescent pink scarf and a fabulous felt cape-coat. When she turns to enquire as to the price of her muddy carrots, she parts perfectly red-lipsticked lips to flash a dazzlingly white smile. I know straight away that she is American, long before her accent announces it. *Those are not European teeth*, I think to myself before she spots me, says 'hello' and tells me that she works with Lego Man.

The American is bursting with addictive energy and

---

16 Really – my town has nothing so fancy as a farmers' market.

informs me that as well as working full time as a designer, she teaches a dance class and that I should try it. She is totally at ease with her body and happily illustrates the following sentence, in the street, in broad daylight: 'The class is a mixture of martial arts –' cue taekwondo-style chops – 'modern dance –' this is accompanied by some impressive hip-wiggling – 'and healing arts, like yoga,' she adds finally, as her hands come to rest in the prayer position. 'It's called Nia and it's every Wednesday night.'

'Sounds great!' I blurt out before I have time to think this through. Mostly because I like her and I am a Massive People-Pleaser.

When I first moved to Denmark, I took up all manner of new pursuits in an attempt to settle in to my surroundings and meet people. And it worked. I joined a choir, made friends and kept busy. And then I had a baby. And Lego Man's travel schedule went turbocharged. And I couldn't make it to enough of the choir practices needed to learn the songs we were supposed to sing in concerts, scheduled throughout the year. It turns out that 'winging it' when you don't read music and aren't entirely familiar with the language you're trilling in can throw your fellow choristers off their top C and create some pretty unorthodox harmonies that not all of the audience appreciate. It wasn't fair on my teammates, I told myself, so I stopped going.

'But if I'm going to carry on working as a freelancer,' I chew it over with the dog back at home, 'I could do with getting out more and interacting with the world. You know, to ensure I remain a sane and a civilised member of society rather than a mad woman who just talks to a dog all day . . . oh . . .' The dog reaches a paw to his nose in a canine approximation of a facepalm, but eventually concedes that I may have a point. If I'm supposed to be starting over, I should make sure I have all the building blocks of a happy, healthy existence in place. Having time to myself to pursue interests outside of work, and being brave enough to step out of my comfort zone to try new things, is an important part of this. Because hobbies are good for us.

Researchers at the Australian Happiness Institute have found that having a hobby gets us out of work on time and improves quality of life, productivity and even the likelihood of career success. Challenging ourselves to do something different creates new neural pathways in our brain and learning a new skill can even make us happier, according to research from San Francisco State University. A British study published in *The Oxford Review of Education* found that participation in hobbies and lifelong learning had a positive effect on well-being – and subjecting ourselves voluntarily to new challenges can even boost creativity. American psychologist Scott Barry Kaufman at the University of Pennsylvania discovered that openness to experience – one of psychologist Ellen's Big Five OCEAN test criteria from the introduction – is the personality trait most consistently associated with creativity.

As a writer, creativity is crucial. So being open to new experiences is something I should get better at, I think. And if I can overcome my resistance to entry-level, extra-curricular mini-challenges, maybe I can be a bit braver when it comes to the big things, too . . .

Like kindling for the fires of change or a starting-over spark plug, hobbies are an easy, instant way to ignite something in our everyday lives and feel refreshed – childlike, even.

Whether it's joining a club, learning to sing or taking up a new craft, as Seneca said: '*As long as you live, keep learning how to live.*'

'Seneca? Wasn't he a racing car driver?' Lego Man asks when I share this nugget.

'No, you're thinking of Senna.'

'Oh.'

'This guy was a Roman philosopher,' I say, dredging up an image on Wikipedia. Lego Man looks doubtful, then gives a nod of approval.

'That makes more sense,' he says, before unzipping a hoodie and dropping his tracksuit bottoms in the middle of the living room to reveal a startling black and white Lycra onesie-slash-mankini.

'Wow!' I have no idea what's just happened. 'Strong look.'

'Thanks,' he says. 'It's new. Paul and I are going on a bike ride, remember?'

I assure him that I had remembered he was out cycling with his friend this afternoon – and that were there ever any danger of my forgetting, the image of him dressed like an orca has now been seared on my mind for evermore. Then Little Red runs up and presents his father with a Duplo killer whale to underline the sartorial similarities. *That's my boy.*

Cycling makes Lego Man happy, I reason. *So who cares if he looks cuckoo?* His other hobbies include building things out of plastic bricks; playing with power tools; wood bothering; and spending an inordinate amount of time and money on fancy design wares and lighting solutions (see 'Liberace'). These are his *thing*s. And, impressively, he always manages to make time for them.

I, on the other hand, suffer from a strange sort of puritanical guilt – a distrust of leisure (and pleasure) that I've been conscious of ever since becoming a parent. There's always laundry, cooking, cleaning or some other domestic or emotional labour that I feel I could be doing – like organising the family's social life or sending thank-you letters (see 'martyr-like tendencies'). Nobody tells me I *should* be doing these things. I may have been conditioned to believe that they are 'women's work' by watching one too many episodes of *Little House on the Prairie*, but no one is making me behave like this in my own home. And yet most mothers I know are terrible at 'hobbies' and making time for anything so indulgent as a non-work-related pastime. Many child-free friends also 'forget' to prioritise their own interests or hankerings to learn new things outside of office hours. A recent UK study found that the average woman gets just seventeen minutes a day to herself. Although perhaps the 'gets' should be replaced by 'takes'.

I should have a hobby, I tell myself: *Lego Man isn't travelling too much for the next few months – and there are such things as babysitters* . . . Deciding that it's about time I did something just for me, I sign up for The American's very next class and pay before I have time to think about it too much.

Nia originally stood for 'Non-Impact Aerobics' and first came about in 1980s California as a rejection of the 'no pain no gain' school of exercise and a move towards 'wellness' of mind and body. Already building up a mental image? Yeah, me too. And it's less Jane Fonda leotard-clad sex kitten ('curl your pelvis like a scorpion!') and more friendship bracelets and tie-dye.

What I'm actually faced with when I arrive at the dance

studio, salubriously located above our town's second best kebab shop, is a room illuminated by fairy lights filled with ten barefoot women of various nationalities. The American is wearing Lycra flares and sweatbands, which, apparently, are a thing in Nia (classes take place all over the world and you can now buy merchandise and clothing online. God bless America). Our teacher welcomes everyone, explaining that Nia is about self-expression and using all of our body, no matter what size or shape we are.

'We're also learning to be fluid,' she tells us, 'so moving out of any pain and towards pleasure.' This sounds like exactly what I need to reconnect with my body beyond 'pillar for head, rucking pack-horse, HIT-machine and occasional receptacle for Snickers bars' status. But then she adds: ' – with an edge! Think "new-age-ninja".'

I am going to be very bad at this, I think.

'It's not about being "good" or "bad".' The American reads my mind. 'If you feel like you're "not doing it right", that's not coming from me. No one is judging anyone else.' She explains that Nia employs fifty-two basic movements (*fifty-two? I don't think my body knows fifty-two movements, basic or otherwise . . .*) and that for today's practice, the focus will be our feet.

I've got feet, I reason, *maybe I'll be fine . . .*

We're encouraged to say our names, where we're from and what's brought us here and I'm relieved to find there's another Brit in the room, who looks almost as daunted as I feel. There are some Italians, talking with their hands, a few Danes looking surly, and two Australians, grinning at the madness and taking it all in. We march and cha-cha-cha to warm up.

So far, so a-cha-cha-cha-ivable.

Then we're told to move around the room, 'expressing ourselves through our bodies' and 'shaking it'. Unfortunately, post-body-makeover, I haven't got as much to shake as I used to. My tautness, which was a source of pride just half an hour ago, is now, I see, a hindrance. The American has curves and knows how to use them and when she moves, she is the dictionary definition of 'sensual'. By contrast, I am all elbows. I learned ballet as a child and my main mode of movement currently involves weights or a rucksack. There is nothing arousing, or even rousing, about my dancing and I feel stiff, angular and hopeless. We 'step in' ceremoniously to begin our 'practice', then work our way through a warm up and some choreographed songs with moves that range from *toddler-high-on-cake* spinning to karate kicks. Then the music is turned up a notch and gets 'a bit more bang-y' (put it this way: there's no chorus) before The American says two words guaranteed to strike fear into the heart of any sober Englishwoman: 'Free dance.'

Oh dear God. The world of expressive dance has managed perfectly well without me for the past thirty-six years. Why is this happening to me now? Whyyyyyy?

I manage, somehow, not to spontaneously combust. Instead, I pulse with anxiety and scuttle up and down like a terrified crab.

'Listen to the beat of the music!' The American tells us. 'Now play with each instrument: let the saxophone inspire the movement of your spine. Express the flute with your arms. Let your feet play with the sound of the piano,' she calls out, whirling around the room: 'How does the piano feel?'

How does the piano feel? I have no idea how a piano feels!

145

I think. But the Italians do. They embrace their inner piano with gusto, stomping around, then tiptoeing, staccato style. The Brit and I cleave to the walls, embarrassed, with an unspoken agreement not to make eye contact.

It's like I'm having to do Dr Dance's improvised dance moves, in public! I shrink inwardly. *And I haven't even had the chance to power pose first.*

The next track involves some sort of horns.

'Like traffic!' says The American. 'Let's see if we can *be* traffic, moving around the space. That's right. Now, you're *angry* traffic! You're in a jam!'

I am near paralysed by this point, when an Italian juts past me, somehow managing to look simultaneously 'like traffic' and also sexy.

How is that possible?

I wonder whether I could make it to the door and out of there in one swift automotive acceleration, but there's a strapping Viking who's *really* committing to 'being' a bus and an Italian emulating an erotic motorcycle in my way.

After an hour, we are released, shell-shocked and pale, back out on to the streets.

'How was it for you?' The American asks. The Brit has been rendered mute by the experience, so I answer for both of us: 'Um, unusual . . .'

She asks what I want from my 'practice' and, rather than giving her my first answer ('A lie-down in a darkened room with some Valium . . .'), I manage: 'I'd like to be able to get better at this whole "liking my body" thing and being able to use it. Enjoy it even.'

She tells me that Nia is great for helping people lose their inhibitions.

I tell her I like to know where my inhibitions are at all times. But I am aware that getting out of my 'comfort zone' is supposed to be A Good Thing.

The idea of pushing ourselves beyond what feels entirely safe dates back to an experiment from 1908, when psychologists Robert M. Yerkes and John D. Dodson flung some mice into a maze. To 'help' them navigate the right route, they were given electric shocks (no one ever said science was fluffy), then monitored, to assess whether they 'learned' faster after being tasered. Turns out, they did. And lo! We now know that getting out of our comfort zone – the modern, humane version of an electric shock – makes us perform better! It's all about finding the sweet spot between paralysing fear and utter relaxation – or 'Optimal Anxiety', as researchers call it. So I need to get back on the hobby-wagon if I want to become a lean, mean, change chameleon.

'The free dance element is also great for getting you to relax into your physical form,' The American goes on, 'to really feel the floor beneath your feet'.

Huh, I think: *I'd like that*.

I'd also like to relearn a sense of play. Little Red's favourite things in the world at the moment are tractors. If there aren't any toy versions to play with, or drawing materials available to sketch one, or real-life ones to look at, he sometimes likes to pretend to be one. My own interpretations have, so far, been found wanting ('Mama no t-actorrrr!' he recently growled at my attempt). 'I'd like to be able to play with my son better. At "being a tractor", just for example,' I try explaining. 'Not a sexy one,' I add, hastily, 'just a normal, agricultural-style one will do . . .' This isn't coming out as

I'd hoped, so I have one last go: 'I'd like to be able to use my body without feeling like a massive idiot.'

I appreciate this is a big ask – to undo years of middle-class habituation and a Catholic upbringing with a weekly dance class. But if Nia can even begin to deliver, then I'm prepared to give it a go.

The American makes some encouraging noises, then dazzles us with her smile until The Brit and I, still ashen-faced, agree to come back again the following week. I plan to do some serious power posing first, as well as seeking out additional techniques to help with confidence.

Neuro-linguistic programming – or NLP – was founded in the 1970s by Richard Bandler and John Grinder at the University of California. They noted that many psychotherapists at the time weren't terribly effective, but the few who were had some things in common. By studying psychotherapists Virginia Satir and Fritz Perls as well as psychiatrist and hypnosis advocate Milton H. Erickson, they came up with a structure for neuro-linguistic programming – exploring the relationship between how we think (neuro), how we communicate (linguistic) and our patterns of behaviour (the programming part). NLP, as it's known, is now a multi-billion-dollar therapy that's attracted fans worldwide, from legions of sport personalities to management consultants and, er, Paul McKenna. Supporters of NLP say that it's an efficient, solutions-orientated technique that allows us to be in charge of our mind and so make successful changes to habits and behaviours.

Critics accuse NLP of lacking in evidence and being, well, *weird*. Its co-founder, Bandler, has admitted cocaine abuse in the past and even stood trial for murder[17]. He exhorts devotees to push negative thoughts away and believes that we can overcome any obstacle if we just *think* hard enough. He famously tells delegates on his NLP masterclasses[18]: 'My mantra for silencing the inner dialogue is: "shut the fuck up, shut the fuck up, shut the fuck up . . ."' (*All right! Easy, Richard* . . .).

And yet, the man is hailed as a sort of messiah by many. Everyone I speak to in the corporate world insists that I 'really must' include NLP in any exploration of change. As though they've all been 'programmed'. Which they probably have. So I'm curious, but sceptical.

Phil Parker is the approachable British face of NLP and works with athletes and entertainers as well as mere mortals keen to make changes. He has *this* many letters after his name: '*DO Dip E Hyp P NLP MBIH Certified Master Practitioner of NLP*' and is currently conducting research into the efficacy of an offshoot of NLP, the Rediscovery Process, with London's Metropolitan University. He's the closest NLP gets to mainstream respectability in the UK and as such, he's just the man for me.

I speak to him over Skype because he's laid up in bed with flu, at the same time as trying to house-train a twelve-week-old puppy. I've been there, and it's not pretty. I dread to think how much his house honks of disinfectant and how

---

17 http://articles.latimes.com/1988-01-29/news/mn-26470_1_ psychotherapist-richard-bandler.

18 Jon Ronson writes beautifully on his experience of attending one of these in the *Guardian* and also documents the 'Shut the fuck up', er, 'technique'. . .

grim he must be feeling, so I'm not expecting much. But Phil is surprisingly upbeat. *Maybe there's something in this, after all*, I think.

He starts by explaining why he rates NLP: 'Traditional therapy is all about "why" something is so – is it due to your upbringing or your parents etc. Whereas NLP is about "how" – it's what we do next, so it's a quicker way to work out how to move on. We can treat phobias, for instance, really well because we look at people who have overcome a phobia and model – i.e. "copy" – the most commonly effective things that they did to get over it.'

'So,' I try to clarify, 'you don't much care why I'm scared of small spaces[19]/dancing sober in public, you just want me to feel better about these things?'

'Pretty much,' says Phil. 'Language is also key: the way people talk about their problems is often contributing to them. If we approach something like starting a new hobby as huge and complicated, when the first problem appears, it reinforces our negative beliefs and we'll feel like giving up. This means that many people are often in the worst state of mind possible for the task at hand. In NLP, we think about what's going on; what you *want* and how to get there. Not, crucially, what you *don't* want. So if you want to start a new hobby, you should just think, "I'm going to do this and I'm going to feel confident and really enjoy myself".'

I tell him this seems too simple.

'That's just your state of mind,' Phil fires back: 'you *think* life's complicated.' He's right, I do. I tell him I feel as though

---

19 I am also a recovering claustrophobic. Welcome to my messed-up
  mind . . .

I'm wading through treacle much of the time. 'And because you're using language in this way, your brain starts to believe things are harder than they need to be.'

'Oh.' *Stupid old treacle,* I think: *holding me up, making me all sticky and scared of dancing like sexy traffic . . .*

Phil saves me from my inner monologue by telling me about a study from the University of Jena in Germany in which neurologists and psychologists used MRI scanners to record the brain activity in volunteers who heard a series of words. When they heard words associated with pain, the pain receptors in their brains lit up. 'They felt pain, because they were hearing about pain,' says Phil. 'It's that simple. Other studies have shown that we can change our white blood-cell count – the cells that fight off infection – just by the way we think.'

This is all very impressive, but other than avoiding negatives, how can we get positive and *stay* positive in the face of fear or adversity? Somewhat cruelly, I remind him that he's currently at home with flu and a puppy that's probably weeing on the living room carpet as we speak. But Phil doesn't crack.

'I'm not passive to these things,' he tells me. 'I am *experiencing* flu, but it's not a permanent state. Same with house-training the puppy. It's a process.'

I don't tell him about the sleep deprivation I suffered at the hands of our now adult dog for weeks, months even. Until I hallucinated colours. I'm not that mean.

'To get more positive,' he goes on after a nose-blow, 'we need to think about what state we're currently in: when you're about to walk in to your first session of something or join a new group, there's a whole lot of stuff in your head, right?'

'Right,' I tell him.

'Like, "Will it be embarrassing? Will it be boring? Is it worth it? Will the room be cold? Am I hungry? Can I be bothered? Isn't there something good on TV tonight? Will I meet anyone I like? Will anyone talk to me?" But once you're aware of these negative thoughts, you can dismiss them: they are unreal. They're not based on any facts. They're just the movie you're running in your head based on your fears, your previous experiences or a small nugget of information you may have. Instead, you need to get into another state of mind: to feel what it's like to be confident. In NLP, there's a shortcut to this state: a process you can use to approach things confidently – to shift your state of mind. So close your eyes. Then think about a time you've ever been very good at something. A time you felt really confident.'

I try, but then hear Phil's voice, scrutinising me via Skype: 'I can tell by your face that you're panicking already here! You're thinking, "But I'm not confident!"'

Stupid old overly expressive face, I think. *Should have got that fixed when Dr Franken-mean gave me the chance . . .*

'It doesn't have to be something extraordinary,' Phil interjects. 'Can you tell the time? Can you tie your shoe-laces?'

'Just,' I mumble, eyes still closed.

'Well there you are – that's something you have a competence in, that you are confident doing. If someone asks you to tie your shoelaces, you can confidently think, "Yes: I've got this. No problem." Right?'

'Right.'

'Now step into this feeling and we're going to do something

called anchoring. Press your thumb and forefinger together on your right hand, hard, and connect to those feelings of confidence. Really feel them. Got it?'

'Got it.'

'Good. Now this works because it's a specific gesture you don't normally use. So next time you're feeling unconfident, you should squeeze your thumb and forefinger together. You can do this gesture and take a moment to put yourself back in that place of confidence.'

'This seems too easy,' I tell him, looking back up.

'I hear that a lot,' he says with a nod. 'It's treacle-thinking all over again! And there's a lot of resistance along the lines of "It's too good to be true", but if you think about it, this is a ridiculous response. What's the opposite? "It's so bad it must be true"? We want change to be more efficient, just like we want our cars and our phones to be more efficient. So why are people so wary of this in NLP?'

He's got a point. But I still don't, deep down, believe it will work. And I haven't seen sufficient evidence to persuade me otherwise. Phil tells me this is because aside from his own research, the field as a whole doesn't get much airtime in academia and is currently unregulated. He explains that while there are things we can do ourselves at home, a properly trained professional practitioner can pick up on unconscious signals that we might miss. 'This can be helpful for more serious issues like depression, chronic pain or phobias,' he says. I wonder whether a phobia of free dance comes under this category but decide to try out self-talking and 'forefinger and thumb pinching' as an introduction to NLP, then wish Phil a swift recovery ('and perhaps an industrial carpet cleaner').

By next Wednesday, I feel ready. In the interests of science (ish) I don't power pose before class as planned – I want to see if the basic NLP techniques Phil taught me can have an impact on their own. I also resist the temptation to have a large glass of wine beforehand (I know: that's commitment. I'm expecting a Pulitzer in the post any day now). Instead I turn up sober as an AA sponsor, and tell myself '*I'm going to do this and I'm going to feel confident and really enjoy myself*'. I repeat this over and over in the car park until I either believe it or am so sick of saying it that I pretend to myself that I do.

After paying and displaying, I press my thumb and forefinger together to 'anchor' myself. Dry leaves skitter along the pavement as I walk to the kebab-house-studio, repeating my mantra; and I don't stop until I've removed my socks and shoes and am saying 'hello' to my classmates.

'Let's think about our spine today,' beams The American, doing something animalistic with hers. When I attempt to replicate this, it looks like I'm doing robotics. My C-3PO may not be sensual (at all), but it does feel good to loosen up and use muscles and movements not normally called upon by sitting at a desk all day, lifting weights or rucking. She encourages us to extend our arms and 'flap our wings' next. 'Like a raven!' The American calls out as she sexy-flaps and I feel like Icarus, mid-melt. I catch sight of my reflection and immediately feel my sinews tighten at how ridiculous I look. So I 'anchor' myself again, and repeat silently: '*I'm doing this and I'm feeling confident and enjoying myself*'.

I'm not sure if the NLP is working, but I do find I really like flapping. Flexing from my shoulder blades down to the tips of my fingers and pretending I own vast, powerful wings that beat the air and propel me forward feels surprisingly good.

After this, we are clocks. The American and the Italians are sexy clocks, obviously, whereas I'm more of a functional, Flik Flak child's starter watch. But I realise that I can do this, as long as I'm not feeling pressure to look cool or sexy.

Maybe, I muse, big hand at noon, little hand at seven, *that's just my thing: playful, functional clocks/traffic/musical instruments rather than the sexy kind.*

With a short segue of simple choreography, our clocks morph into wheels.

'Any kind you like!' The American offers, generously. And so I think about what sort I want to be.

What IS my ideal wheel? I ask myself, possibly for the first time ever. Really, if you've never posed this existential question, you haven't lived. Within moments, I have rejected the more prosaic wheels (*Car? Bor-ing! Lorry? How gauche . . .*) and my mind is filled with Ferris wheels, lazy Susans and – and then it hits me: Patrick Swayze (RIP) and *that* scene in *Ghost*. *Yes! That's it! That's the wheel for me!* I think, spinning now and feeling pleasantly light-headed. And so I 'become' a potter's wheel. In public. Sober. I rise and fall and use my hands in ways I'm frankly horrified to recall but in the moment, while I'm doing it, I don't care.

In common with yoga, there's a wind-down period at the end of a Nia class where we're guided through stretches and meditative movements. We're asked, this week, to think about our childlike selves and what we want to be or do when we 'grow up'. And I realise that I have always wanted to have a go on a potter's wheel. *That could be my next hobby!* I think, still buzzing from all the functional-clock/flapping endorphins. We 'step out' of the practice as a group and there is hugging. And I seem to float out of the studio, immune to the embarrassment I suffered from last time and unconcerned by the half-eaten kebab I almost slip on in the street.

When I get home, feeling energised and inspired, I go online and search for '*pottery courses*' before adding as an afterthought, '*residential*'. This has nothing to do with the desire for a transformative hobby-inspired epiphany and everything to do with the prospect of a couple of nights of unbroken sleep in a starfish position. I find a course I like the look of, check the calendar to make sure Lego Man is around to look after Little Red, and book it. Just like that. This is possibly the most spontaneous thing I have ever done (see 'not at all spontaneous').

My husband is supportive of my pottery mini-break on the understanding that he can cash in his 'culture-lash token', as he dubs it, at a later date on a hobby of his choosing. I tell him that he might want to consider something crafty since a new study from San Francisco State University found that creative activities were especially effective in boosting work performance as well as improving well-being and firing up the right side of the brain.

'Does reading interior design magazines count?'

'No.'

'Oh well, I'll keep thinking then,' he says, pulling out a few lamp catalogues.

Five weeks later and I'm inhaling the scent of lavender and cow dung in an agricultural village in southern France, under the tutelage of a ceramicist who wears exclusively beige and socks with her sandals. I'm already missing Little Red and wondering what on earth I've signed up for. So I remind myself I'm here to boost my OCEAN score – opening up to new experiences to stimulate the creative juices. Then I repeat my NLP refrain: *'I'm feeling confident and I'm going to enjoy myself'*. I try 'anchoring' as I greet my fellow pupils – a woman in her sixties who smells of Strepsils, a man who looks like John Cleese and two women wearing muumuus. By the time introductions are over, it becomes clear that I am the only member of the party who has never been in the Peace Corps and/or Greenpeace. Sorry peace: you have been deprived of my services for too long. But within an hour, we are in the studio, *learning stuff*, and crafting to the strains of Pink Floyd.

I pay close attention to a demonstration of how to use the potter's wheel and, other than wondering at what point 'The Wall' will be swapped for 'Unchained Melody' to fulfil my *Ghost* fantasy (sad times: it isn't), I'm fully 'present', as they say in the green tea community.

Soon the wheel is spinning, just like I imagined it would while cavorting on the floor in my Nia class. I'm pumping the pedal like mad to maintain a consistent speed, and then, *slap!* The clay is on.

'Now, pull it up,' says Sandal Socks. I allow my hands to coax up the now delicate, squirming mass. 'Next, dip your thumbs in to bring it off,' she says. I look around to see if anyone else has a sense of humour as puerile as mine. They haven't. But my pot is rising nicely. *In fact, it's getting pretty high . . . maybe it should be a vase, instead?*

'Okay, now slow down and finish it off,' Sandal Socks says. Cue side-eye to Strepsil Woman. *Nothing.* I try to do as I'm told but can't seem to stop the momentum. My 'vase' is getting taller and taller, so I try to squash it down from the top, until it starts to look distinctly phallic. Next, it keels over to one side and starts careering around like a baby elephant's trunk. And then . . .

Pffft, pffft, pffft, pffft, pffft . . . pffft.

My elephant trunk is no longer on its wheel.

'Don't worry!' I am assured by one of my comrades.

'Happens to us all!' adds another.

'Remember: art has always been about making mistakes,' Sandal Socks reminds me. I'm not sure I'd class what I'm doing as anything so lofty as 'art', but I appreciate the senti-ment – and it reminds me of Ellen's advice at the start of my quest: that I have to make friends with failure and get used to the idea that I won't always get things 'right'. Or be any good. *A bit like the Nia,* I think.

I 'throw' again, and this time I'm supported by all sorts of cheerleading and advice from my more experienced potter-friends.

'Keep it lower this time,' says one.

'And slower.'

'Well, it's certainly *stumpier* . . .'

'Oh!'

'My word . . .'

There is silence. A lone dog can be heard barking in the distance.

'It's impressive . . .' Sandal Socks tails off. We're all thinking the same thing: I have made a vagina. It's a good vagina, but it's a vagina none the less and I don't quite know how I've managed it. I keep trying to improve, as my classmates share their visions of what they're hoping to create.

'I'm making Yggdrasil, the life-sustaining World Ash Tree in Nordic mythology, whose destiny determines the world's end,' says John Cleese, casually, as I slop about with a sponge on a stick.

'I'm taking inspiration from Wagner's Ring Cycle,' announces Strepsil Woman, 'moving between simple shapes and rococo forms.'

'We're recreating T. S. Eliot's poem, the one about cats,' says one of the Muumuus.

I make pots that look like genitalia, consistently, despite all efforts to expand my repertoire (it is amazing how easy it is to make earthenware accidentally look like genitalia), but Sandal Socks tells me this is 'clearly what I need to do just now' and that, 'as long as I'm happy', she's happy.

The next day, we glaze our creations and fire them in a converted oil-drum kiln until they're red hot. Then Sandal Socks removes them with tongs while wearing a welder's mask, that I am on no account allowed to 'have a go' with, she tells me.

This is a blow.

But I want to wear the welder's mask so bad! I think. *SO BAD.*

'You just want to pretend you're in *Flashdance*!' says John Cleese.

'No I don't!' I say. What I mean is: *Yes. This. Absolutely this.*

Several pieces have cracked in the heat, with the cats bearing the brunt of the casualties. My 'good' vagina hasn't made it either, but one of my later, prolapsed versions is imperfectly intact. The pieces are tossed in sawdust to starve them of oxygen and activate the glaze. And then we scrub. There, under the soot, a beautiful glaze starts to glint. A magical alchemy has occurred whereby dirgey pastels have become vibrant – almost luminescent. Resplendent in a crackling, electric greeny-blue, like a dragonfly's wings, is my clay vagina. And I love her.

I have glaze in my hair and soot on my face, like I'm in *Oliver Twist*, but I am thrilled with my prolapsed pot. It is ugly and misshapen and it will never see the light of day, but I've had one hell of a time making it.

And that's the beauty of a hobby – it's just for fun. It doesn't matter. There is no 'wrong' and although scientists may have uncovered a plethora of mind, body and career benefits to having a pastime, the purest and most important of these is surely the joy of doing something just *because* – because we enjoy it and for the sheer heck of it. And indulging in a hobby that doesn't ask anything of me in return, other than the mere fact of taking part, is a tonic.

Back at home, I'm happier and nicer to be around because I've had time for myself. I have recharged. When Wednesday rolls around, I only need to use Phil's anchoring technique for a few seconds to get me off the sofa and out to Nia class. I tell myself, '*I can do this: I'm feeling confident and I'm going to enjoy myself*', and believe it, now. I don't know how much of this is thanks to NLP and how much is down to perseverance – moving through the awkwardness-slash-pain barrier.

But then, I rationalise, *maybe the NLP helped me distract myself from my own inner monologue for long enough to just show up and try something new?*

I can't quite drink the NLP Kool-Aid but I do find myself telling my fellow Brit about the experiment. She looks at me as though I'm only partially deranged and says she'll try it.

And then the music starts up and The American encourages us to do 'wing flapping' again, which I still love and have recently been doing around the house, when no one's watching ('*It's almost as though it gets me from my desk to the kettle that little bit faster,*' is how I explain it to the dog).

The American runs us through a succession of arm movements that help my shoulders loosen, so that by the time she says, 'Free dance! Pretend you're picking weeds!' I find I don't mind so much. I realise that the Italians are far too busy being sassy gardeners to care about what I'm doing. And if I stay in my semi-darkened corner, studiously avoiding the Brit learning to get her funk on in the *opposite* semi-darkened corner, I can – almost – relax.

Lego Man is reading a mountain biking magazine in the bath when I get home.

'How was it? What did you have to be this week?' He loves a Nia update.

'Weed pickers,' I say, turning on the shower and waiting for it to warm up.

'Were they *sexy* weed pickers?'

I nod, pressing my thumb against my forefinger.

'Ahh . . . sex and weeds: together at last! And are you enjoying it?'

'You know, actually, yes. I am,' I say, peeling off my sweaty

T-shirt. 'I'm probably never going to be The American. And I'm never going to be *Italian* –'

'No.'

'Quite. But I can now *writhe*. Sober. In a public place. So, you know – making headway.'

Lego Man sets down his magazine on the bath's edge and reaches out to hold my hand.

'I'm proud of you,' he says.

'Thanks,' I tell him. 'I mean, the class would still be better with wine involved, but you know, I'm getting there.'

'You're a trooper,' he tells me.

Things I've learned about making a leap into the unknown:

---

1. Taking up a new pastime can make us more creative and boost our OCEAN score.

2. Extra-curricular pursuits reinvigorate everyday lives, encouraging us out of the office on time and making us happier, healthier and even better at our jobs . . .

3. . . . but the real benefit of a hobby is the pure, unusable, impractical joy of it. Just. Because.

4. NLP may help with confidence and the drive to get out there and try something new . . .

5. . . . and even if it doesn't, it's a decent distraction technique for pressing mute on The Fear.

6. Getting out of our comfort zone and reaching 'Optimal Anxiety' helps us all become lean, mean, change chameleons.

7. Brits *can* dance sober. This is amazing.

CHAPTER FIVE

FRIENDS

They'll Be There For You (& if they aren't, get new ones)

In which I learn the difference between *Friends* and friends; how Six Thinking Hats can revamp our inner circle; why scientists recommend The Dumpster Test; and how channelling Chicago-style improv to say 'yes, and . . .' turns strangers into new comrades in crime

I've been so consumed with work, working on my relationship and working up a sweat – via HIT, kiln-play and seductive weed picking – that I have rather neglected my friends of late. This isn't something I take lightly. In fact, I'm ashamed to admit it. I'm also aware that if we move back to the UK, I won't just be able to slot seamlessly back into the friendships I left behind. So next, I want to find out about the best ways to improve friendships and maybe, even, make new ones.

My own failings become apparent during a conversation with a friend of eighteen years' standing who calls to check that I'm still alive and ask whether I've heard from our old flatmate. Former roomie now lives alone and appears to spend the majority of her time and resources amassing fancy home-wares and designer kitchen equipment, despite getting takeaways, most nights and only ever using the oven 'for storage'. Her Le Creuset collection makes Lego Man weep with envy. But 'Pans Solo', as she once signed off an email and has been dubbed ever since, has apparently gone off radar.

'Maybe she's on holiday—' I suggest, but am cut off.

'For three weeks?' is the scoffing response. 'She lives in *London*. No one in London takes three weeks off unless they're having a baby or a breakdown. No: something's up. When I last saw her, she'd barely left the house except for work. And her sister's just had another kid so *she's* in newborn-lockdown. And remember how she talked about The Exodus? Well, even more of her school friends left for suburbia at Christmas. I'm worried she's using Netflix and online shopping as a substitute for a life and isn't seeing anyone, so you need to try calling. Okay?'

'Okay,' I reply, 'will do.'

My mother, who can never remember names, always refers to this particular friend (phone girl) as 'the head girl one' and she's not far off in her summation. Head Girl grew up in a military family and went to seven different schools before the age of sixteen. She was always moving. Always starting again. And as a result, as an adult she is not to be trifled with. 'There are only two options when you're on the move all the time,' she told me once: 'you sink or you master the butterfly stroke. You become an extrovert or an introvert.' My friend chose EXTRA-overt and has been taking the world by storm ever since. She is one of life's natural change chameleons – comfortable in any situation and all company, from sailors on a stag do (what a night that was . . .) to landed gentry ('just posh it up a bit – say stuff like, "this is *excellent* butchery . . ." or "rattling good fun" – while speaking like a ventriloquist . . .'). Despite never, technically, making it to head girl status ('I was robbed by a girl named Eleanor Pickering,' she has told us on more than one occasion), she is confident and caring and the kind of friend you always want in your corner. So when Head Girl tells me to 'try calling', I try calling.

I FaceTime and watch my features contort at the mercy of my phone's fish-eye lens until it looks as though I'm staring into the back of a spoon. This goes on for a few rings before a message flashes up:

'*FaceTime unavailable*'.

I try Skype next, but there's no response. I'm just bracing for a redial when I see Pans Solo's status change from '*Away*' to '*Offline*'.

So she is there! She's just done the telecommunications equivalent of ducking behind the sofa and turning the lights off to avoid an unwanted visitor!

'Right,' says Head Girl when I report back: 'I'm going round. And I'm booking that trip to see you we've been on about.'

'You can't just *force* someone to embark on international travel at a moment's notice—' I start, then I remember who it is I'm talking to. The North Sea is no match for her powers. With Head Girl in charge, the Vikings wouldn't have stood a chance.

'Lock up your Aperol,' she says, 'we're coming over!'

Friends have always been hugely important to me. They are my scaffolding; my sounding board and my release – just as I hope I am for them. In their company, I can be myself – not anyone's employee or boss or wife or mother or daughter. Just me. And it's liberating. I feel accepted just as

I am, and grateful for the insight, empathy and advice that they can offer.

Experts agree that the idea of a 'best friend' is very much like the notion of 'The One' when it comes to relationships – a fairytale. No one friend – or romantic partner – can fulfil all of our needs, so having several close friends offers a buffer, in case one of the friendships ends. This has certainly been my experience, so I can't wait to see Pans Solo and Head Girl – two funny, sweary girls who are among my favourite people on earth but who I don't see as often as I'd like any more.

When we met at university, the lazy days of studenthood stretched endlessly before us. But then *life* happened and we became busy with work, relationships and families. Suddenly we had more *memories* than actual time together. So we had to schedule in more of it. Daily WhatsApp chats help bridge the gaps between meetings. Here, we can discuss everything from the best type of cheese (*'Gorgonzola? Are you MENTAL? Brie. Every time.'*), to exciting life developments (*'Made it to my hairdresser's Instagram feed today: hitting all my life goals!'*) as well as the serious stuff like illnesses, loss and heartache. We have 108 years of combined living experience between us, so if one is having relationship problems, the other two will have something supportive to say. If another has a nightmare at work, there'll be a third who's encountered something similar and can empathise. We've known each other long enough not to shy away from the tricky times, too. They can be relied upon to shoot from the lip for a much-needed reality check when I'm being a *'bit of a div'*, as one recently put it.

Because our time together is precious, when we meet up we can TALK. For days. Last time I saw them, we lost five hours into the chat-vortex, over tea that was stone cold by the time the cafe owner booted us out. On a summer visit, there was so much excitement during a reunion at a National Trust property (middle-class alert) that we set off the stately home's resident peacocks, who thought we were squawky new birds encroaching on their patch/peafowl. One of the males came right up to our Marks & Spencer picnic and splayed his plumage until we conceded defeat. Turns out it's hard to tell an anecdote about discovering your ex on a novelty ironing board (true story) with a hundred iridescent blue feathered 'eyes' staring at you. It all got a bit Hitchcock and we were asked to keep it down or leave. So we found a nearby pub and the chatathon continued.

But it's not just that hanging out with friends feels nice: it's good for us, too. As proven by science (thank you, science).

'Research has shown that friendships are vital to an individual's health and emotional well-being throughout their life,' says Irene Levine, psychologist and professor of psychiatry at the NYU School of Medicine, who also runs online advice column *The Friendship Blog*. 'Having close friends can reduce stress and anxiety; decrease your risk of depression; promote a sense of belonging; lower the heart rate as well as reducing cholesterol and decreasing blood pressure. Friendship is a like a behavioural vaccine.'

That's not to say that being a friend, or making a new one, is easy. 'The "rules" of friendship are vague and it's hard to pinpoint exactly when a friendship begins and when it ends,' says Irene: 'Friendships can't be sustained on nostalgia alone and it's important to build new memories through shared experiences.'

This is something I've been aware of since the formal

festivals of friendship started to fizzle out. For years, at school or university, I saw friends daily. Then there were monthly weddings or hen dos. For ten years I was so skint and hungover that I took these enforced gatherings for granted and almost began to dread them. But since then, they've started to thin out. We've only got one wedding this year and on the last hen do I attended, two of the women packed breast pumps. Times have changed.

Now, friends-only weekends are such a novelty that I'm genuinely excited by the prospect of wearing deely-boppers and coughing up £400 to be sick in a canal on the next hen do. And the idea of Head Girl and Pans Solo for two whole days is a total treat. We'll create new memories and stories to sustain us, just as Irene suggests. I just hope Pans Solo is up for it.

What if she just wants some time to herself? I wonder. *What if she doesn't want to hang out with us?* And then an awful thought occurs to me: *What if she doesn't want to be friends with us any more?*

The Oxford University psychologist Robin Dunbar studies social groupings and has discovered that we all need a set number of friends, beyond which we can't compute relationships in any real way. We need five close friends, fifteen good ones and up to a hundred and fifty in our outer circle. Five is considered to be a manageable number for a close grouping – both in humans and the ape kingdom – while fifteen is a jolly-monkey-party or a big night out. And a hundred and fifty is everyone you like and know – really know – to talk to. 'Each of these layers corresponds to a particular level of emotional closeness and to a particular level of frequency of contact: the limits on the layers are at least once a week, once a month, about once a year,' the prof tells me over email when I beg for more information. 'This may be because creating bonds of a given emotional intensity requires the investment of quite a specific amount of time. Drop below that, and the person slips very quickly – within months – into the next layer below in terms of emotional closeness.'

The idea that most of our friends are replaceable may seem harsh, but psychology professors Mark Leary from Duke University in North Carolina and Roy Baumeister from Florida State University have also found the old saying that friends are for a reason, a season or a lifetime to be true. They discovered that if a relationship dissolves, the bond can be replaced with a connection to another person fairly easily.

This means that if Pans Solo has been avoiding us, there's a very real possibility that she's casting us out of her inner circle.

'Irene?' I plead, 'Is there a way we can know if someone's had enough of us? Is there a mental checklist or something we can use to establish whether a friendship has run its course?' I'm hoping she'll say 'no', preferably followed by:

'Don't be daft! We may only be loosely acquainted in a purely professional context but I can tell already that YOU are UTTERLY delightful and no one would EVER want to break up with you! Haven't you and Pans Solo got a peacock anecdote together? I mean! Really! That's a bond for life right there!'

To which I'd reply, 'Yes! Exactly!' and then 'Phew!'

What Irene actually says is this: 'Major life events – such as leaving a job, moving to a new neighbourhood, getting married, going through a divorce or becoming a first-time parent – can topple long-time friendships.'

Crap, I think: *she's changed jobs, I've moved countries and had a baby and Head Girl's been through a divorce. This isn't looking good . . .* Has the gulf between us become too wide to cross?

'Changes in circumstances can create so much distance that those friends no longer share common ground.'

Great. Thanks, Irene.

I think about this and realise I have a few friendships that may have run their course, too – relationships where the petrol light is on and we're running on vapour or memories. I think through the table plan at our wedding and realise that I haven't seen 50 per cent of the guests since we got hitched.

'I'm so glad we shelled out a hundred quid for them to eat salmon and dance to The Cure . . .' says Lego Man when I inform him of this fact.

I like to think I've worked to preserve the friendships that are important to me. But perhaps I've also invested too much in ones I should have let go. I've flown 1,000 kilometres to see friends who couldn't be bothered to drive half an hour down the road to see me the next time I was in town. Then there was the girl I made an effort to meet up with, suggesting dinner, only to be downgraded to coffee. Or the friend who spent an entire lunch checking his phone and then asked the waiter, 'Is there a Wi-Fi password?' I cheered silently when the waiter told him: 'We don't have Wi-Fi, you'll have to talk to each other like it's the 1990s.' The only thing I have in common with some of these people, I realise, is that we used to be friends.

'If we're alert to the signs that a friendship may be drifting apart, the process of "breaking up" can be far less painful,' says Irene. 'In fact, there may be ways to repair some failing relationships, or to at least prepare yourself emotionally so you don't feel like you were dumped when they reach their end point,' she adds. Which is handy. Because being 'dumped' by a friend sounds like the worst – even more painful than being dumped by a lover, according to a study from Manchester University. I can only imagine the dejected lab technicians consuming litres of Ben & Jerry's and sobbing into their white coats during this particular experiment.

'There are a few major signs that point to a friendship going sour,' says Irene. 'Firstly, you have trouble finding time to see each other. You may have said countless times, *'Let's get together!'* but nothing materialises.'

Oh God, I think: *this is true of Pans Solo and me.*

'You might begin to self-monitor what you say and feel unable to talk about certain subjects – because either you'll get too upset or you think they will,' Irene goes on.

I don't talk about Little Red much in front of Pans Solo because I know how much she wants kids.

But isn't this my problem rather than hers? My own 'guilt' that the years of trying worked out? She has never been prickly about motherhood – the way I often felt when friends got pregnant and I was sticking syringes into my stomach every day for two years. *She's a nicer person than I am,* I think.

'Your friendship could also be out of sync because of a relatively minor, but resolvable, problem that's been allowed to fester,' adds Irene. 'If that's the case, speak face-to-face, and make an effort to get things back on track. Don't be shy about letting her know you miss the way things were, and tell her how much her friendship means to you. If you notice her pulling back, ask what's wrong before things snowball.'

Okay, I think, *that's what I'm doing. We can make this work.*

But Irene has one more friendship red flag.

'Sometimes, time spent together just doesn't feel the same. Conversation used to flow effortlessly but now you might feel self-conscious. If you realise your lives and values have veered in different directions, it may be time to let go and stop feigning a closeness that is no longer there – both of you will be happier this way. Cultivate other friendships and let this one drift – because contrary to the myths perpetuated by movies and TV shows (hello, *Friends*!), most friendships – even very good ones – don't last for ever.'

And, er, how do we know if we're being cast adrift?

There may be fifty ways to leave your lover, but there are, apparently, four main ways to end a friendship, according to Irene.

'There's taking a break; diluting the friendship by seeing a friend less often or with other people as opposed to one-on-one; and then there's the "slow fade" – opting out by not extending or accepting invitations.'

Oh . . .

I wonder whether this is what Pans Solo has been attempting. I've always thought of 'friend-dumping' as a more brutal affair – or at the very least something I'd know about. A bit more like Irene's fourth suggestion: 'Putting things in writing helps you think through the best way to convey a difficult message – your friend will always remember the words you use, so you have to be careful in what you say.' First-person statements that begin with 'I' are advised: 'For example, "I've decided I need a break from our friendship." This isn't the time to unload all the negative thoughts you've accumulated over the years, so just explain that the relationship isn't working for you. If a friendship has consistently been draining and unsatisfying, it's likely that it was also feeling that way for your friend. After they get over the initial pain of a break-up, they often feel a sense of relief. Moreover, they're poised to find new friendships that build upon what they've learned from their past experiences.'

Head Girl 'broke up' with a friend this way a few years back, citing 'irreconcilable differences'. 'Rebecca', let's call her, had always been 'the pretty one' at school and it was a defining characteristic she'd carried with her into adult life.

'You know the sort – sits on the groom's lap at a wedding and only ever does "sexy" fancy dress. A marriage wrecking ball who wouldn't think twice about spreading, or inventing, gossip about other people's relationships. Massive show-off. If you've done a poo, she's done two,' Head Girl told me. 'So I emailed Becky Two Shits one day and told her she'd gone too far. That careless talk costs wives. I said I hadn't been enjoying spending time together for a while, then I told her to take care and signed off.'

'"*Take care?*" Nice touch . . .' This had seemed callous at the time. But now I wonder whether it was preferable to ghosting one's way out of a friendship.

I hope – really hope – that things aren't over with Pans Solo.

There's only one way to find out.

'Better get some hummus in,' says Lego Man as he heaves a two-man tent on to one shoulder and a holdall, bulging with beer cans, on to the other.

'Sorry?' I'm scanning the floor, debating whether or not to Hoover. I decide 'not': *It'll be dark soon, they won't notice . . .*

'Hummus!' he says again: 'For the girls? Women love a chickpea paste.'

'Do they?' I think about this and then concede: 'Yes. Yes, we do.'

'Oh and you might want to get more crisps,' he adds, nodding his head towards the holdall to indicate that he's swiped any remaining stocks from the cupboard. Lego Man is making himself scarce for the night to go 'camping and shouting'. He and his friends think they have invented a brave new method to cure modern man of all his ills, but it's basically a form of primal scream therapy in a forest where no one can hear them holler. They build a fire, grill meat, drink beer and then scream into a black sky filled with sparks until they either feel better, or pass out. He's packed a two-man tent because the dog is going with him. As part of the modern-man cure, his friends have decided that they would all like a dog, too – but only in very small doses. So ours becomes a communal pet for the night and sleeps in the tent with Lego Man. Which we can all agree is A Bit Weird. But the dog loves these trips and is already manic with excitement about the opportunity for a sausage. Lego Man always comes home in a much better mood, albeit stinking of woodsmoke – for days, despite multiple showers – so I'm supportive of these manscursions. And besides, Pans Solo is scared of dogs. *A marauding mutt might push her over the friendship precipice.*

I hate a gender stereotype, but I can't help thinking that Lego Man's friendships are infinitely simpler than my own, though perhaps less rewarding and with fewer opportunities for heartfelt compliments. Like this one, which shrieks into the kitchen like a cheap firework two hours later when the girls arrive.

'Ooh, hummus! Mmm. House looking fab! And what have you done to your hair? I love the colour. It looks like spun gold!' is how Head Girl kicks off, instantly noticing a new 'do' I got last month that has completely passed my husband by. We hug, and then she sniffs, suspiciously. I'm wearing a perfume that Lego Man bought me for my birthday. It smells 'outdoorsy' and has something to do with sandalwood. I'm not massively keen, only dabbing it on occasionally to appear grateful and avoid a Lemonheads meltdown. But Head Girl's not having any of it.

'You know you smell like a deer, right? A *nice* deer, but I just wanted to check it was "deer" you were going for.'

'Thank you, yes. It was a present: Lemonheads avoidance tactic.'

'Ah! Understood. Good work.' She bustles past me so that I can get to Pans Solo.

'Don't break up with us!' I want to howl, but instead I give her a hug, tell her she looks eighteen (she does, excellent SPF use), and offer her tea.

'Got any wine?' Head Girl asks instead.

Pans Solo is, as feared, rather quiet and withdrawn. For the rest of the evening she doesn't give much away, other than to reveal that she's adopted a stray cat she's named Adele who occasionally stops by and watches *House of Cards* with her. At this, Head Girl shoots me a sidelong glance to imply something along the lines of: '*Uh-oh, things are worse than we thought . . .*'

Fortunately, I have a plan. It is a plan devised in haste and inspired by a seven-year-old (always the best sort of plan). A friend's daughter recently gave me an unprompted download of 'school and stuff', as only a self-possessed seven-year-old can, telling me, all in one breath, about how her class had tried a team-building game: 'It's called Thinking Hats and we thought it was going to be like the sorting hat in *Harry Potter*, which tells you which house you should go into and I would be Gryffindor or maybe Hufflepuff, but these are different hats that help you to think about things in different ways like maybe how one of your friends might think about something and you might not and so helps you to understand them better—' She gasped for air before adding: 'I liked the yellow hat best.' Then she ran off in search of something more interesting to do than talk at a boring old grown-up.

After quizzing her parents, I established that she was talking about Six Thinking Hats – a tool devised by the Maltese psychologist and physician Dr Edward de Bono in the 1980s to help promote creativity and empathy. The idea is that as individuals, we tend to think in a rut. But by using de Bono's structured system of thinking, we challenge ourselves to think more creatively, empathetically and honestly. There are six different modes of thinking that de Bono recommends, each represented by a different-coloured hat.

Blue is the 'managing hat' and is used to start the process – deciding what the subject or goal of the discussion should be – then again at the end to look at conclusions and next steps. Other than this, the sequence of hats is chosen at whim. A white hat is worn for gathering information and assembling facts. Red symbolises intuitive or instinctive gut reactions or statements of emotional feeling and the black hat is about discernment and identifying reasons to be cautious and conservative. The seven-year-old's favourite yellow hat is about seeing the positives and identifying benefits to any course of action. And the green hat – the trickiest of all the hat colours to pull off in real life (I've tried) – is used to signify creative thinking and ideas for what to do next. Switching to a different mode of thinking is symbolised by putting on another-coloured hat, either physically or meta-phorically. Everyone wears the same colour at the same time so that they're all on the same page.

The theatricality – and opportunity for new millinery – of this technique appealed and it struck me as an interesting way to encourage empathy and honesty. So I ordered de Bono's book online. At the checkout, a message flashed up suggesting that I '*might also like* . . .' six glitter bowler hats.

Yes! I thought, high on discovery and shopping: *I WOULD like six glitter bowler hats!*

Amazed at how I'd made it this far in life without six glitter bowler hats in my wardrobe arsenal, I added them to my basket before checking out. Then I rounded up a few other headpieces lurking around the house, in preparation.

Now, I've read the book; I've got the hats; and the girls are *in situ*. But I could do with an expert to assure me that I'm ploughing the best friendship furrow. So once Head Girl and Pans Solo are safely tucked up in bed, I make a final call to the US, where it's still late afternoon.

Chuck Dymer, a man who sounds as though he's leapt from the pages of a Jack Reacher novel, was a marketing manager for a software firm when he first encountered

Edward de Bono's theory. 'I read about Six Thinking Hats on the plane from Washington to Kansas City, where I live, and by the time we touched down I was hooked! I arranged to meet with de Bono, persuaded him I could teach his theory and worked with him as his sole trainer for five years – that was twenty-eight years ago and it's been a huge part of my life ever since.' Six Thinking Hats is now used worldwide in schools and businesses, especially in Australia and New Zealand, and increasingly in the UK and the US. It's such a big deal in Venezuela that children spend an hour a week studying de Bono, *by law*. His method has been used by NASA as well as international corporations including Speedo, Shell, Siemens, BP and IBM. It's said that Six Thinking Hats even facilitated parts of the Northern Ireland peace process. *Fair play,* I think: *three old friends = not a problem.*

I tell Chuck about my plan and my pre-assembled hat collection.

'The hats can be metaphorical, you know—'

'Yes, I know. I just really like hats,' I tell him, before moving on: 'So, what was it about de Bono's theory that spoke to you? What's so great about Thinking Hats?'

'Where to begin!' Chuck is an enthusiastic man. 'It's a great way to get over initial reactions and biases and get to thinking and understanding a little deeper. Most of the time, we're not thinking in the most effective way – we gather information that supports ideas we already have, like reading news that already supports our worldview.' I tell him I'm guilty of this and he assures me that we all are. In our age of social media, more of us than ever are operating in an echo chamber.

'But Six Thinking Hats encourage us to try out different

points of view in a structured way,' explains Chuck. 'Take the red hat, for example: by allowing us to express thoughts and feelings without justifying them, we clearly see what's a gut reaction and what's fact. And when we work through the hats, we often move away from our initial position – it's a very powerful thing. The green hat frees us up from preconceived ideas, and the blue hat clearly states, "This is what we're thinking about" and "This is the desired outcome" – something we often lose sight of in traditional meetings or discussions.'

I can see the advantages of thinking this way in business and even schools. But I'm a woman with a troubled houseguest and a desk full of novelty hats: please tell me this works in our personal lives, too?

'Well,' Chuck starts, 'I've never formally used Six Thinking Hats at home with my wife but sometimes, when I ask for her opinion and she gives me a negative response, I'll say, "Now you're just being Black Hat!"'

'Right. And how does that go down?'

'She'll pause, say "thank you", then we'll move on.'

Chuck's wife sounds very understanding.

'What about friends? Could you use it with them?'

'That's an interesting one,' says Chuck. 'I don't see why not. It should help with honesty and empathy. So if I ask a friend, "Hey, what do you think of my new coat?" If he's a good friend, he may not want to hurt my feelings so he'll say, "Yeah, it's a great coat!" But you know what? He may not be being totally honest: it may not be such a great coat . . .'

'No . . .'

'But with our black hats on, I could say, "I would really appreciate your honest view on this coat"!'

What if we are Pans Solo's unwanted coat? I worry. *What if she just needs to put a black hat on to tell us this?*

'Of course it can work the other way as well: if someone's always negative, you could say, "Let's try the yellow hat, I could really do with your help taking a positive look at something". The coat might help keep you warm, for example.'

I decide I like the idea of a coat as a metaphor for friendship: it keeps us warm, protects us from the outside world and – unless times are tough – we have more than one of them. Plus they can usually be relied on to have snacks and tissues somewhere about them. At least, in my case. *I'm happy to be Pans Solo's coat for as long as she needs me. We'll just have to see if she still has space in her wardrobe . . .*

I thank Chuck and promise to report back on my groundbreaking Six Thinking Hats for friendship session ('You may have stumbled on something there!' he says.)

The next day, pummelled, scrubbed and smelling faintly of patchouli oil ('an improvement on deer,' in my case, according to Head Girl), we sit around a turquoise pool, encased in fluffy robes. Having handed Little Red over to a smoky-yet-content Lego Man on his return from the wilderness, we've booked in to a nearby spa hotel for the night on an off-season deal to do some therapeutic 'lounging'. I'm hoping that spending time somewhere neutral might help Pans open up. When we eventually pad back up to our room in disposable slippers, we're as relaxed as we're ever going to be, so I introduce the idea of the hats.

'Drinking Hats?' Head Girl perks up.

'No, "*thinking*",' I tell her.

'Oh.'

'Although, it is five o clock . . .' Pans Solo looks at her phone as Head Girl starts dialling down to the bar.

I explain that I'd like us to try out de Bono's exercise, 'for research purposes', insisting that they'd be doing me a huge favour and that it's 'for work'. Which is true.

'It would be great to think about friendship, just theoretically of course—'

'Of course!' says Head Girl, clocking what I mean. We are both appalling at subtlety.

Before Pans Solo guesses that something's afoot, I unzip my bag containing a bewildering variety of hats, and tip them onto the bed by way of distraction: 'Ta da!' I explain about the different-coloured hats and apologise that our versions are a little . . . *eclectic*.

'I don't mean to brag,' says Head Girl, 'but I've actually got my own white hat . . .' She pulls a slim plastic packet from her bag and unfurls an exceptionally alluring rubber swimming hat, peeling its sides apart and stretching it over her head. 'I got it free at the airport with my swimsuit. Hot stuff, right?'

Pans Solo reveals that she too has unwittingly come prepared and proffers a scrunched-up black beanie, rolling it down her face as far as her nose.

'Beautiful! Though I'm afraid we start with blue hats,' I tell them.

There is a scramble for the blue glitter bowler hat and Pans Solo wins, so Head Girl makes do with a peaked base-ball cap and I wear a fascinator that I bought a hundred years ago and have never worn (because: fascinator).

'Great! Now, to get started, we need to come up with a

question or a problem we're trying to address about friendship, and a goal. So . . . just off the top of my head,' I start with a bad fake laugh, gesturing to the hideous feathered monstrosity now bobbing in my eyeline, 'I was reading *in a magazine*[20] about what happens when one friend in a group starts to be a bit distant . . .'

Head Girl raises her eyebrows and gives me a *'Really?'* look that tells me I'm fooling no one. But Pans Solo just drinks wine, studiously, so I press on.

'Perhaps we could think about, say, how a group of friends could best support each other. Because we all go through tough times, don't we? But I feel like we're not always great at asking for help. So this is an exercise in, er, making us.'

I'm pretty sure Chuck would have explained things better than this. Or even his wife. *Just act normal, everyone! Nobody freak out!*

'So, the starting point is how we can support each other better?' clarifies Pans Solo.

'And we have to take a sip every time we speak?' adds Head Girl: 'Ooh and we have to drink while we think! So no stalling?'

'That isn't exactly how it works, no—' I start, but then notice that Pans Solo has already necked her glass and think that perhaps it might not be such a bad idea. *If it helps her open up, why not?* 'Okay, fine,' I relent, aware that I would make a shockingly bad supply teacher. Head Girl refills our glasses, points out that the bottle's nearly empty and offers to fetch another from downstairs. She comes back with two

---

20 The universally accepted lie utilised by experimental spouses everywhere . . .

('to save time later'). By this point, the glass I've already imbibed on top of a post-massage cava ('It's tradition!' Head Girl had insisted, though nobody was quite sure whose) is catching up with me and I feel fuzzy.

I attempt to wrest back control of the situation: 'So, we all live apart, and we want to think about how we can better support each other as friends. That's our jumping-off point. Then we're aiming for, say, ten ways in which we can help each other out more. Sound okay?' There are nods. 'Great. Now, let's switch to red hats!'

I'm already making for the pile on the bed, but I'm too slow: Head Girl snatches the red glitter bowler; Pans Solo takes the impulse-buy trilby that I've never had the guts to wear outside the house; and I'm left with a bobble hat that shrank in the wash and so now merely perches on my head. 'So with our *red* hats on –' I consult my A4 printout – 'we're going to "*express our honest, unfiltered feelings*".'

I hope that doing this within a framework will deperson-alise it and allow Pans to say things she might not normally feel able to. I explain that red hat thinking is limited to around thirty seconds to make sure we all share exactly what's on our minds without editing it first. 'How about we all say the one thing we're currently struggling with? Remember, it's our instinctive, gut response. It doesn't have to be rational, it's just how we feel. Who wants to go first?'

'Well . . .' Head Girl starts, then shakes her head and downs the rest of her drink while spluttering, 'Not editing! Just thinking! And drinking . . .'

'All right, well I suppose I can go,' I say. 'I feel stressed and scared about the idea of relocating and all the things we'd have to do to prepare for it. And I'm shattered. All the time.' This is not new, or news, but I'm keen to get the confessional ball rolling.

'Good one! Now: drink!' chants Head Girl. I remind her that this isn't that sort of game ('THINKING hats!'). 'Ah, yes. Right. Okay. Well, I've got one,' she says: 'I'm a bit bored. Work's okay but it's hardly setting the world on fire. And I went on a date last week with someone whose party trick was reciting capital cities.'

'God, I'm sorry . . .'

'S'okay.' She nods, eyes closed, as though acknowledging that yes, this was pretty horrific. 'But don't worry: I've got a plan. I'll tell you about it when we get to the green hat part.'

Of all the people to have fixed their own problem before the rest of us have even had the chance to even air ours, it was always going to be Head Girl. She refills everyone's glasses. Again. Until we're all fairly lubricated.

'My turn?' asks Pans Solo, sounding very small. 'Um, okay.' She takes a large gulp of wine. 'Well, sometimes, when Adele's not around—'

'Who the hell's Adele?' Head Girl is practically heckling now.

'The *cat*,' I hiss, 'keep up!'

'It can feel a bit, well, *lonely* . . .' Pans Solo backtracks almost immediately: 'but work's busy and there's always loads of people around and I live right in the middle of things—' She stops herself from saying any more. But it's already out there: lonely. The word has a sting – a power to it – and saying it out loud has an effect that none of us were quite prepared for. Pans Solo goes on to describe a weekend when all her plans fell through and she didn't see another soul from 6 p.m. on Friday until 8 a.m. on Monday.

'Not even Adele?'

'Not even Adele.'

'My love, that's awful!' Head Girl bounces along the bed to get closer and puts an arm round our friend. 'You should have called me! I would have come over or we could have gone out—'

'I did, remember? On the Saturday? You said you were hungover and you had a crime scene period so would I mind if we rain checked . . .'

Head Girl's eyes flick left, trying to summon the memory: 'Oh God, yes. I remember. I'm so sorry—'

'It's okay.' Pans Solo shakes her head slightly. 'I watched some pretty good TV. I've taken to Sky Plus-ing *Home and Away* – the sunshine always cheers me up – so I had a bumper stash to work through—' She stops as Head Girl and I both stare at her. 'Oh no, that's bad, isn't it?'

'No!' we say in unison. What we mean is: 'Yes.'

When your friend is lonely you feel like a bad friend. And the fact that she lives in glittering London doesn't help much either. There's a particular quality to city loneliness. It's more taboo somehow – or made more painful, perhaps – because everyone else seems to be out there having a lovely time. Right in front of you.

'It's like I'm stuck behind glass all day at the office then again at home. I feel as though life's sort of happening all around me, on the other side of the pane,' is how she puts it. 'I look out at everyone, having a nice time, and think: *Why isn't that me? What's wrong with me?*'

We both leap in to tell her: 'It's not *you*' – and mean it, too. Because dodging loneliness seems to be more of a lucky break than the norm. Something we'll all face at some point. I have a toddler and a dog who like to follow me everywhere and demand things from me during my every waking hour, so it's hard to imagine being alone. But lonely? I remember times when I have been. Maternity leave was tough and rural Denmark has nothing as fancy as NCT. I only knew two other women with babies and strangely, they didn't go for my idea of setting up a kibbutz where we could all live together and share the ~~misery~~ 'wonder' of the first three months of sleepless nights and sore nipples.

I'm saddened that Pans Solo has been suffering in silence. Far from wanting 'out' of our friendship as I'd feared, she needs more from it than we've currently been giving her.

Lots of us experience times when we're too low to ask for help – which is just when we need it most. 'No news' isn't necessarily 'good news' when it comes to friendships and an unusual radio silence should have been a warning sign that all was not well. During my own low patches, it's the friends who've reached out, demanding nothing in return, who have really made the difference. The phrase 'no need to reply' was generously used by one of my oldest friends during The Stormy Summer Of 2007 (see 'starting over hat-trick') and her texts, emails and letters kept me going when all else was disintegrating. *So how could I have forgotten to use it now?*

And the cat! I think, *where was Adele all this time? That's the trouble with cats: too independent. Not needy and ridiculously happy to see you all the time, like a dog . . .*

Pans Solo presses at the corners of her eyes as though trying not to cry. 'Anyway, aren't we supposed to have a costume change around now?'

'Well, yes,' I say, realising that we've already broken Chuck's thirty-second red hat rule, 'but are you sure you want to?'

She nods. 'We've got an experiment to do! And anyway, I want to wear THIS.' She picks out Lego Man's 'barbecue chef's hat' that was once white but is now a dingy grey, with the faintest of ketchup stains down the left-hand side. Head Girl squeezes into her talc-lubricated swimming cap, so I take the opportunity to nab the spangly bowler hat before realising, with some disappointment, that it makes me look a disco-butcher.

'Okay then,' I plough on, 'the white hat is all about facts – so what do we know about the topic?' I read from my piece of paper to make it sound official and to stop Pans Solo from feeling self-conscious: 'It has to be verifiable information that we've either experienced first-hand or seen an official report on or something. So,' I continue, setting the paper down and looking at Head Girl for support, 'just for example, we could take loneliness as a *social phenomenon*.' I emphasise the last two words.

Fortunately, the good people at the BBC recently made a documentary on this and Head Girl watched it – so we are *rich* in facts. Britain is apparently the loneliest nation in Europe and social isolation affects one in four. Many of us move away from friends and family for work or to study, and while we may think that we can keep up with loved ones online, this can't replicate the benefits of face-to-face contact.

'Studies have linked loneliness to physical illnesses, like heart disease and cancer,' says Head Girl. 'It's so bad that it even increases the chance of early death by twenty per cent, same as obesity—'

All right, reel it in! I raise my eyebrows at her.

She gets the hint: 'So, basically, we're supposed to be sociable as a species and our brains interpret isolation in the same way as *physical pain*. We did this in biology,' she adds, proudly, always pleased to find a use for her otherwise purely decorative science degree.

'And Skype and FaceTime don't cut it?' I ask.

'Do you humanities graduates know nothing?' She shakes her head, exasperated. 'We have two rewards systems: there's dopamine, so the buzz we get from a message on Facebook or buying casserole dishes –' here she looks at Pans Solo – 'Then there's serotonin – the long-term feel-good hormone, the one antidepressants mess with – and oxytocin, the cuddle drug that mums get with their kids and stuff. When we're cut off, we can get the dopamine from online contact and shopping, but we're not getting the oxytocin or serotonin – which makes us sad.' She looks at Pans Solo. 'Sorry . . .'

'No, it's true,' she says as a fat tear swells and then falls out of her right eye. 'I do feel sad. It just feels so . . . silly to admit it!'

'It's not silly!' I scoot over so that Head Girl and I are now flanking her. 'It's perfectly normal. We're just really sorry you've been feeling like this and we haven't been able to help!'

The tears are coming fast now and she snorts slightly, then knocks back another slug of wine before continuing: 'I sometimes just sort of skid into the weekend, forgetting to arrange anything. And then suddenly I'm watching *The Voice* in my pyjamas on a Saturday, alone. Because even bloody Adele has plans.'

That cat! I think: *Talk about ungrateful . . .*

Head Girl has located a travel pack of Kleenex Ultra Balm Tissues (friends = like coats #1) and is now wiping Pans Solo's nose for her, as though she's a small child. *Extraordinary*.

'A weekend skid isn't so unusual,' I say.

'No?'

'If I don't plan anything, it won't occur to Lego Man that Saturday's coming up and that it might actually be nice to see people.'

'Sometimes,' she confesses, 'if I haven't been out for a while, I can't face trying to organise anything. You know?'

I don't know, in this instance. As a freelancer working from home, I am hungry for excursions come evenings and weekends – champing at the bit for an excuse to brush my hair and talk to people. But I appreciate that this isn't the case for everyone. And even Head Girl has experience here.

'We did a campaign on this!' she says, spilling wine on the bed in her excitement. Head Girl works in PR (you'd never guess . . .). 'Half of us avoid seeing friends once a month because we're bushed or can't be bothered. Then we end up feeling as though going out is too much of a big deal. And the more worried we get, the more we think socialising is harder than it is, so we stick to the simpler online stuff and quick fixes that don't make us happy long-term.'

'So what do we do about it?'

'You're the one with the printed-out plan!'

'Oh yes!' I consult my sheet. 'Um, now we do black hats!'

I pull on a witch's hat from Halloween and Head Girl picks up a small black disc.

'Is this a *kippah*?'

'Yes, Lego Man got it at a friend's wedding.'

'So I see.' She reads: '"*Sally and Aiden, 2011*".' Is that kosher, wearing it for fancy dress?'

'You try finding eighteen hats at a few days' notice!'

'Don't worry, I can beanie it,' says Pans Solo, rolling on her knitted number and crowning Head Girl with the black spangled bowler, which makes her look distractingly like Sally

Bowles from *Cabaret*. We all take a moment to do our best Liza Minnelli impressions before the exercise can continue.

'Right then,' I go on eventually, 'so discernment: black hat means being realistic and practical about things.'

Pans Solo tucks her hair up into her beanie, ready for action: 'Okay, well I know, logically, that London is a huge city. That it can be lonely, and that everyone is busy. No one's life is perfect – like you say, we all have responsibilities, we're all grown-ups. Lots of my friends have kids – they have their own stuff to worry about. They can't drop everything for a drunken late-night chat. And also, I think I've just had a rubbish few months.'

She's right, of course. About all of these things. But I worry that agreeing too enthusiastically will downplay her pain. *What would Chuck do?*

'City living is busy,' I concur, tentatively, 'and there must be lots of people in the same situation as you. But that could also mean there are some simple solutions—'

'I thought we were meant to be in black hat mode?' Head Girl interjects. I give her a pleading look and she changes tack: 'On the other hand, who doesn't love a yellow hat? How about we raid the minibar for munchies, then crack on?' (Friends – like coats #2).

Pans Solo is diverted by the promise of a Pringle so I abscond to the bathroom for a power wee, emerging moments later (I'm a very efficient pee-er), resplendent in elasticated plastic glory.

'Are you wearing a shower cap?'

'I couldn't find enough yellow hats –' I point at my head – 'and I've got blonde hair.'

'So?'

'That's pretty much yellow. I wasn't going to fork out £5.99

for another *Fireman Sam* hat.' I nod at the child's helmet that Pans Solo is now sporting.

'All right, Little Miss Sunshine, we'll forgive you. Pans has ordered pizza and garlic bread to go with the Pringles, so bagsie you have to open the door when it arrives.'

'All the carbs, excellent. Will do.'

I scout around for my A4 printout telling us what to do next, and then see Head Girl holding it aloft.

'Okay, "yellow" thinking.' She picks up the free hotel pen and doodles to get the ink flowing. She's so used to being in charge that she now appears to be leading the exercise. 'What are the benefits to the way we live now?' Head Girl exudes a natural authority I can only dream of, so I leave her to it.

'Well, like we said, there are lots of people who must be feeling the same way in a big city,' says Pans Solo.

'And you're more likely to find opportunities to go out and do interesting things there,' adds Head Girl. 'Plus it's better to be alone than coupled up with an arse or living with someone who steals your yoghurt.' We all exchange a knowing look as we remember The Great Unsolved Dairy Heist of 1998. 'Although if you did want to meet someone new, there's a bigger pool to choose from in a city.'

This is true, and I feel glad that Pans will be spared the delights of Craig from High Wycombe, or 'Mr Cock Shot' as Recent Dumpee now refers to him.

'Also, most of your friends live close by,' I go on, 'even the ones who've moved out are only an hour away. And friends with kids are *precisely* the people you can call drunk at 5 a.m., because, chances are, we're already up. And knackered and in need of some solidarity or news from the outside world.' Head Girl and Pans Solo both take a moment to absorb this. 'And you live really close to three different airports so you can come and visit me whenever you like!'

'Great stuff,' says Head Girl scribbling notes, 'but now we're in green hat territory. Shall we move on?' She selects an oversized velvet leprechaun hat from St Patrick's Day. Pans Solo gets the bowler prize with a lime-coloured creation that is now shedding its glittery load all over our bed, as I balance a leftover cracker hat on my crown.

'So the green hat is meant to be about energy and ideas – think new shoots and springtime—' I start.

'We want creative solutions, ladies!' Head Girl jumps in.

I sink back into the soft downy pillows, resigned to being a passenger on this one, and shout out suggestions.

'We could do three-way Skype! Like we're in a bad split-screen teen movie!'

'Or we could have a code word, like with kinky sex, for when we need help!' says Head Girl.

'Um –' I scan the room for inspiration – '"Leprechaun"!' She looks at me.

'We can finesse these later,' placates Pans Solo.

'Okay, how about scheduling in more meet-ups, weekly calls, check-ins—' I suggest.

'You could rent a dog!' Head Girl yelps.

'I don't like dogs.' Pans Solo looks perplexed.

'I could rent a dog!' Head Girl is standing now. 'You see adverts: "*Dog walker wanted, one day a week*". I would *love* that!'

'Good for you!'

Head Girl suggests they both try a Tinder-style platonic 'mating' app ('like "Hey! VINA", which, FYI, has nothing to do with wine . . .' she adds, in case we were in any doubt).

I encourage Pans Solo to join a running club or a choir – both of which release endorphins. 'And doing them as part of a group helps foster a sense of belonging. Studies show we're more likely to show up and stick at something if we do it with other people because we're mindful of letting our teammates down,' I tell her. 'What? I wrote an article about it. I'm fully geeked up.'

Head Girl has some geekery of her own to offer: 'So as you know I am practically a medic, having studied biology for three years—

'Funny, you never mention it.'

'Well, according to *neuroscience*, the best remedy for loneliness is human touch. Hugs release oxytocin, so we need as many of these as we can get. Obviously no one's recommending indiscriminate groping. . .' She looks at me here. *Me! As though I have form in this area!* (I do not). 'If there's no one around you can hug without getting sued, or fired, *massage* has been shown to up serotonin by thirty per cent. And decrease stress hormones. And raise dopamine. But mainly, whenever possible, bag yourself a hug 'cos they're free and quicker,' she concludes before launching herself across the bed and on to Pans Solo.

There is more wine. And then pizza. And then someone suggests seeing how many hats we can balance on our head at any one time. I lose, and we pass out shortly after this, collectively collapsing in the king-sized bed, still in our fluffy robes, until morning. We wake up dribbling, with varying degrees of hangover and imprints of terry towelling all over.

'Put the telly on?' croaks Head Girl. Pans Solo is ordering room service and I'm liaising with Lego Man on what the rest of the day looks like.

'The TV's all in Danish,' I warn, throwing her the remote.

'Doesn't matter.' She wipes at the dried mascara under her eyes with the cord of her robe. 'I just want something to look at while I sweat wine and eat scrambled eggs.'

Once we've checked out, Lego Man, Little Red and the dog meet us for a walk on the beach, bringing welcome supplies of strong coffee in a giant Thermos. Seagulls caw, waves crash and the air smells clean and ever so slightly sulphurous. Pans Solo tries to avoid the dog and Little Red runs around in circles shouting 'Tractorrr!' into the wind.

'Is he normally like this?' asks Head Girl.

I nod.

'God. It's like he's on speed.'

'I know. More coffee?'

I refill Lego Man's camping mugs and we drink until I have tiger blood. Pans Solo admits to me that she's going to 'reach for her red hat momentarily' and confess something.

'I was worried about coming this weekend. I really want *this*.' She waves at the scene ahead. 'Not the dog,' she clarifies, 'or the backnote of rotting fish . . .' She wrinkles her nose at the saline air, 'but the rest of it. And I wasn't sure if I could handle seeing it all when it feels so far off for me.'

I don't know what to say. I'm hugely grateful for what I have, but I want her to know that it's in no way perfect.

'Would it help if I told you that Lego Man and I have been tired now for almost three years? How we row loads? Or how my son debagged me in the kitchen yesterday while you and Head Girl were having a lie-in? I was wearing pyjamas and all the lights were on, so everyone on the street saw my bottom.'

She thinks about this.

'Yes, that helps a bit.'

'Good.'

'Has she told you about how the dog sits under her desk and farts all day while she works?' adds Head Girl, helpfully. 'Or how she has to dance in public *without wine* and be a sexy clock to get her kicks around here?'

'You dance sober now?'

'Big time.'

'Respect . . .'

I tell her that I get envious, too: 'All the time! Of people who get pregnant easily, when it took us ages and we can't seem to repeat the trick. Of people who don't realise how lucky they are. Everyone gets jealous sometimes.' I look to Head Girl for backup.

'Well . . .'

'Oh come on!'

'What? I have many undesirable qualities but jealousy just doesn't happen to be one of them. I'm with Taylor Swift here.' This is not where I thought we'd be going. 'It's "Shine Theory" – celebrating friends' successes as you would your own.' She's referring to the expression coined by US podcasters Ann Friedman and Aminatou Sow after a friend told them: 'I don't shine if you don't shine'. 'So in my mind, I've totally written books –' Head Girl nods at me – 'won at digital marketing –' she gives Pans Solo a gentle arm-punch – 'designed a whole new line of toys—'

'You know that's not what Lego Man does,' I try to explain. Again. But she shakes her head as though this is mere detail.

'He's one of Santa's elves, we all know that. The point is, I feel as though I've totally done all these things – as well as running PR campaigns for pants brands, charities and a Grammy-award-*nominated* musician.'

I'm reminded of something Irene told me, about how it's natural to compare ourselves to our friends and how it's not necessarily a bad thing: 'Because friends can be role models who inspire us to become our personal best.' I feel lucky and proud to have these two in my gang.

'There's one thing we forgot last night,' Head Girl says, unfolding a crumpled piece of paper – the A4 guide to the Six Thinking Hats that has now been annotated to within an inch of its life with scribbles and what looks like a drawing of a dolphin eating a pizza. 'I got really hungry while we were waiting for the quattro formaggio,' she adds, by way of explanation.

'And the dolphin?'

She shrugs. 'I'm a big fan of dolphins.'

Under a film of Pringle-dust and green glitter, I can just about make out a numbered list.

'We didn't get round to the second blue hat session – the overview,' she says, flipping up the hood of her navy parka and announcing: 'so I shall recap on our Ten Point Friendship Manifesto, now.' She clears her throat and reads:

'**1.** *Drunk-dial friends with kids at 3 a.m.* ☺'
'That's not exactly what I said . . .' I start, then give up.

'**2.** *More mini-breaks to Scandi-land/wherever.*'
'Thanks very much.'

'**3.** *Three-ways—*'
'On Skype! You left out the crucial words there!'
'Oh right, yeah, I'll type it up and circulate it when we get home. Next:

4. *Code word: "Leprechaun—"'*
She breaks off. 'Any advance on this? Otherwise we're
going to have a lot of chat about Lucky Charms. I'll work-
shop it.

5. *Rent a dog* – that one's for me. And, aww, look – I've
even drawn a paw print!' She shows us.

'**6.** *Try friend app . . . possibly . . .*

7. *Join a running club. Endorphins etc. Ditto choir*

8. *Hug*

9. *Massage!'*

'That's only nine,' I point out.

'That's because we never got round to my green-hat plan,
what with all the crying and the Pringles.'

'So what are you going to do?'

'I'm going back to school – I'm doing an MBA, so that I
can basically take over the world. And I've signed up for
trampolining classes.'

'Right. That should do it . . .'

'So number ten.' Head Girl clicks out the hotel pen, spins
Pans Solo around and attempts to add another line to the now
sea-sprayed paper, using our friend's back as a leaner: '*tram-
po-lin-ing*,' she sounds out: 'and *M-B-A* . . . there! Done!'

Pans Solo straightens up and links an arm through mine.
'What about you? How are we going to get you less stressed?'

'Oh, well . . . Times like these help me,' I say, gesturing

all around. 'Just hanging out with you lot and the fact that we're still close even though I'm miles away make me feel as though everything will be okay.'

'Ahh! That's so nice! Watch out, I think I'm going to have to hug you again.'

Head Girl bundles on me with such ferocity that I lose my balance, grabbing at Pans Solo for support and taking her down with me. With a faceful of cold, wet sand, I look up to see Lego Man, poised with his phone's camera to capture the inelegant scene for all time.

'It's a framer!'

By the time I wave them off at the airport that afternoon, the world has been set straight on its axis once more. We have all agreed to dispense more hugs, make tea, mop tears, send out leprechaun signals to help each other through those '*bloody hell I'm drowning*' moments. And, I hope, we've also made sure that Pans Solo doesn't feel so alone again.

Back at home, I feel centred. As though I know where I stand with old friends and have the tools to cultivate and curate existing friendships more confidently.

But I'm still going to need new ones, I think: *actual friends wherever we end up living*. I thrive on social contact and while I'll happily make the effort to travel and see good friends at the weekends, I'm going to want some support closer to home.

Taking a leap in friendship is never easy. It's a delicate social dance – a negotiation of needs and desires and personalities. And you have to be proactive. Five-year-olds can just say: 'Do you like swings? *I* like swings! Let's be friends!' or, my favourite opener overheard recently: 'Have you ever played Hungry Hippos?'

But for adults, it's complicated.

There is texting and WhatsApp and email and Facebook and having to do things you may not want to. Like the Tupperware party I felt obliged to attend in an attempt to make new Danish friends – or the time I lost Lego Man for a night when he was roped into flyering for a local drum and bass night, despite not being entirely clear on what drum and bass was ('A type of marching band, perhaps?'). But our efforts paid off and I formed a tight-knit group of brilliant boys and girls in Denmark, in addition to the old-timers in the UK.

Psychologists confirm that it can be liberating to make new friends as an adult – based on who we are now rather than our teenage self – as the process requires us to be vulnerable. Dr Brené Brown, research professor at the University of Houston Graduate College of Social Work and all-round excellent human being of TED talk fame, has found that vulnerability is imperative for anything approaching a truly happy, authentic existence. So although the idea of making new friends is scary, it's always worthwhile. But just as there are rules for dating (see Chapter Two), there are guidelines for making new friends as a grown-up, too.

'Firstly, don't succumb to the myth that everyone already has their friends,' Irene tells me: 'Friendships are dynamic; people constantly accrete and lose friends. Secondly, if someone does turn you down, don't take it personally. It may be that their proverbial dance card is already filled right at this moment.' Just as mine was in London – and is pretty much again in Denmark. But it won't be if we move.

Since I don't know quite where we'll be living yet, I decide to do a 'trial run' and make some new friends where I am now.

'Isn't that a bit mean,' asks Lego Man, 'making friends with someone if you're thinking of buggering off?'

My husband can be quite the poet. But I realise he may have a point.

'What if,' I propose, 'I'm really open about our plans? What if I tell people we may have to move soon? Then it's up to them. And actually, lots of the new arrivals work between Denmark and London anyway . . .' A fast-growing percentage of internationals are now pursuing a LON:DEN existence – like a dyslexic and less glamorous version of the well-established NY:LON commuter category. 'So I could still be friends with them in the UK, if I meet any good ones,' I tell him.

'"Good ones"?! You're nice . . .'

'What?' It's hardly my fault if I have high friendship stand-ards.

'As long as you're upfront with them.'

'I will be,' I promise.

The more I think about it, the more it's a no-brainer: *Making new friends here and now will require all the same skills and mastery of my inner fears, but I'll be doing it in a place I'm at least familiar with. It's like a friendship step-ping stone! Or water wings!* I tell myself. But where to start?

There are some new faces at my Nia class the following week and one girl gives me such a warm smile that I worry she thinks I'm someone else. She's wearing an outsized black T-shirt and giant hoop earrings – a plucky accessory choice for a limb-thrashing dance session and, already, I admire her chutzpah.

After class, emboldened by her apparent friendliness and the experience of dancing like 'sexy wind' (an oxymoron, surely), I say 'hello'. It emerges that she's new in town, so I suggest coffee sometime ('Like an actual brave person!' I tell Lego Man afterwards).

'Or we could grab something to eat?' she suggests.

'Okay! I mean, "sure".'

She suggests inviting a few others she's met recently to 'make a night of it.' And we are on!

Dr Steven Howell, a psychology professor at Keystone College Pennsylvania in the USA, has studied the science of establishing new friendships and, after some presumably pretty rigorous research, concluded that 'a night out' is a good place to start. Exchanging confidences and taking risks together is apparently essential and a 'bonding analysis' study found that a drinking session is an excellent way to facilitate these. I'm not sure that academics should be condoning alcohol consumption as a means to making friends but, having found the technique effective in the past, I'm not about to argue. Researchers discovered that those who drank together and tackled a crisis together – even something small, like how to get home – were more likely to become close than people who didn't drink and avoided such shared dramas.

'*The guy or girl – it works worldwide for both genders – with the black eye who drags you out of the dumpster after the bar fight is the true friend,*' Dr Howell told *The Sunday Times* in August 2015.

Steve moves in some pretty racy circles . . . I think. But, ever a slave to science, I steel myself for A Large One.

'When you arrive get to the core of the group,' advises Head Girl when I call for counsel, 'so the kitchen at house parties and the middle of the table at a dinner, as everyone knows.'

'Do they?'

'Yes. Obviously! Otherwise you'll be stuck in no-man's-land talking to someone dull about their painfully gifted offspring.'

'Top tip, thank you.' The last thing I need is a 'your child doesn't eat kale? My child LOVES kale . . . and Proust' type – the kind that flock like moths to my '*Tractorrr!*'-shouting child-flame (coming up in Chapter Six: 'competitive parenting'. There be monsters . . .).

As well as Irene's guidance and Head Girl's advice on seating, I'm keen to find out whether there are any established tools or techniques to make new friends and start over. Then a scroll through my Twitter feed throws up a *Saturday Night Live* gif and I get an idea.

'Hello, is that Charna?'

'That's me!' says the unmistakably actorly voice on the end of the line. Charna Halpern runs iO *Improv* theatre group in Chicago, where Seth Meyers (or 'Seth', as Charna calls him) and Conan O'Brien ('Conan') hire their writers from. She's worked with Tina Fey, Amy Poehler, all the greats – and now she's agreed to help with my experiment. Charna is giving me a crash course in a fundamental theory of improvisation that I hope will help with my quest to turn Hoop Earrings-style strangers into friends.

'"Yes, and . . ." is really the philosophy of improv,' Charna starts. 'The basic idea is about saying "yes" to each other. It's about truly listening: staying in the moment and then offering something more to progress the conversation or the action. So it's useful for businesses and all social relationships. You say "yes, and . . ." to whatever's thrown at you – so you're agreeing and moving forward.'

Actors and comedians use this technique to improvise effectively, working with their fellow performers, rather than blocking them or competing. It helps them remain focused, positive and open to new trains of thought and experiences. 'It's about making each other's ideas work, because even the worst idea can lead to something brilliant. And being supportive is key,' adds Charna. I mention that this sounds a little like Head Girl's 'Shine Theory' and she whoops in agreement: 'It fits beautifully with Shine Theory – because "yes, and . . ." is about making other people look good, which in turn makes you look good. If you engage in "yes, and . . ." you make people around you more confident and more apt to offer a suggestion. It makes for a more creative, interesting environment. So you can have a crazy idea and say, "all right, let's try it!" Which of course facilitates friendship, as you're collaborating and forming bonds in a positive environment – so you get everyone's best side by treating each other with respect and enthusiasm.'

I'm guessing there's also less likelihood of a stonking hangover here than with the Keystone researcher's advice of 'getting so drunk you fall in a skip'.

Charna assures me that 'yes, and . . .' should work brilliantly to build friendships – even between the most unlikely of bedfellows: 'I was once hired by the US Embassy to go to Cyprus to work with both sides of the Turkish Cypriot border to help negotiations and take down the border,' she tells me: 'I ran improv classes each side and eventually the border came down and both groups became friends!' The internet confirms that Charna is indeed the improv world's answer to Ban Ki-moon and that she was even hired by CERN to help nuclear physicists collaborate more effectively. A night out for tapas should be a cinch.

'Just remember: great things happen when you say "yes, and . . ."!' she tells me as a parting rally cry.

Okay, I think: *I can do this.* If I can be traffic, sober, on a Wednesday, then I can sure as hell channel my inner Tina Fey and be a Chicago-style improviser, with wine, on a Thursday.

I get to the restaurant at exactly seven thirty, as Head Girl instructed: 'Forget fashionably late or you'll get stuck with the kale-bore. Arrive on time and sit somewhere decent.' Hoop Earrings is already at a candlelit table and beckons me over, gesturing to the seat next to hers. I shuffle in, trying not to set fire to my hair (this happens more than you might expect in Denmark, the candle capital of the world) and we wait for the others to arrive. They do. And they seem *okay.* One looks grumpy but another has big, backcombed hair and is wearing a jumper with a horse on it that I'm already admiring. There's also a man who has the best 'unimpressed resting face' (*'URF'*) I have ever seen but his eyes crinkle when he smiles and he seems jovial.

Tumblers of gin with cracked black pepper and cucumber appear, then I hear the satisfying hiss of several tonic bottles being opened. The results taste sublime, but I ask for some water, too, aware that I'm a horrific lightweight.

'I can't drink much, I've got a deadline tomorrow . . .'

'Oh you'll be fine, have some ham,' Monsieur URF tells me, gesturing at the wooden slabs laden with tapas being lowered on to the table. He turns to the waiter: 'What she means is "please may she have some more alcohol, thank you very much."'

So in the spirit of 'yes, and . . .', I agree.

'Let's get drunk and say stuff we shouldn't,' he whispers. 'Cheers!'

After this, things get boozy. Quickly.

Within half an hour, my cheeks ache with laughter. I have already discovered that Hoop Earrings has a bullshit radar I can only aspire to and knows all the words to Yazoo's 'Only You'. Grumpy Girl is less fun. During Horse Jumper's anecdote about the time she saw two tortoises in coitus ('it was the necks, straining so *slowly*, that I still remember to this day . . .') she remains boot-faced. Someone tells a story about a piano-playing pug and she checks her watch. When it comes to pudding, she announces to all that she never touches the stuff and is starting a juice fast tomorrow.

She and I will not be friends.

Once our sticky-toffee-covered plates have been cleared away, Hoop Earrings confesses to me that she's undone the top button of her jeans because she's eaten too much and that I must remind her to do them up again before we go home.

'Or we could go on somewhere . . .' Horse Jumper suggests.

Oh God . . .

I am tired. So tired. But I can hear Charna's words ringing in my ears: '*Great things happen when you say "yes"!*'

'Let's do it!' I say.

So we pay up and we go OUT out. There are smoke machines. And disco lights. And what may or may not be a vodka luge. And there is dancing. Drunk dancing, which I have long excelled at, mostly because I'm too inebriated to feel self-conscious. And I'm having such a nice time that I, apparently, demonstrate my 'sexy weed picker' moves to a nightclub full of twenty-year-olds. On a SCHOOLNIGHT!

Inevitably, our party ends up in the ladies' loo, where lots of women are hoicking up tights, applying lipstick and saying to each other 'He's not worth it!' I love a ladies' loo. There is a general consensus that shoes are overrated, so we all take ours off, sinking down a few inches until we're on the same eye level as any passing hobbits. And then Horse Jumper pulls out of her handbag two aluminium cylinders. With a can of Elnett in each hand like a cowboy in a western, she tips her head upside down, flips it back up and sprays until the mirror is obscured by a million glue particles. Drunk, shoeless and now suffering from mild asphyxiation, I pronounce that I've never seen a mane more fabulous.

This is womanhood!

We emerge, light-headed from fumes, shoes in our hands and arms round each other for support (moral and physical). Deciding 'air' might smell nice after all that gin and glue, we make our way out to street level.

'Mind yourself on that step, pet, it's slippery,' Hoop Earrings warns me, as I sidestep some bile and a stream of steaming urine flowing from a hunched figure in the corner.

'Ahhh, thanks. You're so nice!' I tell her. Playing it cool.

We pick up Monsieur URF and outside, the four of us move as one – weaving like a carnival dragon along the pavement. Somewhere just past the kebab shop, someone starts humming and we break into a drunken chorus of Yazoo.

I don't know what hour it is, I only know that it's a long way past my bedtime and that I'm going to feel Very Bad Indeed in the morning.

But it's worth it, I think: *this one was for you, Dr Steve and Charna!*

I have successfully embraced my inner Tina Fey – and she's a blast.

I fall through the front door, delighted with life, and sleep for a whole three hours before Little Red wakes me with a joyful battle cry for the day ahead:

'Mama? *Tractorrrr!*'

Things I've learned about friends and change:

1. It's okay to end friendships that just aren't working any more . . .

2. . . . as long as we do it nicely . . .

3. . . . though it's worth fighting for them first.

4. Six Thinking Hats helps cut to the friendship chase – improving honesty and empathy as well as depersonalising awkward chats.

5. Making new friends is hard, but worth it.

6. Embracing 'yes, and . . .' with your inner Tina Fey is a great place to start.

7. We don't have to get so drunk that we fall into a skip to have a good time (as Jermaine Stewart's lesser known B-side goes).

CHAPTER SIX

FAMILY

Much Ado About Puffins

In which I learn about Enmeshment Theory and building belated parental 'boundaries'; what happens when FBI hostage negotiation techniques are applied to toddlers; and how to project manage an extended family using the ADKAR technique

We wake on Sunday morning to news from the home front. My mother's gentleman friend – a lovely Robert Wagner[21] lookalike – has *proposed!* And they are to be married!

This is, obviously, HUGE.

My mother last got married in 1977, when petrol cost eighteen pence a litre and the Queen celebrated her Silver Jubilee. A lot's changed since then. Including, it seems, my mother.

'Of course we'll have to start looking for somewhere else to live,' she tells me breathlessly over FaceTime before the screen freezes, as it always does, thanks to the woeful Wi-Fi

---

21 Circa *Heart to Heart* rather than later, more weathered iterations. It's an uncanny similarity first pointed out by Chapter One's Stephen Powell, just FYI. Good with interrelational diagrams *and* celebrity doppelgangers.

and broadband package she was mis-sold sometime in the internet's infancy.

'What? Move? Why? What's wrong with where you live now?'

'We can't possibly live here!' Her face is mobile once more and she gestures theatrically around her beautiful rustic cottage, conveniently located within London's commuter belt. 'There isn't room!' There are, in fact, two bedrooms, a living room, kitchen and bathroom. But these, seemingly, will not suffice. 'Anyway, you get a lot more for your money if you move further out. We were thinking Wiltshire somewhere, maybe Devon . . .'

I see myself frowning in miniature, framed by a neat rectangle.

'*Devon*? Did you say *Devon*?'

At this inauspicious moment, the screen goes black and a message appears: '*Poor connection. Video will resume when connection improves.*'

'Arghhh!' I yell in frustration. 'Get better broadband!'

Lego Man appears in the doorway, leading a merry band of cross-species males who have taken to following him around instead of me at weekends. 'Everything okay?' He has a dog chew in one hand and a spanner in the other. I don't ask.

'I think my mum just said she's moving to Devon. As well as getting married. And then her Wi-Fi crashed. Again.'

'Wait, *married*?'

'Yes.'

'*Devon?*'

'Yes.'

'Devon!'

'Will everyone just stop saying "Devon"!'

In case you're rusty on the West Country, all you need to know is that Devon is A Long Way Away from where Lego Man and I are considering moving to and its USP is cream teas. Now, I love a scone as much as the next girl, but I wouldn't relocate for one. And I can't help thinking we've messed up here. *I'm planning a move back to the UK to be closer to my mother and she's moving to sodding Devon?* I'd been planning to tackle 'family' as one of my year-of-becoming-a-change-chameleon experiments, but it never crossed my mind that it might not only be me making changes.

'But Devon's miles away!'

'I know!'

'Oh well, it's her life.' Lego Man can be irritatingly rational.

'I know that, too. It's just a shock, that's all.'

'You are happy for her, aren't you?'

'OF COURSE I'M HAPPY!' I protest, far louder than is necessary: 'I'm DELIGHTED!'

'Okay, then. Good . . .' Lego Man backs out of the room and his entourage follows suit. 'Come on,' he says to them. 'I think Mama needs some time to process the new strategic developments.'

'Don't you management-speak me—' I start but lose energy and think that perhaps it might be wise to take a moment. I'm surprised by my reaction. It seems disproportionate. Childish. Petulant, even. And I don't know why.

I'm not some tweenager negotiating a new stepfather: I'm a thirty-six-year-old woman with a family of my own. Of course my mother should get on with her life. I just always rather expected that she'd do it nearer. And not change anything . . .

In common with most human beings anywhere, ever, I have been guilty of taking a parent for granted. My mother has always just been there, day after day, like the weather. My earliest sense memory of her is a whirlwind of Laura Ashley and Issey Miyake (it was the 1980s) talking into a curly-corded landline while simultaneously stirring a pan of soup and making play-dough from scratch. She worked full time, but still managed to be on the parent–teachers' association and nail the mums' race at Sports Day. Every year. Until it got embarrassing and there was discussion about imposing some sort of handicap ('Could she *hop*, maybe?'). As a single parent, my mother did everything – handled everything. I grew up in the shelter of her love and even during her leather-trousered Notting-Hill-Carnival phase, she was always there for me. *So isn't it about time that she started living for herself rather than you, you massively spoilt brat?* I reproach myself.

Psychologists have long had a field day with the parent–child relationship and the inevitable 'split' that must occur for us to become our own person, separate from them. This split can occur at any age, though it's fair to say before thirty-six is typical. Lego Man has vivid memories of his own coming of age Rudyard Kipling moment, aged seventeen.

'We were on holiday visiting a puffin colony in the Outer Hebrides,' (this tells you almost everything you need to know about my husband's upbringing) '–when my dad got his big SLR camera out and started taking pictures. So I took a few on my wind-forward cheap Kodak one. We had them developed back home and they came out really well. Dad mentioned he was going to enter his puffin portraits in the village show's annual nature photography competition—' (this is North Yorkshire in the 1990s – there wasn't much on) '—so I said I would, too. And I won! Dad was livid. But from that moment, he treated me differently. I really started growing into my shell—'

'Not "coming out of your shell"?'

'No, *growing in*. Like a hermit crab. From then on, he's asked for advice on stuff, taken me seriously – even let me choose the cheese at Christmas.' In Spartan culture, the passage from boy to man was marked by the killing of helots. In my husband's family, it was marked by being put in charge of buying the cheese at Christmas. Post-puffin victory, he was a man – an autonomous adult, capable of making his way in the world (allegedly). 'I learned a lot about family life from those puffins,' he once told me wistfully as I tried very hard not to laugh.

Well, look who's laughing now, I think.

I can't help feeling I'm coming to all of this a little late. Despite having left home at eighteen and lived in different places for the past few years, I am like my mother in many ways; and I can feel myself resembling her even more as I get older. I now like to make sure that everyone has been to the loo and has gloves on before they leave the house. Even in summer. Just yesterday, a friend debuted a pair of faux-leather leggings and I heard myself muttering, audibly: '*A recipe for thrush . . .*'

My mother's father died when she was six and mine left when I was three. Not having grown up with one of these mythical creatures around, neither of us has ever been entirely sure how 'dads' work and Lego Man is forever reminding me that I don't have to 'do it all'.

'It's what my mum did,' I habitually tell him.

'Yes but what about me? What's my role?'

'Oh . . . Yeah. That.' I have 'issues' with control. Lego Man travels a lot for work, so I'm often in charge on my own. And then he comes back, expecting a slice of the parenting pie, and I have to learn to 'share' all over again.

But there are also generational differences between my mother and me. I grew up expecting a career as well as a family, whereas few of my friends' mums worked. My mother, were she to put on one of Edward de Bono's red hats, would probably admit that she still doesn't see why I don't want to spend all my days finger-painting. 'Why bother having a baby if you're just going to work most of the time?' is a question that has been levelled at me in various guises on more than one occasion. Lego Man has never received such a grilling.

My mother was raised at a time when emotions weren't flaunted – and any that occasionally seeped out were bottled up sharpish. One of her favourite tricks to this day is to pretend she's upset about something unrelated by way of catharsis. 'I'm not crying,' she once told me crossly, through distinct sobs, 'it's just that the kingfisher chicks have hatched on *Springwatch*. It's very moving.' After a tense lunch some years back, I tried to have a conversation about why you could have cut the atmosphere with a butter knife when she launched into a spontaneous rendition of 'The Hills are Alive' from *The Sound of Music*. I relayed this to a friend, who said: 'That's nothing – my mum shut down talk about Dad's suicide attempt by telling me the daffodils were early this year.' Lego Man's father once evaded talk of his own mother's serious illness by announcing: 'The dog's not well'.

I like to think I'm better equipped to express my emotions than my mother's generation, but in common with the rest of my wonderful, mad family, I use humour as a defence mechanism wherever possible. We don't scream and shout: we simmer; find the funny; then NEVER SPEAK OF IT AGAIN, leaving underlying issues happily undisturbed – until the next disagreement over appropriate gift etiquette.

The German psychotherapist Bert Hellinger believes we all unconsciously repeat our parents' mistakes or re-enact their pain out of a misplaced sense of loyalty – imagining that we can alleviate their unhappiness by sharing it. Scientists have found that genes can, essentially, retain memories of past experiences and pass these on. This is called 'transgenerational epigenetic inheritance'. An influential 2013 study from Emory University School of Medicine in the US found that a traumatic event could affect the DNA in sperm and alter the brains and behaviour of subsequent generations. Okay, so this study was on mice, but, you know – *mammals*. Dr Brian Dias of Emory University told the BBC at the time: 'There is absolutely no doubt that what happens to the sperm and egg will affect subsequent generations.' Researchers from Mount Sinai Medical Center in New York also discovered that children born to women who were pregnant during the 9/11 attacks were more likely to develop post-traumatic stress disorder (PTSD) and become distressed in response to new stimuli. So the experiences of a pregnant woman can be transmitted to her unborn child.

We can't do much about the genes we inherit – more's the stumpy-limbed pity – but we can change how we behave to improve familial relationships. Close family ties have been proven to be one of the biggest predictors of happiness and a Harvard University study found that the quality of our connection with our parents even affects our health. So to be happier and healthier, I'd like to get this right. And I haven't got for ever.

In the past year three friends have lost a parent and four more are now caring for chronically ill family members. The family friend with a terminal illness is now in permanent pain and there have been many more judicious 'no need to reply's employed of late.

We may all live longer and enjoy the wonders of penicillin in the twenty-first century, but we aren't invincible. Despite the general role reversal post-puffin-gate, Lego Man still can't get his father to adopt a healthier lifestyle – and none of Little Red's grandparents can move as fast as they used to. So it feels important to weatherproof our relationships and ensure that the time we have left with our nearest and dearest is spent well.

Researching child–parent relationships, and whether it's possible to make changes as an adult to these most complex of bonds, I come across the theory of enmeshment – a concept introduced by Argentinian family therapist, Salvador Minuchin, to describe a lack of boundaries and an inability to cope with distress. A child who is enmeshed can feel co-dependent and carry their parent's feelings and worldview into adult life, allowing these to outweigh or even eclipse their own. The idea strikes a chord and I wonder if this might be why I feel so discombobulated by my mother's new life.

Harley Street psychologist Will Napier is the UK authority

on this and has even developed his own brand of therapy to tackle it. So I Skype him; tell him everything ('*Devon! Scones!*'); and ask for help.

Most psychologists speak in a calm, low voice and avoid revealing too much personal information, despite persistent attempts at prying on my part. Will and I, however, Get Stuck In. We chat at length, and volume, about all manner of topics. Were there any peacocks nearby, I suspect they'd have a field day.

Will, I discover, was working at the Priory when he began to look more deeply into enmeshment. 'I had one client who had everything going for her objectively – she was a lovely person, totally undislikable,' he tells me, 'but she was miserable. We traced this back and I learned that her mother gave up work to look after her and would say: "All we ask of you is that you're happy." Which, if you think about it, is an enormous pressure. The daughter felt guilty and ungrateful and so became deeply *un*happy. If her mother had known the effect this would have, she wouldn't have said it,' says Will, adding: 'It's perfectly understandable why parents say things like this: you want your kids to be happy. But although it's hard to watch your children suffer and not do anything about it, it's a crucial part of growing up – life isn't without pain. And many, *many* people miss out on learning how to handle it. They are enmeshed.'

Will began working with this theory and identified two distinct kinds of enmeshment: '"Wet enmeshment" is when a parent becomes overemotional and rushes in to make things better if a child is upset. This looks as though the parent is being very caring – by offering intense attention. But actually, the parent is addressing their own psychological needs rather than the child's – they are being over-the-top to make them-selves feel better and soothe themselves. "Dry enmeshment" is when the parent avoids distress by dismissing the issue – ignoring; telling a child to "snap out of it"; or "not to worry". Parents who practise dry enmeshment tend to be overly cheerful, telling someone "not to be upset" or that something can be "fixed". That everything *must* be "fixed". So if a pet tortoise dies, a dry enmeshment dad might tell his child, "Don't worry, I'll buy you another!" People who are dry-en-meshed tend to self-medicate – buying things or getting drunk to forget about the pain or cope with stress,' Will tells me: 'Which, obviously, doesn't work.'

'Obviously . . .' I think of Lego Man's addiction to designer lamps and my love of a good glass of Pinot Grigio after a hard day at the gravel pit and wonder whether we may have a problem. 'And, er . . . is it possible to be dry-enmeshed and wet-enmeshed at the same time?'

I recall times growing up when I was encouraged to sing songs from *The Sound of Music* through the pain of some pretty serious upheavals, and other occasions when I was wrapped up, literally and metaphorically, in numerous layers of protective padding. Early family bereavements and bouts of illness between the ages of three and seven meant that my mother was vigilant about my health and naturally wanted to protect me – from everything. I had asthma inhalers at the ready; a bedroom stuffed with humidifiers; and more Vicks VapoRub than would have been needed for a whole army of sickly children. So was my enmeshment wet *and* dry?

'We can indeed experience dry and wet enmeshment at different times,' Will confirms, 'and being aware of the roles we play and the stories we inherit is an important start to un-enmeshing yourself, as it were. But the real solution is to discover that it's okay to be anxious. To offer yourself what you didn't get from your parents and make room for the inevitable suffering of daily life.'

I tell him he makes life sound like a ball.

'It's not *all* suffering, obviously,' he assures me: 'but this aspect of life will always be there. We need to learn how to handle it as adults if we didn't learn it growing up from our parents. And many, *many*,' he emphasises the word a second time, 'of us didn't.'

So we can improve our relationship with our parents on our own? Without having to 'change' them?

'Exactly – it's part of growing up and taking responsibility for our own lives.'

Will explains that there are three stages to admitting and acknowledging pain in ourselves as well as in others. We have to tell ourselves:

1. I *get* that you're suffering

2. I *mind* that you're suffering

3. I can *handle* that you're suffering

'Think of an aeroplane experiencing turbulence,' he says. 'If you're on a flight and things get a bit bumpy, the captain doesn't just come over the intercom and shout, "Arrgghhh! We're all going to die!" does he? Or she?'

'Hopefully not . . .'

'Well it's the same with enmeshment – you're telling yourself you can "handle" the suffering, just as a pilot might say, "We're going through some turbulence but we'll be okay",' says Will. 'The pilot thinks: "I've got this. I've experienced it before." I encourage clients to "use their pilot's voice" when they experience pain or stress or suffering. You're acknowledging that anxiety is part of reality – that it's not a threat. And that it's okay *not* to be okay sometimes: that's normal. That's part of life. You'll get through it: you're tougher than you think.'

I can feel another slogan mug coming on – because he's right. Over the past couple of years, I've realised that I am stronger – mentally and physically – than I ever grew up believing I could be. I can go for a run in midwinter without catching pneumonia. I can leave the house without a vest on and no one will die. I can endure break-ups and career upsets and push an *actual human being* out of an impossibly small orifice and survive. (Just.) I can stand on my own two feet.

From what Will's told me, I feel certain that I and pretty much everybody I know is enmeshed to some degree. *Philip Larkin wasn't joking* . . . Head Girl's parents still expect her to go on holiday with them. It's assumed that Pans Solo will call her dad daily and visit once a week. Recent Dumpee often bails her parents out financially. And Newly Unemployed Friend could function as a full-time handyman for his mother, should the cheese bubble burst. With a growing number of twenty- and thirty-somethings forced to live at home, thanks to the crippling cost of housing, more of us than ever must be suffering from enmeshment. So I ask Will whether there's a way of testing this.

'Ooh, like an "Am I Enmeshed?" quiz?'

'Yes!'

'Okay, well, how about: "Your mum calls, she mentions you haven't visited in months and asks you to go to a party she's hosting."'

I'm already picturing a *Bridget Jones*-style turkey curry buffet.

'Do you a) say, "Great! Sounds super!" and put the date in your diary, b) wish you could say "no" but go anyway, c) stay home but feel guilty, or d) feel calm, thank her for the invitation but tell her you won't be coming this time?' Will is courteous enough to allow me to contemplate this in the privacy of my own head before going on: 'An enmeshed child will go to the party even if they don't want to, feeling they "should" because they don't want to appear ungrateful and want to make their parent happy.'

'Isn't this just "being nice"?'

'*Is* it, though?' *Uh-oh, I'm being psychologist-ed.* 'Many of us feel it's our job to look after our parents and make sure they're okay and not lonely. But it's not our job.'

This is something I struggle with. I often worry about whether my mother's looking after herself properly and the last time I opened her fridge, I found it bare but for a bottle of cava and a family-sized bar of Cadbury's Dairy Milk. I offered to do a food shop, but she assured me, 'No need! I've got peas and half a pie in the freezer!'

'We're often trained to feel guilty and responsible for our parents' happiness, and reversing this is like turning around a tank,' says Will: 'So in the case of the party, it's not actually about whether you go or not – it's *why* you're going. You can *not* go and accept the guilt, or you can make a decision despite that guilt. You can go to the party for your mum, even though you know you've been guilt-tripped into it, and rest assured that when you're standing at your mother's memorial service and asking yourself, "Did I do a good job of being my mother's child?" you can say, "Yes".' Being a dutiful daughter or son is all well and noble – it's what most of us would like to 'give back' to the parents that raised us – but it shouldn't be everything. We can't live *for* other people and psychologists agree that to be truly happy/successful/non-resentful of annual turkey curry buffets, we have to find meaning in life for ourselves. And to do this, we must make choices.

'You can decide, "I'm only going to go to two of my mother's social events a year" and then communicate this to her in a kind, but firm, way,' suggests Will. 'If it's a parent who expects you to call several times a week, you can say, "I really enjoy talking to you, but let me call you every Sunday –" for instance – "when I have time to speak and we can have a proper catch-up." It's about being in control, setting boundaries, and deciding what you can authentically offer without resentment. Resentment is the litmus test here – and the key way of knowing whether or not you're being authentic. In any relationship. Take my wife, Jenny—'

Crikey, I didn't think we'd be veering into this territory . . .

'Come and say hi, Jenny!' At this, Will twists his laptop until I see a smiley lady with cropped hair who I had no idea was in on our conversation. It looks as though Jenny is putting away shopping in the kitchen, but she doesn't seem to mind being roped into her husband's discussion.

'Hello!' She waves, cheerily.

This is all very jolly!

'So Jenny and I are going cross-country skiing in Norway soon.'

'Oh, lovely . . .' I have no clue where we're heading.

'I'm glad you think so.'

Huh?

'Then, she's making me go cycling in the Loire Valley.'

'Do you *like* cycling?' I ask, doubtfully

'Well I can assure you that these aren't holidays I would have chosen.'

'Oh.'

'So why do you think I agreed to these trips?'

'Um . . .' I think about how this dynamic would work in my own household: 'Are you storing up two holidays' worth of "tokens" for future use?' (see 'culture lash').

'Well of course there is some reciprocity expected –' Will gives his wife a look here – 'but the point is, I've accepted these holidays and I am open to the experience. If I didn't completely *own* the decision to go on these trips, I'd feel resentment. See?'

'I think so.'

'And resentment is a horrible feeling that can be really destructive. So if you take the quiz and realise you're enmeshed, in common with many (*many*) grown-up children, then you need to take action. You need to get better at self-soothing; setting boundaries, and learning what you can authentically offer. Then stick to it. Enforce those boundaries, using the word "no" more. Because if we don't use "no" enough, "yes" becomes diluted – it doesn't mean anything.'

This is fascinating. Although . . .

'My mother rarely asks me for anything these days. I'd

like to be able to help her more, or for her to call more – or do more for her. I have little need to say "yes" or "no" to her, but I still have guilt. All the guilt. And I want to "fix" things for her.'

Will nods: 'You may be reverse parenting – a lot of clients do this. It's about learning that her pain isn't your pain and going back to the three-point guide: using your pilot's voice to tell *yourself* next time you feel guilty or anxious: "I see that you're not okay; I mind that you're not okay; I can handle that you're not okay." You're acknowledging those feelings but recognising that they're a sign of enmeshment. This is how you change an enmeshed relationship.'

This makes sense. 'Fixing' my mother is not my job. It's never been my job and now that she's getting hitched and buying a house with the lovely Robert Wagner, it's definitely not my place to interfere. Even if she does move to (sodding) Devon. I realise for the first time that she doesn't 'need' me. She loves me. She likes having me around. But she doesn't need me. Which, really, is how it should be. I'd hate the idea of a grown-up Little Red ('Big Red'?) feeling indebted to me or as though he had to look after me. We should aspire for the people we love to want us rather than need us.

'So all I need to do is "let go" a bit more and practise my pilot's voice?'

'That's it!'

We arrange to speak again the following week after I've tested Will's theory. And then I get a message from my mother.

She tells me she's having a clearout and asks whether she

can donate a few boxes of my teenage miscellany still loitering in her loft to the charity shop – 'Or the tip?'

Rather than indulging in my natural impulse to feel rejected and hurt and as though life is terribly unfair – essentially, my inner adolescent – I switch on my virtual flight-deck intercom. I tell myself: *I can see that you're not okay with this; I mind that you're not okay; but I can handle the fact that you're not okay . . .*

Next, my mother mentions nonchalantly that she's decided to retire a year early and is just off to look at a new three-piece suite. Instead of panicking about her finances and cross-examining her on the prudence of this, I breathe deeply. *It's not my job to fix my mother. She is separate from me. She can make her own ~~mistakes~~ 'decisions' . . .*

I do this a lot over the course of the next week. And I start to believe my own pilot's voice. And, actually, I have less to worry about if I'm not spending my limited concern-tokens on a capable, happy parent who doesn't want or need them anyway. *Pilot's voice, pilot's voice, pilot's voice*, I tell myself. On loop.

Un-enmeshing myself is one thing. But considering the implications of this for our impending move is quite another. Because if my mother doesn't need me, it means moving back is all of my own choosing.

Lego Man's parents have always had each other. As well as a dog. And chickens. And a timeshare on a canal boat. When they're not mucking out a menagerie or *Rosie and Jim*-ing it along England's waterways, they recently let it be known they're more than happy to keep doing their own thing and visiting us biannually in Denmark ('We're very taken with the pickled herring . . .'). In addition to this, my mother in law has finally fathomed 'Face-Time-telephoning'. So we're not moving back for them.

My mother will have Robert Wagner. If for some awful reason she had to go into hospital again, he would be there – right *there* – with her. Not 320 kilometres or, worse, 1,000 kilometres away.

But what if something happened to Robert Wagner? I worry.

Well, then he's got his family, I rationalise.

But what if they got sick . . .? I catastrophise my way through a series of increasingly outlandish scenarios, like a Channel Five documentary speculating on who's next in line to the throne and working out that, eventually, if enough people cark it, Simon Cowell will be king. *Enough*, I tell myself: *if by some strange kink of fate, Armageddon strikes (sodding) Devon before anywhere else and my mother needed me, I'd find a way to get there . . . by road, rail or air. From wherever we are.*

This means I will have to make a decision about what I want and what's best for my immediate family, which feels like a tremendous responsibility. *No wonder most of us stay enmeshed for so long*, I think: *being a grown-up is hard.* I've been thinking about a big move as something I *should* be doing – something that's almost been determined for me. I've also been quietly consoling myself with the idea that change, on a grand, cross-border scale, will 'fix' all the other less-than-perfect parts of my life. Or at least eclipse them, keeping me so busy I won't have time to think about them. But it can't. And it won't.

I need to learn to make smaller, well-thought-through changes to the life I have, too. I need to grow up. *Shit . . .*

Pilot's voice, pilot's voice, pilot's voice . . .

'Will my virtual inflight intercom ever become automatic?' I ask Will when we speak again.

'That depends,' he tells me, 'on how enmeshed you are!'

Oh.

'Most people need to practise their pilot's voice for some time. But it is doable. Of course, you can avoid all this in future by trying not to enmesh your own child!' he adds, jauntily.

'Ha!' I try to sound equally carefree: 'Yeah!'

I thank him, hang up and stare out of the window while the dog snores and dream-runs under my desk.

Crapsticks. I hadn't thought through this part.

I knew all about children before I had one. I felt certain I'd worked out what all my parent friends were doing wrong until I became one and realised I knew nothing. And that it could be seriously tough.

Even after years of trying to get pregnant and elation that it was possible for us, I hated the experience. I felt sick for the first six months and only wanted to eat chips. Ligaments loosened until my cervix gave up, so that every step I took felt like someone was stabbing me between the legs. Which was good preparation for childbirth. Part of me still hoped that the baby might slip out like a Slinky. He did not. Seventeen hours into active labour, I saw a bright light and thought, 'Oh thank God, I've died!' But they were just examining my bits in more detail. My 'birth notes' for this period read:

'Helen is very upset that she is not dead.'

Becoming a parent is one of those life stages that society regards as a peak of female happiness. But despite the heart-swelling weight of a newborn on my chest, I also had a web of stitches that didn't heal for three months. I mimbled about like a stretched ghost, near-lunatic with exhaustion, breaking things because I was too sleep-deprived for hand–eye coordination and throwing away excessively soiled babygros that I was too tired to 'empty' and scrub clean.

What didn't help was the multimillion-pound parenting industry, keen to capitalise on a new parent's anxieties. I felt as though I had a choice between full-on Gina Ford routine-based 'newborn management' or baby-led attachment parenting[22]. Either way, society seemed to say, I had to choose and then Stick At It. Meticulously. Otherwise it would all go a bit *We Need To Talk About Kevin*. In reality, science shows that super-strict adherence to any doctrine is a dreadful idea. Psychologists at the University of Mary Washington in Virginia, US, have found that intensive parenting ideologies of any persuasion made mothers significantly less happy and three times more likely to experience depression.

After six months of maternity leave, I *had* to get back to work but also, honestly . . . a part of me *wanted* to. I knew how to do that: I was good at it. I didn't know how to do this new thing and I didn't appear to be terribly good at it. What I only realise now is that no one is naturally 'good' at it. Most people felt the same way that I did, but they didn't talk about it. Instead, they lied about how much sleep they were getting, all the while crumbling inside like a house with dry rot. And then they felt guilty if they went back to

---

22 A term coined by two evangelical Christians keen to entice women back into the home . . . just saying.

work and guilty if they didn't. Research shows that more than half of mothers who work feel guilty about leaving their children, but for the most part, it's unfounded. In Scandinavia, the vast majority of mothers work; 85 per cent of Danish mothers are back in the office before their child is one – and Danes aren't all scarred for life. Studies from Harvard Business School show that working mothers are more likely to raise successful daughters and caring, empathetic sons. What's more, working women today spend nine hours more playing with their children each week than their non-working 1960s counterparts. For me, working meant that every spare moment I had to spend with my son was treasured. I already loved him beyond belief, but suddenly I could enjoy him, too.

Fast forward eighteen months and parenting has become easier, though no less ridiculous. What started as a white bean on a hospital monitor is now an 84-cm tall living, breathing person whose weight in my arms now requires a shift in balance. I picked up a six-month-old the other day (a friend's, not a random one) and nearly launched her into space, she was so light compared to Little Red. Our mini Viking is now scaling the furniture and changing daily. My aunt recently enquired as to whether or not he was still into trains as she'd seen a T-shirt she wanted to buy him. 'Yes,' I said, 'but I can't guarantee he will be when we see you next. He could be over them and into Batman by then. Or joyriding . . .'

Time has flown and I haven't done half of the things I planned – like updating the baby book or signing him up for swimming lessons or any of the educational activities I've seen on Pinterest. My life is nothing like a Pinterest board, and whenever I start to harbour secret hopes that it could be, hubris strikes. Just this morning, I was playing on the floor with Little Red and having a fleeting moment of, 'Ah, this is nice! This must be what Hallmark films are made about!' when the dog was sick an inch from my head. Great grey puffy clouds of undigested Pedigree. That never happens on Pinterest. Recently added to my list of 'Things I Never Thought I'd Say Before Becoming a Parent' are:

'Try not to jump in the sick'
'That is not an official wrestling move, that's just sitting on my head'
'You can't ride the dog'
and:
'Please don't lick the wheelie bin . . .'

I don't bother with competitive parenting, and while friends' toddlers can tie their shoelaces and count to twenty in three languages (really), Little Red does a cracking impression of a tractor. He has a limited vocabulary but loves to shout and run and jump and climb. This often makes me nervous, but I'm trying hard to be okay with it, because: enmeshment. Parents who are overprotective make children more anxious, according to a study from Sydney's Macquarie University. And if we're afraid to let children 'vocalise' (i.e. '*shout*') or experience adverse emotions, we encourage them to hide their feelings, making it harder for them to read other people's emotions and develop empathy.

'So we have to let him express himself—' I tell Lego Man, only to be drowned out by the sound of a two-year-old 'being a tractor' around the kitchen before trying to ride the dog. Again.

'I wouldn't worry too much.' Lego Man blows air out of his cheeks before attempting to break up the brouhaha.

For the most part, Little Red is a joy to be around. But when he loses it, in solidarity with toddlers worldwide, he Loses It. We're talking epic James-Cameron-disaster-movie-style meltdowns.

'*No!*' is how it starts.

'*No!*' is how it always starts. We've walked into town to buy milk and now we're heading back.

'It's time to go home for lunch. Wouldn't you like some lunch?'

'No!'

'You can have a banana?' Lego Man goes straight in there with banana bribery. *Amateur*.

'No!'

I try to lift him, but he makes his body rigid and straight like a board so that I can't carry him. When I set him back down he goes floppy, so that his feet won't be planted. This up-down game continues until he wriggles free, throws himself face down on the cobbled street, and screams.

'Argggghhhhhhh!'

Passers-by exchange judgy looks and an elderly woman who had been enjoying a flat white in the cafe opposite holds a finger to her mouth and motions: 'Shh!'

'Arggghhhhhhhhhhhhhhhhh!' is Little Red's response. Elderly Woman tuts and shakes her head.

'Raisins?' Lego Man tries another enticement: 'I'll get you *raisins*!' His voice goes up at the end with a note of desperation.

At this point a chugger, identifying a captive audience, accosts him about setting up a direct debit to save some donkeys.

Low blow, I think: *collaring a man while his toddler's down.*

I'm just trying to reason with Little Red (ambitious) when a man with a cross-body satchel and an armful of pamphlets also spots low-hanging fruit and asks whether I'm friends with Jesus Christ.

'Argggghhhhhhhhhhhhhhhhhh!' Little Red continues to scream, getting up and heading, at speed, towards the town's fountain.

'It's complicated,' I yelp and give chase, making it just in time to stop my son from leaping into the water.

Lego Man pays off the chugger and is just enrolling Little Red in a seminary to buy our freedom, when – as suddenly as it started – the child stops screaming. He beams, the past five minutes forgotten, and we walk a happy '*Tractorrr!*'-shouting two-year-old back home.

After lunch, I find Lego Man on the NHS website.

'It says here that toddler tantrums "can occur daily" from the age of eighteen months but that "by four, tantrums are far less common . . ."'

'We've got TWO MORE YEARS of this?'

He reads on: '*If you think your child is starting a tantrum, find something to distract them with straight away. This could be something you can see out of the window. Say, for example, "Look! A cat!" Make yourself sound as surprised and interested as you can.*'

'A cat? A flipping cat?'

Lego Man isn't convinced either, but we bookmark the page and six hours later, when it's time to brush Little Red's teeth for bed, we instigate Project Cat-Watch.

'Arrrggghhhhhhhh!' Limbs thrash, skilfully disarming his father of both toothbrush and toothpaste.

'Look!' Lego Man points out of the window at the neighbour's randy tabby: 'Is that a cat?'

'Arrrggghhhhhhhhhhhhhh!' the protests continue.

'*Miaow . . . purr . . .*' Lego Man tries to *be* a cat, in the hope that this might pique some interest.

'ARRRRRGGGGHHHHHHHHHHHHHHHHHHHHHH!' Little Red notches up the volume to demonstrate his disdain.

'We're going to need a bigger cat . . .'

After another ten minutes of shouting he finally stops, accepts that it might be quite nice to sleep now, and I put him to bed.

Trooping downstairs, I find Lego Man lying on the sofa, broken.

'I see now why they call it the terrorist twos—'

'I think it's "terrible"—'

'Well *exactly*. And you can't negotiate with terrorists, can you?'

'I'm not sure,' I mutter, '. . . but you may have given me an idea!'

'Hello? Is that Gary?'

An avuncular-looking man in his sixties has answered my Skype call on the first *blob blob blob*.

'Gary! I need help.'

I explain that I'm researching into change theories, tell him about tantrum-gate, and say that I'm after a practical technique to diffuse a toddler-shaped bomb.

'Okay,' he tells me, 'we can work with this.' And I believe him. Because Gary has dealt with some of the toughest conflicts in the world, handled extreme behaviours and coped with frustrated toddlers of all ages during a thirty-year career as the FBI's former chief hostage negotiator.

Yeah, that's right: I'm not mucking about here. I've called in the Feds.

Gary Noesner – pronounced '*Nes-ner*' – joined the FBI aged twenty-two and describes it as 'more of a calling' than a job.

'All of life is a negotiation,' he tells me, 'so yes, everyday life can very much mirror the dynamics of the stand-offs I faced in the FBI. Each of us is called upon to negotiate stressful situations in social encounters and the techniques can absolutely be put to use in family life.'

While at the FBI, Gary developed a five-step 'Behavioural Change Stairway' model for negotiations that he assures me anyone can use. The steps are 'active listening', 'empathy', 'rapport' and 'influence', all leading to the end goal of 'cooperation'.

'Because what we really want from criminal hostage takers – as well as children – is their cooperation in the moment,' says Gary: 'While you hope that every interaction helps develop long-term positive behaviour, the immediate goal is to stop the tantrum and obtain cooperation.'

Active listening is the most critical step, apparently, 'as well as the easiest to implement: because everyone wants to talk about themselves,' says Gary: 'So the most powerful tool you have is to be a good listener.' To show you're paying attention, he recommends adding in the occasional 'Really?' or 'How interesting'. 'Repeating the last word or phrase the person said is also good.'

I explain that my son's lexicon is limited but he insists

that the method will still be useful. 'Emotional labelling is a really important technique. If you give someone's feelings a name, it shows you're identifying with how they feel and that you understand.' Helping children label their emotions has been proven by psychologists to result in fewer behavioural problems, stronger social skills and even better physical health, according to research from Dr John Gottman (of Four Horsemen of the Relationship Apocalypse fame in Chapter Two). A further study from Australia's Melbourne University and MacKillop Family Services found that when a parent talks to a child about emotional experiences, they develop knowledge and skills to respond not only to their own, but also to other people's emotions.

'I use this approach with my grandkids,' says Gary. 'It's about getting down to their level, sitting on the floor and asking them open-ended questions about what they're up to. I say, "Oh that looks interesting, tell me more!" or I help them find stuff out, or I make them laugh. The one thing you should never do with kids is underestimate them. It's amazing what's going on in their little heads. So if your son's face down in the street and you're stuck there, tell him "You seem as though you're feeling frustrated",' suggests Gary. 'Articulate his feelings to help him understand them and tell him you want to help. This works in hostage negotiation as well as when resolving conflict, because you catch people off guard. It's very disarming when someone's expecting screaming and shouting and you say "You seem like you're very upset. Let me help you."'

'There's nothing inherently difficult about relationship-building,' Gary assures me, 'it just takes an investment of time and emotion. If you're pressed for time, it's going to show in your intent. Anyone who's ever tried to get a kid dressed and out the door will know that.' I tell him I hear him. Especially in sub-zero Scandinavian winters when Little Red has to wear fifteen layers of technical outerwear before he can leave the house. Gary nods. 'A kid will pick up on impatience. Just as employees or people in a hostage situation will. I've had instances at work where a member of the team has come to me at a really inconvenient time when I'm busy. But I've always welcomed them in, turned my phone off and closed the door to show that I'm making their needs a priority: that I'm listening.'

I say this sounds as though it takes superhuman reserves of energy and patience.

'Ha! I think I'm pretty patient,' says Gary, 'although my wife Carol doesn't . . . It takes practice – I'm sixty-five years old now and I still have to work at it. But I'd say two thirds of people can get really good at this if they try. And if it works ninety per cent of the time with hostages and in conflict situations then you should be able to use it to de-terror a toddler!'

And so, the next morning, when the Weetabix bowl is upturned and its contents flung against the walls to stick like serrated concrete[23], I roll up my sleeves. As Little Red nose-dives from his chair to fling himself dramatically to the floor, spoon still in hand, I tell him: 'Okay kiddo, you're getting Gary-d.' Mostly because admitting that I'm applying FBI hostage negotiation techniques to my son seems harsh. Fair, but harsh.

---

23 A friend of mine recently cut her hand open on congealed Weetabix while clearing up the remnants of her one-year-old's breakfast. The stuff should come with a health warning.

Step one: active listening.

I crouch down and look at Little Red but don't say anything. This throws him and the wailing halts. He un-presses his nose from the floorboards and turns to look at me, resting his cheek on the wood.

'How are you doing? Do you want to tell me how you're feeling?'

He does some pretty convincing babbling, complete with conversational lilts and percussive bashing of the spoon on the floorboards.

'Uh-huh . . .' I show I'm paying attention, adding an 'Oh really?' that I hope makes sense in his stream-of-toddler-consciousness download.

Step two: empathy with a side order of labelling.

'You seem upset,' I start, 'are you feeling upset?'

He nods slightly, suspicious.

'Do you feel frustrated because Mama wouldn't give you another banana?' He would happily subsist on them if he could and constipation didn't intervene.

'M-yeah,' is the noise he makes, the side of his face still glued to the floor.

Step three: rapport. I'm not entirely sure how to build rapport with a two-year-old without capitulation, so I lower myself down until I'm lying on the floor as well. It's not massively comfortable and I notice from this angle that the skirting boards are filthy, but I'm prepared to forgo a spotless home in the pursuit of experimental parenting.

'You know, Mama gets upset and frustrated sometimes too. It doesn't feel nice, does it?'

'No . . .'

'But you know what? It's okay to feel like that. It's *okay* to get cross sometimes.' I'm mixing up my Will and my Gary advice here, but it seems to be working: he raises his head slightly. So I keep going and try my hand at step four: influence. 'When you're feeling better, if you help me wipe up the Weetabix then maybe we could go and play with your train. What do you think?'

'Tractorrr!'

'Or your tractor, yes.'

At this, he puts down his weapon (the spoon) and rests for a moment.

Bingo!

Time for step five: cooperation.

'So how about we get up now? If we clear up, then we can play!'

Slowly, carefully, Little Red pushes himself up into a very respectable plank position. Then he looks around, checking that the tractor and the train are in sight.

The clock ticks.

A lorry thunders past.

Come on Gary, I think: *don't let me down. We can do this!*

As the second hand approaches twelve, Little Red leaps up and runs to the sink. He pulls down the dishcloth by one corner, then tears back to dab at the crusted cereal. His wiping-up skills leave something to be desired but he makes a decent fist of it. Then he drops the cloth, takes my hand and pulls me off to play: 'Tractorrr!'

'Everything okay?' Lego Man materialises from the loo, conveniently post-commotion. 'I thought I heard shouting.'

'You did, but we're okay now. I think Gary might have nailed it—'

'You mean *FBI-parenting?*'

'Yes,' I sigh, bracing myself to say it: 'FBI-parenting.'

We practise FBI-parenting regularly over the next few weeks and it seems to work at mellowing the meltdowns, as well as – perhaps – reducing their frequency. Because he's feeling listened to and understood, as well as getting help to label his emotions, Little Red seems less frustrated. As are we. By tuning in to our toddler, things become easier. Everything takes longer – because I'm 'negotiating' with him to put his shoes on rather than squishing them on myself. But we walk more, rather than strapping him into the buggy or taking the car, and I notice things I've bustled past before. Children are an excellent defamiliarisation device and with his hand in mine I'm reminded that yes, tractors *are* big. Bark *is* interesting. The side door of the apartment block a few doors down that has been off its hinges for a long time *is* an 'uh-oh!' Ditto the used condom that's appeared in the bushes outside our house. He notices things, and so I do, too.

I wonder whether I've cracked this whole 'family' thing. Until a friend comes over who has a twin sister, three other siblings, a daughter, a stepson and a whole kettle of familial fish I haven't yet thought about.

'What about big, extended families?' she asks over lunch, after I've eulogised about Will and Gary's methods.

'*Mmm?*' I have a mouthful of couscous.

'Well it's all very well thinking about mesh ment—'

'*En*meshment.' I try not to spray her.

'Sure, and FBI-ing your kids. But I have a gazillion relatives – I can't talk down all of them, one by one. My brother has two kids and my sister has one of her own and is seeing a guy who has three. And my uncle hates kids. And he's not

my real uncle anyway . . . And Aunty Sue's just a teensy bit
. . . racist. And my mum's . . . well, my mum, and Dad's on
his own planet. We all manage to be civil for about an hour
but by dinnertime it's war.'

'Umm . . .' *Gary never said anything about taking on a*
whole army. How do you FBI-whisper a whole marauding
gang?

As an only child I have no experience of this. I haven't
had grandparents since 1998 and although my mother has
sisters and a brother, they're as adept at muffling ancient
resentments under everyday pleasantries and *Springwatch* as
she is. Lego Man's parents are only children and his beloved
grandmother celebrated her last Christmas, smacked up on
shortbread and sherry, in 2013. Our tribe is small, so The
Twin's family intrigues me.

'God, so how does it work when you all get together?'

I'm imagining family gatherings along the lines of *The*
Sound of Music's choir contest scene. Though with fewer
Nazis.

'You can meet them all if you like, see for yourself.'

'Can I?' I don't want her to think I'm abusing our friendship by demanding an audience with her extended family for
research purposes. I've already done a lot of staring at her
and her matchy-faced sister whenever I've seen them together.

'We're renting a place over the holidays since we can't
fit everyone in at ours, and I'm bribing friends to come
and dilute the madness. Really you'd be doing me a favour
– I'm staring down the barrel of six days and nights of
no mobile signal and no escape. If you can come up with
ways to minimise the bloodshed, you're more than
welcome.'

'Well in that case, I'd love to! I'll find you the best "extended family anti-destruction technique" known to womankind!'

I realise as soon as I've said it that this is a big shout. Lego Man shares his scepticism as we make coffee and hiss at each other so as not to be overheard.

'What makes you think you'll be able to help? You don't know anything about extended-family management or the challenges of step-parenting—'

'Have you been reading my *Psychologies* magazine again?' I glance at the stash of mags on the kitchen counter.

'I might have brushed past it . . . Did you know that one in three Brits is now a step-parent, stepchild, step-sibling or step-grandparent?'

'I did not know that.'

'But seventy-two per cent of remarriages with existing children end in divorce.'

'Oh brilliant, I'll tell her that . . . [I won't]. Milk?' He passes the semi-skimmed as I start to worry I've bitten off more than I can chew. 'Well, I'll make sure I do my homework and find out all about blended families—'

Lego Man makes a buzzer noise as though I'm a contestant getting the answer wrong on a shiny-floored game show: 'We don't call them *that* any more.'

'Don't we?'

'No. It's offensive. It implies that you're aiming for some kind of family smoothie – as though anyone who isn't finding it easy is a failure.'

'Oh.'

'Do you think maybe you should have thought this through first?'

'No . . . *Yes*.'

'Everything okay?' The Twin is standing at the kitchen counter.

'Fine!' I try to sound bright, seizing the kettle. 'Biscuits?'

The Twin and I have talked before about her experiences of step-parenting.

'It's just . . . different,' is how she put it: 'everything requires an extra level of thought. Like what to call myself for starters.' Before she and her partner were married, his son would describe her as 'Dad's girlfriend'. 'But that sounded too teenage – like I was the babysitter shagging their dad. So we tried saying nothing. But then, people assumed I was his mum and he'd correct them, like: "She's not my mother!" It happened at the dentist once. Made me sound like I'd abducted him or something and taken him for plaque removal. Then we got hitched and I became his wicked stepmother. Which was nice.'

She also struggles to balance the needs of her daughter and stepson. 'I don't do the discipline for him and it's not me he wants if he's upset,' she told me: 'I don't get to ration his pick 'n' mix the way I do my daughter's. Which, obviously, she thinks is massively unfair.' Then there are the exes to think about. 'You know how in life you generally try to avoid seeing the people your partner was in love with before they met you? Well, imagine being contractually obliged to see them once a week. For ever. As well as the person I *actively* chose to divorce. Oh, and then there's all the organising of trips back and forth between houses – and the packing! Some weeks it's the packing that finishes me off.'

I speak to a few divorced-parent friends (welcome to your

mid-thirties!) who agree that it's the 'negotiating with someone who really annoys you', missing children when they're with the other parent and 'semi-constant packing' that are most gruelling on an ongoing basis. But these experiences aren't unusual. There is no 'normal' any more and there isn't just one type of family unit.

'Even among my siblings I see different set-ups – and we all have different ways of doing things, which can be . . . *interesting*', The Twin tells me. As someone still struggling to adapt to the traditions of my in-laws at Christmas and Easter (no chocolate before 5 p.m.?! Presents *after* lunch? What cruel truculence is this?), the idea of an extended company of characters under one roof sounds like a recipe for unrest. The UK charity Relate found that 68 per cent of us predict arguments over the holidays, and diffusing tension once you've exhausted all topics of (safe) conversation sounds like a Herculean challenge. I ask The Twin how she'd like family life to be, in an ideal world.

'Well . . .' She leafs through a copy of *Hello!* magazine as she contemplates this before saying, with some certainty: 'A cross between The Waltons and The Kardashians would be great.'

What I want to say is: *'Are you out of your tree?!'* But I manage a nervous laugh and an 'I'll do my best . . .'

Lego Man finds me lying on the living room floor later that afternoon surrounded by his brightly coloured management books.

'You might get more out of them if you actually open one.'

'I'm hoping the theories might seep into me, like osmosis.'

He sits down and starts stacking books, one on top of

each other like a primary-colour-bricked wall. *Once a Lego builder, always a Lego builder,* I think.

I close my eyes, only to experience a weight being placed on my stomach. Using all my recently acquired muscles, I crunch up to look at what's been placed there.

'Try ADKAR' he tells me.

'I'm not trying anything else with an acronym.' I feel suddenly weary.

'You're missing out. I bet it's what The Kardashians use . . .'

So I sit up, seize the book and read.

The Prosci® ADKAR® Model was created by engineer Jeff Hiatt, founder of Prosci Research, in the mid-1990s to help organisations change more successfully. The first 'A' stands for awareness – helping participants understand why change is necessary. 'D' is for desire – getting people on board with change and appreciating that there are consequences if they refuse to comply (sounds a bit Kim Jong-un – apparently, *totally acceptable*). 'K' stands for knowledge – making sure people know how to change and giving them a role model to emulate where possible. The second 'A' is ability – ensuring change is possible and that participants have a realistic time-frame and the resources they need. And finally, 'R' is for reinforcement – making sure the change will be maintained and offering suitable rewards.

An example of ADKAR in action can be found in hotels worldwide. The little signs asking us to reuse our towels create awareness, by reminding us that millions of litres of water are wasted by washing extra linen. Next, we're told that we can help make a difference with very little effort on our part – creating a desire for change. Knowledge comes after this: we learn that we need to place our towel back on the rail if we're happy to use it again. Ability is taken care of – we're all able to do this tiny thing. And finally, change is reinforced: we feel warm and fuzzy for having done 'the right thing' (reward); we're making a measurable, if small, difference to water waste. On top of this, some hotel chains have started offering drink vouchers or loyalty points for participating.

ADKAR is most commonly used in business but it's also implemented in the sports world (you know, throwing balls and stuff *better* . . .) and, intriguingly, in family life[24].

'Organisational change theories for companies should work well on family units because, historically, they were the same thing,' says Tim Creasey, who works as Jeff Hiatt's chief innovation officer at Prosci in Fort Collins, Colorado: 'In agricultural economies, the composition of an organisation was literally made up of family members. Using ADKAR can be helpful because it's based on the building blocks that anyone, anywhere needs to make a personal transition change successfully. And by using a common language you can take the heat out of the situation.'

So the potential awkwardness of launching into a structured management theory with your nearest and dearest actually becomes an *advantage*?

'In a way, yes!' he says. 'It helps take change from a nebulous concept to something with concrete outcomes. And because it has a focus on the individual, it takes in our differences. So, for instance, my two kids, both boys, raised

---

24 Disclaimer: there is no evidence that The Kardashians have ever partaken in ADKAR. Lego Man was just trying to lure me in. But, you know, Kris: worth a go . . .

the same way, are hugely different. I employ ADKAR at home to focus on what motivates them as individuals – one of them is motivated by physical play and the other likes video games. These are what work as rewards for them. In business, when we talk about reinforcement, we mean understanding what kind of praise or reward will most motivate an individual – will this be from a manager or from their peers, for example? In families, the same applies – one person might respond better to a patriarch or matriarch figure while someone else would prefer a pat on the back from their siblings.'

Interesting. Although this sounds like a lot of work, I tell him: establishing what motivates each individual family member – or employee – and tailoring the approach to them.

'It does take some effort to start with,' he agrees, 'but it saves you work later. It's a more efficient way of doing things.'

And doesn't everyone just get the giggles and feel silly?

Tim assures me that, in his experience, the answer is 'no': 'It can be done fairly naturally in a non-work setting – I often say I'm "putting on my ADKAR glasses" at home and we try out the method when we need to make a change.'

Okay, so how would you segue from normal life into ADKAR with your family?

'It's pretty easy – I start with "A" for awareness. So I tell them what the change is I'd like to explore and then my two-year-old will usually ask "Why?" – the natural reaction to change. We all want to know "Why is this necessary?" The "project manager" – me in this case – will then give him a WIIFM—'

More acronyms?

'. . . this stands for "What's in it for me". Then it really is as straightforward as running through each of the letters in turn. And watching out for the most common mistakes.' These, I learn, are failure to effectively communicate the need for change and failing to remain visible and engaged throughout the project. 'It's important to remember that resistance to change is the norm, not the exception,' adds Tim. 'To manage resistance, you should listen and understand objections; remove barriers; provide simple, clear choices and consequences; show the benefits of change in a real and tangible way; and convert the strongest dissenters. Usually the two-year-old in my case . . .' I empathise with him on toddler dictators and sign off, steeling myself to try ADKAR next weekend.

We are in the mother country to remind Little Red what his grandparents look like, and we take a detour north. The car is full to bursting with child- and husband-related paraphernalia, Lego Man having invited himself along for the ride as soon as he learned the location.

'That's prime puffin country!'

When I pointed out that he hadn't technically been invited, he made me text The Twin to ask/beg.

'*Sure – the more the mental-er,*' was her reply.

So we loaded the car with a trousseau of travel cot, stroller, multiple changes of clothes and enough Duplo to build a small fort, and set off.

The scenery changes from towns and villages to open country – green fields in neat squares and horizons pierced by the odd tree. Dark clouds roll in behind us, so I rest a little heavier on the accelerator to outstrip them. As we reach the crest of a hill, we spy the sea.

'That,' Lego Man tells Little Red, 'is where we'll see puffins!' He whips out a pair of binoculars.

'Where did you get *those*?'

'These? I've had these for ages.' This is a lie. 'They'll be handy,' he adds, scanning the road in acute detail. 'In fact, I think I see the house – yep, there's someone on the door-step.' He waves.

'We're half a mile away, they can't see you.'

'Oh. Yeah . . .'

When we finally pull up outside the house, The Twin is huddled under a ramshackle porch, glass of wine in one hand, cigarette in the other, sheltering from the rain.

'Thank God you're here.' She exhales and stubs out the cigarette, looking around to check no one's seen her. She sounds stressed and speaks rapidly: 'Most people have only just arrived because my family like to be late, which is fun for those of us who try to schedule mealtimes. Come in, I'll help you find a room.' She leads us inside and up a narrow staircase: 'I think these are all taken, so we'll go to the next floor.'

'Classic puffin,' Lego Man whispers: 'each colony is sub-divided and early arrivals take control of the best locations, the most desirable nesting sites being where take-off is most easily accomplished.' He nods to the exit, now disappearing from view.

'That one might be free, depends on how tonight goes. So, my racist aunt and my uncle who's not really my uncle aren't together any more but they like coming along for big family stuff and sometimes bunk up.'

'*Textbook* puffin!'

I shoot Lego Man a look.

'What? Birds are usually monogamous, but this is the result of fidelity to their nesting sites rather than to their mates – they love returning to the same burrows year after year!'

We find a room where we're unlikely to be disturbed by estranged puffin uncles and set up camp. Lego Man struggles to assemble the travel cot while I rifle through my bag to find the carton of milk I've packed for Little Red's pre-bedtime snack.

'The colony is at its most active in the evening,' narrates Lego Man, doing his best David Attenborough impression: 'the creatures give bi-parental care to their young and the male spends time maintaining the nest while the female is more involved in feeding the chick . . .'

This could be a long night . . .

We put Little Red to bed, wait out a few protestations, then head downstairs. In the kitchen, vats of food are being prepared. The windows are steamed up and we're greeted by flushed faces.

'You've met my mother,' The Twin offers, signalling to a well-upholstered woman wearing pyjamas. She rests her bulk on the counter and flirts outrageously with Lego Man.

'Has your mum been napping?' I whisper to The Twin as I help her chop vegetables.

'No, she just likes to get into her pyjamas when she arrives somewhere new.'

'Oh.'

We work in tandem as she gives me a diplomatic-style briefing on each new arrival.

'Aunty Sue,' she whispers, as a slight woman with a neat white bob appears. 'Likes: talking about people we should all apparently remember; pretending she's a vegetarian. Dislikes: the French.'

'Got it.'

A man in a turquoise jumper sidles in, nods to Lego Man, then wordlessly flicks the top off a bottle of beer and hands it to him.

'That's my brother, Al. After Capone. We think he was in jail last year, because no one heard from him for three months. Plus he stole my bath mat last time he came to stay. In fact . . .' She sets down the knife down and accosts him. 'Is that my jumper?'

'No, it's my jumper.'

'No: it's *my* jumper! The label in the back will clearly say size twelve.'

'So?'

'So, men's clothes don't come in those sizes. Show me the label.' The Twin lunges at him.

'No! Get off!'

'Show me!'

She tries to forcibly remove the jumper. When this doesn't work, she reaches up a sleeve and tugs the hair on his forearm until he squeals.

'My God, is this a *fight*?' Lego Man moves in next to me for protection. 'An actual fight?' The rain ramps up outside until a crack of lightning punctures the clouds and a roll of thunder shakes the house. Lego Man and I look at each other. We have both watched television before: we both know that Something Bad Is About To Happen. Just then, a man wearing baggy cords with a newspaper tucked under his arm ambles in, rolls up the paper and swats at Al, distracting him long enough for The Twin to slip out of a headlock.

'Thanks Dad.'

Children appear and everyone behaves a little better for a while. The Twin's daughter is shy and reserved, and as a result gets left out of the games. The Twin's twin looks, unsurprisingly, just like my friend only crosser. Her son and stepdaughters sit separately and frown at iPads.

'We disagree on how to raise our kids so they all do their own thing – stay up as late as they like, smoke crack . . . whatever,' The Twin says, straight-faced. 'But for tonight, at least, I want us all to eat together. To get through one meal without arguing. Think ADKAR can manage that?'

Actually, I'm not sure. But I run her through the basics and hope for the best. The Twin drains her glass, finishes Lego Man's beer, then carries a cauldron of spaghetti to the table and summons the rest of the family to join her.

It's at this point that the excuses start.

'Be there in a bit,' shrills Aunty Sue.

'I'll take the kids theirs,' says her matchy-faced sister.

'Got any chicken?' asks Al, scanning the fridge.

'No,' The Twin says firmly. 'I've made bolognese and we're all going to eat it together. I'm not asking everyone to be dressed –' she looks pointedly at her mother – 'I just want us all to sit down. Is that too much to ask?'

There are murmurs of objection but with some herding, the flock are rounded up.

'Now, we're going to play a game. It's called ADKAR and we're using it to set some ground rules for the week.' The Twin is a teacher. She's good at rules. She rattles through a brief explanation of the theory and what the letters stand for and from the open-mouthed gapes around the table, I get the impression that the rest of the diners are too stunned to object.

'So "A" is for "Awareness": I think we can all agree that as a family, we like a row. Everyone remembers last year –' there is tittering – 'so it would be nice if this year we tried to keep things civil. To do that we need to make changes. To how we behave and speak to each other for starters. I'd suggest keeping things clean, so topics to be avoided include: the EU, ex-partners and vegetarianism—'

'But I am a vegetarian!'

'Mum saw you eat a whole rotisserie chicken last Sunday.'

There is a sharp intake of breath before Aunty Sue hisses at The Twin's mother: 'Judas!'

'Next comes "Desire": it would be *nice* not to row, we could be like happy, considerate families –' She holds up a magazine as a visual aid and I cringe inwardly – 'like The Kardashians!'

'I'm not sure this is a realistic goal,' I whisper to Lego Man, who shushes me.

'"K" is for "Knowledge" – making sure we know how to change. Many of us grew up with different traditions and ways of doing things. So we need to find common ground and work out what stuff we can all do together.'

'Uncle' Bill starts picking his teeth with a fork.

'The second "A" is for "Ability", so we're going to put some things in place to help us achieve this. We're going to play more games, go on walks –' there is grumbling at this – 'do *activities* and . . .' she pauses, as though reluctant. Lego Man stares at her, eagerly; ' – and Lego Man has very kindly agreed to lead us all on a puffin-watching expedition tomorrow.'

Tumbleweed passes up and down the table and I pray that there are some takers for this.

'Finally, "R" stands for "Reinforcement" – making sure we carry on being civil to each other and recognising good behaviour with rewards.' There is cheering here. 'Everyone will get to feel like they've *actually* had a nice time and yes, there will be prizes.' She unfolds a list of the week's attendees. Next to each name is a reward she's deemed suitable, from breakfast in bed to foot rubs, Minecraft binges and 'all the wine'.

The Twin asks whether there are any questions and then addresses her family's concerns, one by one:

'No, there isn't any Wi-Fi.'

'Or phone reception.'

'Puffin-watching is optional.'

I see Lego Man's face fall and give his hand a squeeze.

'Is everyone clear?' The Twin takes the silence as acquiescence and for the next fifteen minutes all seems surprisingly serene. People eat and talk and no one tries to put anyone else in a headlock. Or administers a wedgie. Then The Twin slips out to go to the loo and I get up to check on Little Red. When we reconvene round the table, three quarters of the seats are empty.

'Where is everyone?'

Lego Man shakes his head. 'You've just committed the cardinal sin of ADKAR: failure to remain visible and engaged throughout the project.'

'I had to pee!'

He holds his hands up: 'I don't make the rules.'

The Twin ushers everyone back to the table for 'cheese and Mars Ice Cream Bars' – the 'afters' of champions – and we consult on what to do next.

'You have to send a clear message that you mean what you

say,' I read from my notes: '*Find negative stakeholders and create consequences for dissent.*'

The Twin seizes the printout. '*Removing a key manager who is demonstrating a resistance to change sends a powerful signal to the organisation as a whole that says "I'm serious about this change"*. Well, it looks like I'm going to have to throw someone under the bus.' She frowns, then looks at me.

'*Me?*'

She nods solemnly.

'Why me?'

'I can't *actively banish* a member of my family in the middle of nowhere to the mercy of puffins—'

'Puffins are actually very caring creatures!'

'No one cares about puffins!' she tells Lego Man sharply, before turning back to me. 'Look, you're going tomorrow anyway. And this was your idea!'

'You're really going to do this? After all I've done for you!'

'Yes.'

'Wow . . .'

I look to Lego Man for support but he's busy shovelling Stinking Bishop into his mouth. 'I can't stop eating this cheese. I'm getting dairy sweats . . .'

'I'll buy dinner next time I see you,' The Twin offers by way of compensation: 'And I'll babysit, starting now!' She snatches up the baby monitor from the table. 'I'll even make you those muffins you like . . .?'

Lego Man looks up: 'She does make a good muffin.'

'Fine,' I sigh.

'Great!' The Twin takes another swig of wine as we tune back in to the rest of the room. Children are crying, adults are snapping at each other and an overheated atmosphere is brewing in the overheated house. I hear one 'You're turning into your mother', a couple of 'You're not my real dad's, and several 'Well, he/she *would* say that!'s before The Twin leaps to her feet, dramatically, and turns on me.

'How *dare* you say the infrastructure's weak! That's my mother you're talking about!'

'What? I never—'

The Twin gives me a wink.

Oh.

'Yes. Sorry. I did say that. Definitely.'

We all know the rule: we can be as critical as we like about our own family but woe betide an outsider who slags us off.

'Right, that's it: I think you should leave! First thing tomorrow!'

Grudgingly, I play my part: 'What? No! Me?'

'Yes!' She points. 'YOU! We've all committed to working on this, like The Kardashians. But you're not taking it seriously . . .' I look around the table with an expression that I hope appears hangdog, but can't quite bring myself to meet the gaze of her mother. The tension is unbearable. It's like watching someone blow up a really big balloon.

'Sorry . . .' I mumble again.

'I'll take her outside, help her calm down.' Lego Man springs to his feet: 'I can only apologise for her appalling behaviour.'

All right, Meryl Streep . . .

'I have to make it look real,' whispers Lego Man as he frogmarches me from the room.

Deciding that some non-family air might be just what we

need, we pull on coats. The rain has eased off but the night is damp and cold as we walk in silence towards the sea, the backs of our hands grazing each other until he links his with mine.

'I can't believe no one wanted to learn about puffins,' Lego Man says finally. 'Kids today –' he looks perplexed – 'they have everything! I mean, I would have sold a kidney for shoes with lights in them! We barely had lights in the house! What's wrong with people?'

I shake my head and curl my fingers more tightly around his.

'I know, at least you tried—' I start, but he cuts me off with a 'Shh!'

'What?'

'There they are!' He drops my hand and pulls out his binoculars before you can say 'pelagic seabird'.

All I can make out is a few lumps on a rock, but Lego Man is in heaven.

After several hundred iPhone pictures, in the dark, of what may or may not be a puffin, a wet glob of seagull excrement splats on my shoulder and I tell him it's time to head back.

Inside, we find a harmonious scene of family young and old, blood relations and step affiliations, united in balancing items of clothing on a slumped, rotund figure.

'What's going on?'

'We're playing Uncle Buckaroo,' The Twin's stepson tells me as a body twitches under the weight of two coats, a flat cap and several shoes.

'What's Uncle Buckaroo?'

The entire room looks at us in amazement.

'You don't know it?' The Twin sounds surprised. 'You wait

for a relative, usually "Uncle" Bill, to fall asleep, then balance stuff on them until they either move or wake up. You never played?'

I remind her that it was just my mum and me growing up: 'I think if I'd started using her as a human clothes horse she might have noticed.'

'Deprived childhood, explains a lot,' slurs The Twin's mother.

Psychologists agree that focusing on what we have in common rather than our differences can help smooth over familial gatherings. The 'Ability' stage of ADKAR, if you will. And while 'balancing stuff on a relative' might be an unconventional unifying device, it seems to be working. Everyone is playing nicely – not fighting, not on their iPads, not even trading insults. The game inevitably comes to an end when 'Uncle' Bill, trapped under six coats, three hats and numerous woolly jumpers, wakes with a start, convinced he's suffocating.

'What next? Dead Club?' one of Al's boys asks.

The Twin translates: 'You know, where you place bets on the next celebrities you think are going to die.'

'What? That's horrible! Whatever happened to wholesome family fun?' *'Come along children, gather around the fireside, let's guess who'll croak next'* . . .?

'We play it at school!' she says, by way of justification: 'I made a mint on Ronnie Corbett. We've got a sweepstake going. As long as Al doesn't nick it, the winner gets £20.' Still sensing disapproval, she adds: 'What? It's the "R" in ADKAR, for "Recognition" via rewards, see?'

We go to bed after this. But just before I turn out the light, I listen. There are no bloodcurdling screams, no raised voices and no sounds of sobbing. All I can hear is laughter, punctuated by the occasional clink of a beer bottle. I'm not sure this is exactly what Tim had in mind when he talked about putting on his ADKAR glasses, but if it works for The Twin, then I'm pleased for her.

'Kris Kardashian would be proud,' murmurs Lego Man, before passing out for a night of cheese dreams about puffins.

Things I've learned about change and family:

---

1. There's more we can do to improve relations than we might think.

2. Working on our pilot's voice to end parental enmeshment is a great start.

3. FBI hostage negotiation is a legitimate parenting tool.

4. Our family are the people we care about, regardless of blood ties . . .

5. . . . but that doesn't mean we'll all necessarily get along.

6. . . . unless we're The Waltons

7. Treating family like an organisation and ADKAR-ing them can bring everyone aboard the good ship *Change*.

8. Finding something that unites us makes for happier family gatherings. Usually.

CHAPTER SEVEN

FINANCE

Got Money On My Mind

In which I learn how the Japanese philosophy of kaizen can help us face our money fears; what talking to kids can teach us about our finances; how tapping can (and can't) help control spending; and why someone I know is suffering from ADOSOD

We are Going On Holiday. An annual event that always involves a combination of giddy recklessness (Lego Man) and stomach-knotting stress (me).

'I've booked the room!' he shouts excitedly: 'And flights! Just airport transfers to go!'

I hear him tapping away and booking peak-season travel to a town neither of us have ever heard of. All to the melodic strains of Madonna's eponymous vacation-themed hit, which has now been playing, on repeat, for thirty minutes.

'Done!' Lego Man appears in the kitchen, jubilant. He is wild-eyed and ruffled, with a whiff of Caliban about him, had *The Tempest* been set in modern-day Scandinavia. Little Red and the dog pick up on the manic energy now coursing through the house and both start leaping around as Lego Man announces: 'Right, next up: new shorts! For all of us!'

'Do we need new shorts?' I ask, pretty sure we own ample

summer wardrobes in mint condition thanks to the scarcity of truly scorching days in Denmark. You don't wear out a sundress in the land of Nord and Little Red's UV-blocking, SPF100 'sun suit' has seen action precisely twice.

'These will be HOLIDAY shorts!' Lego Man clarifies: 'For our HOLIDAY!'

My husband loves to spend. Money flows through his hands like water: it's there and then it's gone down some metaphysical plughole. Which, when you're living in tax-'em-high Denmark, is tricky. Moving back to the UK would mean we'd be better off financially, since taxes are lower. *But if we ('he') learned to spend less,* I can't help thinking, *we wouldn't need more – of anything . . . We have enough to eat and a roof over our heads: we're lucky. So why is Lego Man such a shopping fan?*

Needless to say, I have my own financial blind spots.

'I could fix that!' has become a catchphrase in our house thanks to my unfailing zeal for adopting a make-do-and-mend approach for everything from pillowcases (achievable, just), to the car (less likely to result in success). I have always been cautious with money and, as the daughter of a single mum who never seemed to have enough of the stuff, I learned that the best approach was to 'squirrel away what you could and try not to look at your bank balance in case it's a jazzy colour'. Talking about money was vulgar and 'nice girls' just got on with things. This squirrel/ostrich approach meant that I could dismiss my failure to negotiate salaries or my chronically poor overdraft choices by saying, 'Oh, I'm just rubbish with money!' as though it were a genetic predisposition, like myopia. I became accustomed to a general feeling of powerlessness when it came to banking fees, car costs or house maintenance. And the precise numbers of pounds in tens, hundreds or – who knows? – thousands lurking in my account was cloaked in mystery. For years this didn't seem like much of a problem and I blindly stumbled from one month to the next. Because, actually, 'I'm rubbish with money' is seen a perfectly acceptable justification for financial illiteracy as long as you're white, middle class and female.

'Men do money; women do YouTube videos of kittens,' is how Head Girl puts it sarcastically whenever I bemoan my inability to perform basic financial admin. Head Girl is good with money. She once took an 'Introduction to Finance' evening class. We all need to be more like Head Girl. But most of us aren't. Many financial companies don't even bother talking to women – assuming instead that all their clients are male. As a result, a 2015 savings survey conducted by YouGov in the UK revealed that men have almost twice as much money put away as women – £74,000 versus £39,000 – a figure that includes home equity as well as bank accounts and investments.

Hmmm, 'investments'. I turn the word over in my head and wonder how one would go about *'getting some of those . . .'*

In my twenties, I told myself I wasn't earning enough to 'invest' or even save. This was probably because I wasn't assertive enough to ask for enough. Women in the UK still earn 19 per cent less than men – a statistic I personally upheld for the best part of a decade until discovering a memo left on the printer one day detailing how a male colleague was earning considerably more than me for doing the same job. In many ways, I was the noughties underachieving, crap-haired, poverty-dodging, publishing equivalent of Hollywood A-lister Jennifer Lawrence. Bear with me: I'll explain.

In her 2015 essay 'Why Do I Make Less Than My Male Co-Stars?' J-Law highlighted the problems that women have with money after the Sony hack revealed she was paid 7 per cent of the profits on *American Hustle* – compared to the male leads, who earned 9 per cent. The film made a cool $251 million at the box office worldwide. But the point wasn't about how much film stars earn. We can all agree *that's* insane. It's about the fact that someone was paid less for doing the same thing as her co-stars because she didn't[25] have a penis. In the twenty-first century. Which is crazy. *And it's partly our fault for not demanding it,* I think: *If only I'd discovered Dr Dance and his fee-doubling power ballad tip in my twenties!*

As my thirties loomed, I finally started getting paid a decent figure. I still wasn't savvy enough to have negotiated this, so can only assume that my bosses took pity on me or became bored by the sight of my threadbare spring/summer/autumn/winter coat, worn season after season. But once my rent had gone out and I'd paid for such luxuries as electricity, heat, water, food and 'maintenance of twenty-first-century lady woman working on a glossy magazine' (a not inconsiderable monthly grooming expense), there wasn't much left. I somehow persuaded myself that these were inevitable overheads and that 'everything would be okay in the end'. Only no one passed this memo on to 'life'. So I was skint.

What makes things trickier is that most of us still don't talk about money. Aside from the nod about my speaking rates, I have no idea what my peers earn, so no way of

---

25 Still doesn't, as far as I know.

checking what I'm worth. The closest I've ever come to having a candid financial discussion with friends, Head Girl's kitten recriminations aside, is a desperately sad conversation with Pans Solo some years back about an insecure boyfriend who couldn't handle the fact that she earned more than him. Lego Man found this baffling, assuring her that far from feeling threatened by the success of a partner, he'd be overjoyed ('I could SHOP more!'). But instead, Insecure Man did everything he could to undermine and punish her: complaining when she worked late, putting her down in public and refusing to even acknowledge it when she got a promotion. Money is power, whether we like it or not. But a culture of silence around the green stuff gives money even greater muscle. *Which needs to change*, I rationalise.

Rather than having an instinctive reaction of fear when I hear Lego Man has spent our savings on a holiday and assuming that we'll soon be destitute, the time has come to take my £-sign blinkers off and empower myself.

Instead of ignoring the outgoings on our joint account (see 'ostrich'), I undertake to observe them. Like an anally retentive hawk. Swapping my finance-bird from ostrich to hawk won't be easy, but my research to date has taught me that the first step on most change journeys is awareness. So as I ponder the best approach to fixing my household's financial failings, I want to understand more about how Lego Man spends and how I save.

I am an anthropologist, I tell myself, as he bounds back in and tells me he's ordered us all boogie boards. ('Boogie boards?' 'Yes! For our HOLIDAY!'). *This is an exercise in observation*, I repeat, calmly: *I am studying the lesser spotted shopping enthusiast known colloquially as Liberace Lego Man.*

This approach lasts until 1 a.m., when I wake with a stomach-churning recollection of the peak-season flights we've just booked. I lie awake fretting to the soundscape of rain *drip, drip, dripping* on to the Velux window above our bed – and, inevitably, within ten minutes, on my head (see 'rubbish landlord'). I know, rationally, that holidays are worthwhile. That we are more productive when we're well rested and the alternative of 'working all year round' is (apparently) bad for us. The British philosopher A. C. Grayling described travel as expanding the mind and spirit and I've read research from the University of Pittsburgh showing that regular holidays cut the risk of dying from heart disease by 30 per cent. There's evidence that taking a break reduces blood pressure and stress levels, too, according to studies from the UK's Nuffield Health charity. And psychologists from Cornell University in the US have proven that it's experiences, not stuff, that make us happy – something my minimalist sensibilities are totally on board with. Spending time with others and experiencing new things have both been shown to improve mental well-being. *Holidays are all about spending time with the people we're closest to and trying new things,* I think, listening to Lego Man breathing deeply, his blond head half submerged in pillow. *Looking at it this way, a fortnight away could be the perfect starting-over research trip* . . . Once I've persuaded myself that it's work-related, I feel less guilty about spending money on it. I make a mental note not to mention this to Lego Man (*NB: don't risk divorce by talking shop on holiday* . . .) before finally nodding off.

Three weeks later, we're sitting in the sunshine looking out over Instagrammable views, reading, napping, and occasionally mopping ice cream from Little Red's face before the ants get to him. We've countered months of seasonal affective disorder at the hands of a severe Scandinavian winter by filling up on vitamin D, and Little Red's UV suit has now had its *third* outing. Spending time somewhere hot and sunny has been a novelty. But financially speaking, it has been a litany of misadventure. Allow me to take you back in time two weeks.

Little Red attracts a lot of attention wherever he goes because he is a) loud, b) ginger and c) very smiley – and Lego Man enjoys this celebrity by proxy. In the same way that men with puppies tend to get lucky in parks, fathers all secretly agree that walking around with a cute kid in tow is a wonderful ego boost. On this particular occasion, we're waiting for the connecting flight to our holiday destination in the departure lounge at Heathrow when Little Red and Lego Man decide to take a stroll. En route, they encounter an actual, twenty-four-carat film star with a son the same age as ours. She is rather taken with Little Red. And Lego Man is rather taken with her. So they get chatting.

Sitting alone with the coats, I see the words '*Go to gate*' flash up on the departures screen without much concern. Ten minutes pass, during which my family has still not returned. When I see the word '*Boarding*' appear next to our flight, I gather up our belongings and go in search of my missing men, tracking them down to just outside the disabled loo.

'Come on, we have to go! They're boarding—' I start. Then I spot the Actual Film Star.

I run through a mental IMDB filmography of her roles to date before managing a smile and stammering something along the lines of, 'Oh! Hi!'

'Hi.' Actual Film Star does not smile at me or even allow her eyes to leave the male members of my family. Instead, she keeps her laser-like focus on Lego Man until he says something HILARIOUS about it being 'time to go now', at which point she erupts into peals of laughter and places a hand on his arm to apparently 'steady herself' from all the LOLing.

Not cool, Actual Film Star, I think: *not cool. You may well be able to pull off a grey marl jumpsuit and look staggeringly beautiful at 8 a.m., but what about the sisterhood?*

Before I can give her my best 'look' to this effect, the words '*Final call*' appear next to our flight. Lego Man tears himself away from the flirting A-lister and we run. Really run, *Chariots of Fire* style, to the gate. But it's too late.

'I'm sorry sir, you've missed your flight, we've had to take your luggage off,' a nice lady in a blue uniform tells us.

There is 'language', during which I cover Little Red's ears, and some marital telepathy is exchanged along the lines of '?!?!' before Lego Man declares he will 'take care of it'. Little Red and I go foraging, the square packaged meal I'd been promising him on the plane now a long way off, at the far end of the runway. When we return, Lego Man announces that he has booked us on the very next flight. At considerable expense.

Eight hours later than planned, we touch down at a different airport and go in search of the ferry we now have to take to reach our final destination.

We sit on the top deck and Little Red screams into the breeze with delight, *Titanic* style.

'I know it hasn't been *ideal*,' says my husband as the boat manoeuvres into position to dock, 'but it feels great to finally

be here, doesn't it?' I do some murmuring by way of response.
'I think this might be one of the "precious moments" my
mum's always banging on about in family life!' he says affectionately, as Little Red starts picking his nose. 'It just feels
great to be away! I'm . . . *this* happy,' he adds, throwing his
hands out wide to indicate 'very'.

As his left arm snaps to full extension, there is a faint
Ting! Ting! Ting! And then, nothing.

'That's weird,' says Lego Man, looking around him.
There's no sign of any loose machinery and we're the only
passengers braving the gusty winds on the top deck. After a
few moments in the crucifixion pose, he retracts his arms:
'Oh dear . . .'

'What's wrong?'

'Nothing! Everything's fine . . . Everything's *fine!*'

No one, in the history of the world, has ever said
'Everything's fine' and meant it. Let alone twice. *I smell a
sea bream.* He starts collecting up our things and scouring
the deck as though we've got some tiny luggage he's worried
we might miss.

'What *is* it?'

'It's . . . my ring,' he says finally.

'Your wedding ring?'

I don't know why I clarify this: he wears no other. Lego
Man is about as far from *The A-Team*'s B.A. Baracus as it
is possible for anyone to be.

He holds up his left hand by way of an answer and reveals
an entirely bare ring finger.

'It doesn't seem to be there any more.'

Lego Man had mentioned that his wedding band felt loose
once before. But never that things were so roomy that a

combination of 'cooling sea breeze' and 'grand gesture' was likely to send it flying. I remain calm and reassure him, 'It's okay, we'll get on to the insurance when we get to the hotel.'

'But it's my wedding ring!'

He's overwrought, so I try to be rational: 'It's a piece of jewellery: it's not our marriage. Yes, it's a shame—'

'I need a new one!'

'Okay, but let's be practical . . . what are you doing? Are you *Googling*?'

'There's a place not far from here, looks all right,' he says, straightening up and holding the device away from him slightly until the map function shows him which direction he's currently facing.

'Can't you wait? We could get one from a reputable establishment once we're back—'

'No, I need it now—'

'What, in case Actual Film Star comes looking for you?' I'm not quite so calm now.

There is some terribly British subdued rowing as we attempt to scoop up our son and disembark without 'making a scene'. Lego Man summons a taxi and shortly after driving off, I notice we're heading in the opposite direction to our hotel.

'Are you—? Is this—? We're not . . .?' I start, before realising that we've pulled up outside . . . a jewellers.

One ring later, we reach our hotel. I put an exhausted Little Red to bed and Lego Man offers to run me a bath. I'm just getting to the last page of a bedtime story when I hear a splash followed by: '*Bollocks!*'

'Everything all right?' I don't really want to know the answer.

Lego Man appears with a wet sleeve and a dripping mobile. 'Dropped it. In the bath.'

Before I can even begin to form the first syllable of '*insurance*', he goes on: 'We'll have to find a phone shop in the morning.'

It's been an expensive twenty-four hours.

We survive the trip. Just. But as soon as I get home, I make a call.

Dr Robert Mauer is the Director of Behavioural Sciences for the Family Practice Residency Program at Santa Monica-UCLA Medical Center and a faculty member with the UCLA School of Medicine. But Bob, as I'm encouraged to call him, is also the world expert in something called 'kaizen'. No, not the baddie from *The Usual Suspects*, but a change theory to do with taking small steps to make a big difference that has been taking parts of the world by storm. Or rather: small localised rain clouds.

'It can be a fairly radical idea to get your head around,' explains Bob when he speaks to me at seven in the morning his time (thank you, Bob) from his base in California: 'But once you do, it's life-changing.'

Bob's introduction to kaizen came when he was working at the UCLA Family Medicine Clinic in Santa Monica, circa 2001. 'This was slightly unusual for a psychologist but it meant I really got to see what physical symptoms people presented with and link them with the mind,' he says. 'I kept seeing people who were really overweight or hadn't looked after their health at all – and I started to wonder why we didn't intervene more before things got so bad. Why was it that we let things get terrible before we tried to "fix them" instead of staying healthy all along? And I realised that there are very few tools for *staying* healthy or helping us make better choices. Most of what's out there is about cleaning up the mess when there's already a problem.'

Bob read a newspaper article about Toyota, the Japanese car manufacturer, who for years after World War Two led the automotive world in terms of productivity and profit. Their secret? Kaizen.

'This is the philosophy of small steps toward improvement that originated in the US,' Bob tells me: 'In World War Two, US car factories were made into tank factories and everyone was asked to come up with small incremental changes that could improve productivity and efficiency. It was about seemingly insignificant improvements as well as worker participation and a humanised approach to increased productivity. After the war, this idea was introduced to Japan when General MacArthur's occupation forces began to rebuild the country. Despite Japan's corporate dominance in the late twentieth century, many of its post-war businesses were run pretty poorly, with low morale. General MacArthur wanted to improve efficiency and raise business standards – because a strong Japanese economy would safeguard against the threat from North Korea . . .'

I suddenly feel astoundingly under-read and resolve to stop fussing about the price of boogie boards and swot up on The History of the World, Volume I.

'. . . So MacArthur brought in US production specialists who emphasised the importance of small steps toward change – because this had worked so well in America.' One of the experts was US statistician and engineer William Edwards Deming, who had such an impact on productivity in Japan that the country's prime minister awarded him the Order of the Sacred Treasure, Second Class to recognise his contributions to Japan's worldwide success.

This 'small steps' innovation proved so popular that Japan adopted it as her own, giving it a far zippier-sounding name – kaizen, Japanese for 'improvement'.

'After the war, no US companies were interested in sticking with this approach – to their detriment,' adds Bob: 'but the Japanese kept with kaizen.'

When Bob read about Toyota's continued (at the time) success, crediting kaizen as the driving force (pun intended – and relished), he had an idea. 'It just hit me,' he says, 'that this was a better way of working. In our personal lives as well as in business.' Bob collaborated with Deming before his death in 1993 to explore how kaizen could be applied in all areas of life. 'There have been seventy years' worth of studies into kaizen now,' he tells me, 'and it *works*.'

Here's how.

Research shows that going to the gym for an hour a day doesn't reduce the risks associated with sitting for six or more hours a day, but keeping moving *throughout* the day brings big results. This is kaizen. New York City applied kaizen to its crime rates in the 1990s by implementing the 'broken windows theory'. This is the idea that if a neighbourhood puts up with minor snafus – like vandalism or broken windows – without taking steps to rectify them, the result is an increase in more serious offences. So police clamped down on smaller misdemeanours and major crime fell as a result.

'The idea that small changes lead to big changes has been practised in the East for centuries,' says Bob, 'Thus the old philosophy that a journey of a thousand miles begins with a single step. It just makes sense.'

So why aren't more of us kaizen-ing it? And why am I only learning about it now?

'Well, in the US at least, we tend to think that big problems need big solutions – and we want large results. But because we're not making small improvements along the way, by the time something becomes a problem it's generally too big to manage in one go. Then we feel we *have* to take big steps,' he says. I ask Bob for an example of this around, say, *money*, and he graciously accepts the challenge.

'Okay, so if we're in debt, there's often a lot of guilt and shame – even anger – attached to it. We might be mad with ourselves and have a harsh inner voice criticising us. To try to quieten this inner voice, we feel as though only a big voice or comeback will work.' He tells me that he's helped a lot of accountants who don't pay attention to their personal finances. 'They're so busy with other things that they forget about their own money. It's the nature of human beings, that unless something triggers the amygdala – the part of the brain concerned with fight or flight – we don't do anything. Unless it gets to be a crisis, we don't change our current course. This is an approach that served our hunter-gatherer ancestors well – it makes sense to keep hunting the same way until something persuades you otherwise. Or eats you. But in our modern lives, it isn't always so great.' Big changes, I learn, not only don't work so well – they're more stressful, too.

To explain why, Bob gives me a quick biology lesson. In addition to my history lesson. *Must sign up for some sort of Open University course and start reading the hard-copy encyclopaedia gathering dust on the bookshelf*, I think. *Starting tomorrow . . .*

Our brain is divided into three parts, Bob explains. At the bottom is the brainstem or the 'reptilian brain' as it's known, which is 500 million years old.

'Wow! That is *old* . . .' I mumble in considerable awe.

The reptilian brain, I learn, is the bit that wakes us up in the morning, sends us to sleep and reminds us to breathe. Useful things like that. Resting on top of the reptilian brainstem is the midbrain, which is three hundred million years old and regulates our temperature, controls our emotions and governs the fight or flight response that keeps us alive should the sabre-toothed cat from Chapter Two come calling. The third section is the cortex – a slip of a thing at just a hundred million years old – which wraps around the rest of our brain and is the place where civilisation, art, science and Lady Gaga lyrics reside.

In the midbrain, the amygdala, Ms Fight or Flight, works by shutting down or slowing other brain functions that could hinder our ability to escape the sabre-toothed tiger. There's no need to look at YouTube videos of cats online if you're about to be eaten by a wild one. It's still handy today, to jolt us if we're about to step out in front of a car, or help us out if we need to run away from an explosion like they do in films . . . Or for when we get into a fight, in a skip – like the binge-drinking friendship researchers in Chapter Five. But for the most part, our amygdala is getting us all het up unnecessarily.

Our bodies haven't quite grasped that we're not in sabre-tooth land any more – or that most 'surprises' in life don't actually require a fight or flight response. So now, every time we try something new or veer away from our usual routines, our amygdala goes on red alert and triggers fear – shutting down the thinking, creative, Lady Gaga-lyric reciting part of us.

'The same thing happens when we're trying to make changes,' says Bob: 'A large goal will stimulate fear and stress – so our amygdala will restrict access to the cortex, shutting down some of our creative and thinking powers. But a small goal or step will bypass the fear, so you can still use your cortex as normal and you're more likely to be successful in your change. By keeping it small and gentle, we keep the fight or flight response in the "off" position.'

The kaizen approach to life can, as a result, lead to creative breakthroughs – and we're more likely to get things done.

'Because what you have to do is minimal, it may seem insignificant – and that's the point. There's no resistance, or reason to procrastinate or avoid the task. It's about going slower sometimes and appreciating the small moments.'

Having spent the past three years embracing the Danish art of *hygge* in all its forms, this appeals to me.

Hygge is a Danish phenomenon that defies literal translation, but the best explanation I've heard is: '*A complete absence of anything annoying or emotionally overwhelming. Taking pleasure from the presence of gentle, soothing things,*' . . . which is starting to sound quite like kaizen. *Hygge* is a lot about celebrating the little things: being present and mindful. Getting my head around this meant learning to rethink my relationship with 'stuff' too. I learned that if I consumed less and really valued the things I had – the seemingly inconsequential moments and simple pleasures – I didn't need to work so much. I didn't need to earn more money to buy more *stuff* I didn't really need anyway. *Hygge* meant I had time to spend with friends and family. If it didn't sound terribly un-British, I might even go so far as saying that *hygge* changed my life. So I think I might quite like the kaizen approach.

I ask Bob where he recommends I start in changing my attitude to money and – if possible – reforming Lego Man's wayward ways at the same time.

'Okay,' he says, 'so if you're feeling ill-informed, you need to find a way to change this. So make it manageable. The kaizen strategy is that you start out by making a very small change, and then build and build on that small change until – eventually – you end up with significant progress. Small actions trick the brain into thinking: "Hey, this change is so tiny that it's no big deal – no need to get worked up! No risk of failure or unhappiness here!" By outfoxing our fear response, small actions allow the brain to build up new, permanent habits.' Because really, he explains, it's never about the money: 'The things driving us on the surface are superficial – the roots are always much deeper and so kaizen is about reprogramming the brain without overwhelming it, using an inner voice on ourselves that we might use on someone we love. It removes the battle between you and you.'

This is a war I've been waging for more than three decades, so calling a truce will be no mean feat. But Bob assures me I can do it – as long as I start small.

'Basically: aim low,' is how he puts it. 'Try saying, "Okay, I'm going to spend one minute a day becoming more financially aware." So you might download an article you see about planning for retirement. It might take a minute to find and download that file – you haven't even read it yet – but you've done your minute for the day so you stop there. Until tomorrow. When maybe you'll read it.'

I can do a minute, I think: *a minute doesn't sound scary at all!*

'Or if you're at the gym on the treadmill, you might make a conscious effort to watch a financial show for two minutes on TV instead of something else.'

'My gym isn't this fancy: we don't have TVs . . .'

'Okay, a podcast then.'

This is more like it. And for Lego Man?

'Well, many of us have a different attitude to finance than our partner and this can be a positive thing – it helps you not to go crazy or be too restrained.' In other words, Bob says, 'relax.' I can just see the Katharine Hamnett T-shirt now. Instead of fretting too much, Bob recommends role-play (not like that).

'If you're more conservative with money and your husband's more impulsive, and you had to, say, research into buying a new car, you could close your eyes for fifteen to thirty seconds and imagine doing something positive and constructive like reading online evaluations of various makes of car, for example.'

'Okay . . .'

'Now, do it. Picture yourself asking the salesman questions, listening to what they have to say, and then walking out of the showroom.'

'That's it?'

'That's it.'

I shut my eyes.

'Now, can you see yourself doing this?

'Yes . . .?'

'And how do you feel?'

'Fine –' my eyes ping back open – 'because it was just pretend.'

'Okay, so you feel:neutral:? You're not feeling afraid of getting into debt as you do this?'

'No.'

'So when you're free from the idea that you'll have to commit – that this is a binding financial decision – you feel better. See? The goal is for you both to make decisions that aren't based on fear or excitement. Ever. In anything. That's how children make decisions.'

'Oh.' *I knew I'd always been in touch with my inner child . . .*

'If you're more cautious, then it sounds as though you have a habit of making decisions out of fear while your partner makes them out of excitement, like a kid in a sweet shop.' This is exactly how we both operate. We are pathetically transparent. 'So you both need to meet in a more neutral place.'

But approaching finance in a childlike way isn't always a bad idea, according to Bob.

'Another useful kaizen technique is to imagine having a conversation with a child you care about who you're explaining something to,' he says, '– so it could be your five-year-old self or even your own child.'

'He's a toddler: his only words are "uh-oh", "no", "Mama" and "tractor". But he's very good at animal noises . . .'

'Even better! He can't answer back, so you can actually act this out rather than having to imagine it.'

I'm delighted to learn that Little Red's reluctance to speak will be an advantage for once. *We might even be able to save for his education, if he ever moves on from farm vehicles, roaring like a lion and making monkey sounds . . .*

'What you're going to do,' Bob goes on: 'is have a conversation with your son and explain to him how you're going to buy a car – or a house if that's what you need next – all in a loving, positive tone of voice. You're going to do this out loud and in a way where your intention is to love and support and educate him. Okay? You should notice that the way you advise him is very different to the way you and your husband handle it. Just try – you'll see!'

I promise I will and as soon as Lego Man gets home, we have a go at Bob's imaginary shopping exercise, tackling the usually fractious topic of buying somewhere to live.

'First, let's imagine ourselves going into an estate agent's,' I say, peeking slightly to check my husband's got his eyes shut and isn't secretly laughing at me. 'We're just looking around. Got it?'

'Got it,' Lego Man says, nodding admiringly (I'm still peeking) at what I can only assume is the impressive virtual selection of properties in the virtual estate agent's virtual office.

'Now, we're going to ask for a few details within our price range –' his mouth twitches at this and he raises an eyebrow, just a fraction. *I know that look: he even wants to blow our budget during a virtual shopping exercise!* I shut my eyes tight to ensure I fully commit to the exercise and stave off any further irritation. 'Now we're going to flick through the brochures, looking at different houses we might like to buy, considering them all objectively.'

'Uh-huh.'

'And then we're going to walk out.'

'That's it?'

'That's it,' I tell him: 'baby steps. You can open your eyes now, by the way.'

'Oh, okay, thanks. Well, that wasn't so bad.'

'No, it wasn't.'

I haven't got a knotted-stress-stomach at the thought of financially committing myself for the next twenty-five years and we haven't veered into blazing-row terrain. This is novel.

Next it's the toddler's turn to play a part in our second kaizen exercise. Only Little Red's a bit busy with his train set at the moment, so we scurry around after him, attempting to explain how soon we'll be shopping for a new house.

'Then we're going to look for somewhere nice to live that has a garden, for you and the dog—'

'No!' is his first response. But then we realise that this is because Lego Man has been standing on a vital piece of track.

'We're going to buy a house of our own that's not too far from where Papa has to work–'

'—or civilisation,' I chip in.

'And where you can have a new bedroom and Mama and Papa can sleep in a room that doesn't leak,' Lego Man goes on.

'And although finding a house might take some time and can cost a lot of money—' I crouch down to explain.

'and Mama and Papa might get quite stressed . . .'

This is an understatement.

'. . . and we'll have to have long meetings about things called "mortgages" where the bank lend you money – it will all be worth it!' I'm telling myself as much as Little Red. 'And we're all going to work together and make it into a lovely home. Would you like that?'

'*TRACTORRR!*' the child shouts, ramming what is clearly in fact a caboose into his father's leg.

'Jolly good.' I creak up to standing.

'That went well.'

'Actually, you know, I think it did.' Explaining the process of buying a house to Little Red has clarified what we're doing in simple terms: it's stressful and costly but ultimately we want a home – so we'll invest time and money to make it happen. Kaizen win.

Next, I want to improve my financial knowledge. Which, even starting from a base point of 'total ignorance', is also surprisingly attainable.

Reading the paper, I come to the end of the features section and prepare to flip the whole thing over, as I have done for years, to get to the reviews and perhaps the obituaries (I love a good obit). I'm just flicking through the remaining pages to make sure I'm not missing anything good when I spot a colour change and a strange section called 'Finance'.

What is this brave new turquoise world?

I spy some £ and $ signs and start to suspect that I may have stumbled on the personal-banking promise land. So, embarking on Bob's sixty-second kaizen experiment, I read from it.

Within thirty seconds I have learned that a sacked Barclays boss is in line for a £500,000 bonus on top of his pay-off.

This is outrageous! I'm incensed.

For the remaining thirty seconds I read about how the chancellor is implementing a tax on pensions that will make us all worse off and how there isn't anything we can do about it.

This isn't making me feel better: it's making me furious! I think. But once the minute is up, I stop. And breathe. And then I do the same thing the next day. And I learn a new word: 'indices' – the plural of index and not, as Lego Man suggests, dice used for insider dealings.

In the morning I scan the financial headlines again. And when I pass an animated Bloomberg billboard that afternoon, announcing some merger or other, I'm vaguely aware of what's going on.

'Oh yeah, that's because the stock price was falling,' I drop into conversation, just casually. The child, the dog and Lego Man all look at me in shock. 'I do *know* stuff!' I protest.

By day four I'm feeling genned up enough to call up a pension provider and ask: 'Please may I have one of those?'

And they say 'yes'! So I start one.

'I've got a PENSION!' I greet Lego Man when he comes home from work. 'Did you get my email? Telling you? About my PENSION?'

'Yes, I got your emails. All of them. Well done you. That's great news.'

'Thanks!' I reveal proudly that my pension has the princely sum of £200 in it so far.

'Two hundred quid? You can't retire on that.'

'Yes, thank you, Captain Obvious. But it's a start,' I tell him, and begin thinking about how to build on this financial nest egg.

Savings, I think. *I should see if I have any money hanging around my current account earning precisely nothing and put it in a tax-free ISA. And maybe* – I'm feeling daring now – *I could think about investments!* So I spend my sixty-second windows over the next few days keeping an eye out for '*how on earth to go about doing this*'. Until my search yields fruit.

I find out about managed funds and DIY jobbies (I only have a minute – I can't be expected to know all the jargon just yet) as well as what's doing well and what isn't. We have people over for dinner and I find myself regaling our lucky guests with fascinating facts about how the drinks giant Diageo has increased its dividend every year since 1999 and would therefore make an excellent investment. 'What's more, they make GIN! So we could actively contribute to their future success!' This warrants a toast all round.

Bob has been a boon. I'm already feeling okay about trying out his suggestions – purely because they are so small and manageable. But I'm not sure whether his advice is helping Lego Man curb his spending.

My husband's latest tactic, now that the holiday is over, is to upgrade our homewares on the sly. On Saturday I come back from a run with the dog (I know! Get me! Thanks, Chapter Three's Jim . . .) to a cardboard-box den, constructed from two weeks' worth of Lego Man's accumulated online purchases. As well as the usual – records, books, *Inspector Morse* DVDS[26] and various bits of mountain biking para-phernalia – there are several large brown boxes that he insists are 'nothing to worry about' and that I should 'go and treat myself to a relaxing bath. With Little Red . . .'. When I emerge, dripping and cold (a bath with a toddler is a far cry from 'relaxing'), Lego Man can be heard trundling around in the loft.

---

26 Despite the fact that we've already watched every episode of Endeavour's crime-fighting series.

'Everything okay up there?'

'Fine!' he yells from the roof cavity.

'*Fine?*' Uh-oh.

I trudge downstairs in search of coffee but discover that our coffee machine is missing. In its place stands a space age chrome contraption with a large protruding lever like a one-armed bandit.

'Er, what's this in the kitchen?' I holler up the stairs.

'Oh, new coffee machine . . .' I hear the screech of the loft ladder being put away and wonder what else he's got stashed up there. 'Didn't I say?'

'No, you didn't "say" – and why do we need it? The old one worked perfectly well!' More importantly, I'd just learned *how* to work it.

'This makes for a nuttier blend, according to the readers of *Which?* magazine . . .' He leans over the bannister to address me and the blood rushes to his head.

Baffled by the new machine, I open the kitchen cupboard to take down a glass for water. But instead of the assorted tumblers we've accumulated over the years, I'm faced with a veritable wine bar display of squeaky new glassware.

Arghhh!

Peering into an empty fridge (rich in glasses: poor in food), I decide it's pasta for lunch again and so reach into the depths of the under-hob cubbyhole to fish out a pan. As I retract my arm, handle in hand, I meet with more resistance than expected. I assume the pans have been weighed down with other items of cookware during one of our more slovenly 'tidying' sessions, so use both hands to lift it out and look. To my surprise, it is empty. I wonder fleetingly whether I'm perhaps suffering from a horrible wasting disease whereby my upper-body strength has been suddenly depleted. So I pick up another and try again, only to find the same thing. Then I look more closely. The pans are far shinier than my ex-Woolworth's creations of eighteen years' service have any right to be. And that's when I see it. The logo.

I'll kill Pans Solo for telling him about these . . .

Bracing myself, I heave the rest of the pans on to the kitchen floor for inspection, much to the delight of Little Red, who starts bashing them like a one-man steel band, then stomp back to the bottom of the stairs.

'Where are my PANS?' I bellow. Very much like a fish-wife.

'Oh, yeah . . .' he says, 'I was going to mention—'

'But you didn't.'

'No. Well, it was your friend who said how great Le Creuset pans were . . .'

You're not the one who flipping uses them! I think. And neither does she!

'I can scarcely lift them. Empty. How am I supposed to cook anything in there? Are we going to eat salad, for ever?'

Little Red adds to the drama with some frenzied bashing and the dog starts barking. Lego Man comes downstairs, looking shifty, and tries to assure me that these are 'design icons' that will 'last and last'. He also adds his old failsafe: 'At least I'm not a gambler. Or a cheater. Or a golfer . . .'

I nod, aware that these fates would be worse.

'You can build up your strength, in the gym – you'll get used to them!'

'But it shouldn't have to be like this! I shouldn't have to do weight training to boil pasta.'

'No,' he says, 'sorry, they were just so . . . shiny . . .' He confesses that he's already taken all of our old pans and glassware – as well as our faithful coffee machine – to the charity shop. 'Oh but I kept one pan, I thought Little Red might like it, as a toy,' he says, going over to the mini plywood kitchen he recently bought for our son and retrieving a tiny, one-egg receptacle that I first took with me to university in 1998.

I look at him.

'*Are you serious?*'

'Or . . . I could just make lunch instead?' he offers, knowing when he's lost.

'I think that would be a good idea, yes.' I hunt for crisps in the snack drawer to tide me over. 'And tomorrow's,' I add through a mouthful of ready salted. 'I've got to "build my strength up"'. I hold up the packet to indicate that I mainly intend to do this via Kettle Chips and leave him to it.

Three more things happen to push me over the edge.

First, I discover that the memory stick I keep on my keyring for work has been upgraded ('It's titanium!' he tells me. 'I don't care!' I tell him). On Monday, our street has to be shut down for a lorry to deliver a pallet of shelves that Lego Man has ordered – shelves that we don't need and that I didn't know about, for a house we only rent. The pallet is so big that it blocks our front door. What's more, the shelves prove so heavy I can't shift them. Then it starts to rain. I cover the cardboard boxes with bin bags pinned down, to stop them blowing away, with a crate of empty bottles ripe for recycling – so that it looks as though several alcoholics have set up camp outside our house.

'*THIS HAS TO STOP,*' I text Lego Man at work with a picture of the tramp-boudoir currently blocking our front door.

'☹' is all he replies.

When he gets home, he's apologetic and quickly clears our emergency exit. But at bedtime I see that our electric toothbrush, a perfectly adequate whirring Braun affair, has been upgraded to a sonic number. Our new, sleek, black brush operates at a frequency only detected by the dog and our toddler. Both of whom object to it so much that they howl, in unison, as soon as it's switched on and don't stop until it's turned off again.

The din is so bad that I resort to using a manual toothbrush (oh the humanity!). But Lego Man persists and finds that the protests are lessened if he brushes at the far end of the bathroom with his entire head covered by a towel, as though he's eating an ortolan songbird – a sight too gruesome to be witnessed.

I fume my way to the bedroom and have a final scroll through my social media feeds before bed. There's not much to report on Twitter, but one slightly woo friend who believes in fairies (true fact) has shared an article on Facebook about how some real-life science types are now endorsing tapping. This is the controversial alternative therapy inspired by Chinese acupressure whereby you tap your fingers on various meridian points on the body to 'cure' everything from cancer to chronic depression and addictions – including the urge to splurge. I click on the link and learn that researchers from Staffordshire University in the UK have commended the effectiveness of tapping, otherwise known as 'Emotional Freedom Technique' (EFT).

'Emotional Freedom'? I'm British, I think: *is that even possible?*

Professor Tony Stewart of Staffordshire University thinks so. He led an evaluation of EFT at Sandwell Primary Care Trust in the UK and has stated: 'EFT is a new and emerging therapy that has been used to treat a wide variety of conditions.' Another study found that an hour-long tapping session reduced cortisol levels by up to 50 per cent. Though to be fair it's not clear whether the experience of having a nice calm sit-down somewhere for an hour might have had the same effect and, understandably, not everyone's convinced.

The British Association for Counselling and Psychotherapy insists that 'considerably more research into this intervention would be required before it would be possible to draw any robust conclusions,' while another study found that tapping was no more effective than a placebo.

But if our mind can control how we feel, I wonder, *then is trying something that's free, easy and accessible really such a bad idea?*

When Lego Man emerges from his sonic-protector towel, I tell him we'll be trialling tapping next to gain mastery over 'our' relationship with money. By which I mean 'his'.

'Sure, I can do that,' he says, and taps the side of his head.

'What are you doing?'

'I'm tapping.'

'I think there are official places you're supposed to do it.'

'Oh. I thought it was just like a gentle reminder.' He raps his temples again: 'Like a sort of, "Oi! Don't buy that! Stop spending!"'

'I'm pretty sure there's more to it.'

He shrugs and gets into bed. 'We'll see.'

The following afternoon, I dial up Lori Leyden, a psycho-therapist turned tapping evangelist who is also an expert in psychoneuroimmunology. No, me neither, but turns out it's the study of the mind-body-spirit connection. Since few tapping practitioners seem to possess mainstream qualifica-tions (in anything), I'm interested in speaking to someone who comes from a solid science background to find out how the woo-theory won her round.

'So, er, Lori,' I start, envying the sun streaming in as she speaks to me from her home in Santa Barbara, California, over Skype: 'Why tapping?' I stumble to find a polite way to ask how, as a psychologist, she's happy to champion something that the rest of the world sees as decidedly wacky.

'Because *it works*,' she says, simply, 'quickly and effi-ciently. That's why it's so great. For me, I can reach and help more people with tapping than I ever can with psycho-therapy.' Since 2007 Lori has worked with genocide survivors in Rwanda as well as those affected by the Sandy Hook school shootings in Newton, USA, offering counsel-ling and tapping for PTSD. 'Despite all my knowledge about psychotherapy,' she tells me, 'it was through EFT that I was able to take practical steps to help people and make a difference.'

So why aren't more of us into it?

'Well, we've got four thousand years of testimonies to the effectiveness of Chinese acupressure and only twenty-five years of research into tapping – so it's relatively new. Plus people get put off tapping because it looks funny. People are wary of appearing "silly". And it does look weird,' she admits, 'tapping your face in lots of places. But it's effective – for trauma as well as general self-care.'

'Can it stop my husband shopping?'

She smiles, displaying yet more excellent American dentistry.

'Well, it's never about the money, first off,' says Lori, echoing Bob, 'just as it's never about the food, if that's our crutch, or drink if it's that. It's about what we're trying to soothe with money, food or drink. You're viewing money as something to soothe yourself with.'

'You mean, my husband?'

She shrugs, barely perceptibly, as if to imply, '*if you say so*' before adding: 'We *all* have our issues.'

Ouch. Maybe it's me, too, I think, *although I'm not the one who installed a home gym of shiny new pan 'weights' in our kitchen cupboard* . . .

I explain my own anti-spending impulses and describe what I'm up against with Lego Man's tendencies.

'Titanium!' I tell her. 'I mean, really!'

Lori nods in the understanding way that those working in psychotherapy have down to a fine art and says finally: 'It sounds as though what he may be suffering from is *ADOSOD*.'

ADOSOD? Could it be that Lego Man has an actual syndrome?

'It stands for: Attention Deficit . . . Oooh Shiny Object! Disorder.'

'Oh,' I tell her: 'I love it!'

'You're welcome. So with people who like to spend, it's not about the stuff – it's what the money represents. If you grew up poor or financially unstable, then money is likely to mean freedom from something. If you really think about your issue with money, the likelihood is you'll get to a pretty deep place – an "Aha! It was all about my mother or my father!" moment,' says Lori.

Despite a typically recession-tarnished 1970s upbringing, Lego Man never wanted for anything growing up. But his parents were very into carob and cagoules (see 'puffin-watching holidays'). Stories from Lego Man's childhood invariably involve home-made granola, hemp, goats or lighting fires to keep warm. He had no television growing up and the first time he saw a leather-jacket-clad David Hasselhoff in *Knight Rider* at a friend's house, it blew his mind. Since then, he's felt horribly torn between wanting desperately to acquire all the 'shiny things', as Lori refers to them, and harbouring an appreciation for his rugged, rural upbringing. Hence the 'hiding new purchases in the loft' game, upgrading us by stealth and an obsession with camping. So shiny things are Lego Man's ongoing rebellion against his parents – who are now, ironically, also into shopping in a big way since cruising into retirement. *So who are you sticking it to now Lego Man, eh?* I think, and then remember: *Oh, it's me. The big old party pooper who doesn't want a titanium memory stick or a sonic toothbrush that makes babies cry . . .*

So what can we do about this?

'In EFT, we get people to tell the truth about how they are feeling about a problem,' says Lori, 'so you're not burying your head in the sand and saying "Oh, everything's great" if it's not. So in your husband's case he might say, "Even though I have this problem with spending . . ." then we pair this with a statement we *want* to believe, like: "I deeply love and accept myself". This is the set-up statement where you tap out a karate chop –' she demonstrates, tapping the fingers of her right hand into the fleshy part of the outside of her left hand as she repeats the statement a few more times. I try this and it feels strangely soothing. *Though the martial arts reference might be overselling it a bit . . .*

'Then you tap eight key points from the top of your head down your torso – around five times on each spot.' She starts with the centre of her parting, where she taps with two fingers, five times, before moving down to the inner corner of her eyebrow. Next is the outer corner of her right eye, followed by the bony area under the right eye, an inch below the pupil. The philtrum comes fifth, and she taps lightly on the area just under the nose. Then the groove between the chin and the bottom of the lower lip. Moving downwards, Lori taps the indentation between her collarbones, before finally twisting slightly to show me the last pressure point of the basic tapping sequence: the side of the body, a few inches below the armpit.

'The tapping sequence is something you can do anywhere, at any time, so when you feel your psychology start to shift, or you feel like you want to soothe yourself by spending – in your husband's case – you just start tapping,' she says.

I'm pretty sure Lori has pinned down Lego Man's issues with money, but then she swings the spotlight on me.

'It might also be helpful to explore your own core issues and limiting beliefs,' she says: '– so if you're reluctant to spend or talk about finances, maybe you think "I don't deserve money and shiny things".'

This winds me as I realise she's right: I don't feel, deep down, as though I am worthy. Lego Man earns more than me. I don't like this, but it's true. And although we 'share' everything, I wonder whether a part of me always feels indebted somehow. Even though our bank account is (usually) in the black, there's a sense that I shouldn't spend any of it. Which is illogical, impractical and a little 1950s suburban housewife for my liking.

'Hypothetically speaking,' I ask, 'if I wanted to "fix" my approach to money –' I try to sound breezy – 'would the basic process be the same?'

'That's right – it's the beauty of tapping, you can adapt it to whatever you need.' Lori tells me that a beginner, starting out, should notice some positive changes after doing it for just a couple of minutes a few times a day. So I decide to have a bash, despite my doubts.

'Even though I don't feel I deserve money and shiny things, I deeply love and accept myself,' I repeat, karate chopping and then tapping my eight pressure points just before I visit a craft fair for work (really). One-on-one financial interactions normally leave me stiff with stress – from paying the babysitter to buying anything with cash. But I find I can stand there, looking at the wooden wares of women in crumpled linen and chunky jewellery, without the familiar sensation of spine-furling awkwardness.

'Even though I don't feel I deserve money and shiny things, I deeply love and accept myself,' I think to myself when someone compliments me on my top. 'Thank you,' I manage to say, instead of firing back a customarily self-deprecating, 'What, this old thing? £5.99! Topshop, 2004!'

Thinking about money, properly, for the first time, has been a revelation. I've stopped feeling as though discussing cold hard cash is somehow gauche or – horrific phrase alert – 'unladylike'. Because that's nonsense: money is important.

And we should talk about it – rather than letting it fester and assume a significance it doesn't deserve or letting it rule us.

I feel calmer and more in control. And I have A PENSION!

Lego Man's financial outlook is more of a challenge. I teach him the basics of tapping but can't shake the feeling that he's not taking it seriously as he paws at his head and body indiscriminately.

'You're not King Louie in *The Jungle Book*!'

'I'm tapping!' he tells me, embarking on an enthusiastic rendition of 'I Wanna Be Like You', much to Little Red's amusement.

I wonder whether I'm going to have to get Lori to give him a good talking-to. 'What you're doing is buggering about! Come on, at least give it a go.'

Lego Man tries out his 'studious face': 'Okay, run me through it again? One more time.'

'Karate chop your hand and repeat after me, "Even though I have this problem with spending money, I deeply love and accept myself".'

'But isn't that basically saying "It's okay to spend money"?'

'I think the point is that you spend money to soothe your-self, so saying this regularly and tapping might be a healthier alternative. Shopping shouldn't be a substitute for something else. You're not Imelda Marcos.'

I remind him of the tapping points and hand over a printout detailing what he should do and when.

'You can even do it on the loo – it only takes a minute . . .' *'and Lord knows you have enough of these going spare each bathroom visit . . .'* I manage not to add.

Lego Man says he'll 'have a go'. And for a whole week, no men in boiler suits attempt to hand over rain-sodden parcels and I'm not asked to sign for any mysterious packages.

Could it be, I wonder, *that he's 'cured'?*

Then the weekend rolls around and he offers to do 'the big shop'. *We need food,* I reason, *so this will be okay. This is sanctioned shopping. What can go wrong between here and the supermarket?*

Answer: A Lot.

Four hours, ten plastic sacks and three smart cardboard bags later, and my Liberace husband is home again, beaming.

'Shall I just get in the bath now while you hide it all?'

'I think that would be wise, yes,' he tells me, adding: 'I'll bring you up a cup of tea . . . in one of our new NEW cups!' He pulls out a set of six mugs that we don't need and that I don't like. I bite my tongue and climb the stairs.

Maybe this is the thing about change, I ponder as I reach the landing: *you can only do it for yourself.*

I make my way to the bathroom and turn the bath taps on full pelt.

Maybe, I think, *it's like Dr Benjamin – behavioural change expert and biscuit fan – told me at the start: external pressures don't work. It's only internal motivation that can bring about change.*

I did promise to take Lego Man for richer or for poorer: In ADOSOD sickness and in health. *Perhaps he's putting me to the test.*

The tea arrives, accompanied by a pastry from my favourite bakery. 'It's an apology bun,' he tells me. No wonder I couldn't give up sugar long term: my family express emotion almost exclusively via cake.

'There's just so much . . . stuff.' I try to articulate my feelings about his spending and seemingly insatiable urge to fill our house, then upgrade its contents: 'You do know we're meant to be moving soon, right?' Whether this is to the UK or not, we both agree that we don't want to be in Leaky Windows House for much longer, but I wonder whether Lego Man is in some sort of denial. Resisting the change and uncertainty that lies before us by accumulating more 'shiny objects' that he can *feel*, and *touch*, and that can *belong* to him, here.

'I know I may shop slightly more than other people – ' I nearly spit out my tea at the 'slightly' part – 'But it makes me . . . happy.'

'But don't you see? That's *weird*.' I suspect that this isn't exactly how psychologists would recommend phrasing this sort of marital 'feedback' but I'm all out of empathy on this one. 'Don't *we* make you happy? Little Red and me?'

'Of course you do, but it's different.'

'How?'

'I'm not sure. But I don't think you *telling* me not to buy things is going to help.'

Then what will? Sectioning? I want to yell but manage not to. Mostly because I now have a mouth full of flaky pastry and don't want to waste any.

He leaves me to my bubbles soon after this and I start thinking about our belongings and what they mean. I can't get over the idea that we have too many of them, so next, I resolve to declutter and address the full horrifying scale of all that we own. Something that I suspect is going to come as quite a shock to Lego Man . . .

***

Things I've learned about changing our approach to money:

1. Buying 'stuff' is seldom about the stuff.

2. Small steps are less nerve-wracking than big ones – and more effective too.

3. Money is power, so being in the dark about it isn't doing anyone any favours.

4. A minute a day can change our approach to finances (and even bag us a PENSION!).

5. Tapping may look silly but it's free and easy – so if it helps, it's worth a try.

6. We can't change other people or their spending habits. More's the pity . . .

7. Money can't buy us love but it can buy enough glasses to open our own bar, close roads and create a home gym in a kitchen cupboard.

***

CHAPTER EIGHT

HOME

Gonnna Build A Lego House

In which I brave The Loft; attempt The KonMarie Method; execute Kurt Lewin's Operation Ice Tray; embrace The Danish Art of Decluttering; and explore why *hygge* is an essential life skill

A spider abseils down a single strand of silk as I set foot on the first rung of the ladder. Cool air makes my skin tingle and sounds of traffic from the street can be heard more clearly now, thanks to flimsy insulation.

This is the first time Lego Man and I have jointly lived anywhere with a loft. Our damp Edwardian flat in London had no such luxuries and the glass house we rented in the middle of actual nowhere for our first two years of living Danishly was more 'art installation' than useful living space. When we moved to a 'proper house', I foolishly delegated loft management to my husband and since then I haven't set foot up there (see 'ostrich'). But now the time has come to tackle my roof cavity demons and I'm genuinely scared about what I might find. I've read *Jane Eyre*. And this isn't my first attic rodeo. I once interviewed a woman who found out her husband had been living a double life after a trip to the loft revealed a separate phone, pictures of his 'other family' and an extensive collection of vintage pornography.

Fortunately, the first thing I see at the top of the ladder isn't porn, but Little Red's paddling pool – deflated and stored after last year's two-day summer. Then there's the Christmas box, stuffed with carefully wrapped baubles. And then shelves. Rows upon rows of them – as though I'm in a very ordered stockroom.

I'll give him this: Lego Man keeps a neat loft.

As well as dozens of clear plastic boxes containing various wires and tools, there's a designer bird feeder I've never seen before; a 'spare' barbecue (*who needs a spare barbecue?*); a shiny red bike frame; and enough Lego to entertain our son until his dotage. But other than that? It's mostly *our* stuff – photo albums from the time when people had photo albums; books; and baby things we have no need of any more. There's the bouncer I used to put Little Red in when he was a few months old so that I could treat myself to the occasional shower. I would sit him in it and bounce him with a wet foot while I scrubbed off sick/milk/puréed carrot and sang Blondie songs. Mostly because I was too tired to learn/remember any lullabies – though also, because: Blondie. There are toys, a bassinet, and boxes of baby clothes that we can't quite bring ourselves to pass on, just in case, after the miracle of Little Red and a further two years of failed fertility treatment, the unlikely happens and I get pregnant again.

It hasn't.

And probably isn't going to.

But getting rid of our baby kit means admitting this.

'Maybe,' I suggested some months back, 'it's like going to the loo in a restaurant or lighting a cigarette in the olden days – it always makes the food arrive!'

'So what, if we give away all our baby gear, you'll get pregnant via Sod's Law?'

'Yes!'

But Lego Man wasn't sold. So here it remains, a monument to what was, and to what we are immensely grateful for, but would quite like again. Despite the madness of it all. Because there's nothing quite like the scent of a newborn's head, or the wobbly wide-eyed wonder of an infant, or the hilarity of a toddler. And because we're greedy like that.

Gulping down a lump in my throat, I move on to the dusty boxes of paraphernalia from our former lives. There are reference guides; books and more pens than a woman could ever want. I drag out a corkboard displaying an invitation to the Chanel show at Paris Fashion Week, a London 2012 Olympic cycling ticket and a picture of Benedict Cumberbatch looking like an otter. Then there are the notebooks. As a journalist, I'm legally advised to keep my notes for at least a year, but I'm also partial to a journal and a committed tearer-outer of articles and images I like the look of in maga-zines and newspapers. Before life got busy, I would keep these scraps and stick them into hard-backed Black 'n' Red books that doubled up as diaries. So when I find one from the year I met Lego Man, I open it.

Turning over pages thick with Pritt Stick and newsprint – clippings now crinkled like Braille – the pictures are both strange and familiar. Perching on the edge of a plastic box, I look at a blueprint of the life I thought I wanted. This mainly seemed to involve living somewhere picturesque and occasionally rollicking around in a camper van.

Dust particles dance in the sunlight, streaming in from the tiny window, and time seems to slow down. It's soothing, somehow, up here in the eaves of the house – far from my computer or phone or the needy dog. As though no one can bother me.

I can see why Secret-Family-Love-Rat liked it up here . . .

Looking at what 'home' used to mean for me, I realise I've changed. We all do. Some changes have been small and imperceptible – kaizen style. I can't recall the day, for instance, when I stopped caring about camper vans. Others have been monumental: the day I became a parent will forever be etched on my mind and body. The physical 'things' I've kept from each stage of my life aren't necessarily objects of beauty in themselves – they're nostalgia cues.

Just as Lori said: it's never about the 'stuff'. It's about what it means to us. *And possibly*, I think, *just possibly, I'm just as bad as Lego Man when it comes to hanging on to 'stuff' for sentimental value.* I hear Lori's voice telling me: 'We all have our issues.'

We're hoping to make a change by buying a house of our own some time soon – a blank canvas that we'll turn into a home . . . somewhere. So wouldn't around now be a good time to work out what we actually want to take with us? Because – note to self – the answer definitely isn't 'everything'. The sheer volume of our belongings feels like an obstacle, stopping me from thinking clearly. I waste time asking myself 'What are we going to do with that weird ceramic arm that Lego Man bought from a charity shop?' or 'Where shall we put the old school desk he found at a reclamation yard?' when I should be thinking about the bigger questions, like, 'What do we actually want in our lives?'

'We have probably hit peak stuff,' said none other than IKEA's head of sustainability, Steve Howard, in a debate for the *Guardian* newspaper in January 2016. And when the flatpack-furniture-and-impulse-buy-tealight people say we've got a problem, things must be serious. Looking around me, I realise old Steve was right. The 'paperless' workplace we were all promised is still a long way off and despite everything getting smaller and faster, we've accumulated more of it. I still have dozens of concertina files, but I also have a titanic digital archive. Lego Man not only has all of his music in its original CD form, he also has a fit-to-burst iTunes library and *three* record players.

Simon Rego, director of psychology training at Montefiore Medical Center in the Bronx, New York, is an expert on 'stuff'. So when I eventually tear myself away from the crinkled pages of my past life and make it down the rickety loft ladder relatively unscathed, I call him.

'Why have I got so much stuff? Why have we ALL got so much stuff? How can we declutter? Help!'

Simon is calm. You'd like Simon. Simon says (calmly), 'Some amount of stuff is normal –' *exhales deeply* – 'and collecting things is an impulse that cuts across all ages – you see it in three-year-olds and you see it in people in their nineties. There are a variety of theories about why we end up doing it. I follow the cognitive theory that it's often down to themes or beliefs that people hold – so they'll tell themselves "I don't want to waste this" or "this picture I drew when I was seven has sentimental value". It's natural to want to hang on to objects that trigger memories, but some people confuse letting go of the object with letting go of the person or memory,' he tells me.

Photo-hoarding is another common issue: 'Millennials often become digital hoarders, so if you've never thrown anything away in Hotmail or on iPhoto, then you may have a problem.'

'Wait, what?' I have never thrown anything away on iPhoto.

'Okay – but can you still access the pictures you want in the way they were intended? Can you actually enjoy them?'

'Er, no.'

'Right . . .' Simon sounds less calm now. 'Well, many people have many more pictures now than they used to, but they don't actually "have" any of them.'

He has just described my photo history perfectly. For the first seven years of life, I spent summer holidays with a much-loved aunt and uncle while my mother worked/ recovered from nailing it at Sports Day. My aunt and uncle didn't have children yet, but were avid documentarians of my own development. There are dozens of pictures, lovingly pasted into faded sugar-paper albums covered with sticky-backed plastic, charting my summers aged two to seven. Then their own kids came along. The first is well documented, the second less so and the third is practically a phantom – with parents too busy running around after the other two to bother locating the camera. As a result, my youngest cousin is largely absent from the family albums and my own pictorial record halts abruptly, aged seven, picking up again around the age of eighteen when I took lots of 'hysterical' pictures involving traffic cones and curries at university. Everything stops again in 2008 when I bought my first digital camera – and I haven't queued in Snappy Snaps since.

Now I keep all my pictures online in the hope that one day I might have a spare six months to create PhotoBooks of the past decade. Only this seems increasingly unlikely with each passing year – and the virtual backlog is wasting precious brain space, according to Simon.

'Clutter – including digital clutter – can feel like a weight on your mind and cause stress, so it's worth addressing before it goes too far,' he tells me.

And, um, how can you tell if it's already gone too far? I look at my husband's collection of vinyl, next to his collection of magazines, right by his collection of Lego replicas of historic landmarks (honestly, I'm almost ready to open my own model village).

'So, the tendency towards acquiring excessive things is pretty common, and most of the reasons used for hanging on to "stuff" will have a grain of truth in them – there is a utility in most things, you just may not need a jumper five sizes too small. But someone else might be able to make use of it. It's about learning to let go. Only a small percentage of people – around two or three per cent – cross over into the psychological disorder of "hoarding". This has been diagnosed in North America since the 1980s, but there's even a mention of hoarding in Dante's *Inferno* – so it's been going on a long time. If you have so many possessions that there are rooms in your home you're no longer able to use because they have so much *stuff* in them, that's classed as hoarding. If there's an increased risk of falls or fires or other hazards because of the amount of *stuff* you have – then you have a problem.'

There have been no falls or fires – and our rooms are, so far, serviceable. But my husband comes from a family of stuff-fans. We lost the dog under a pile of crochet during the in-laws' last visit and didn't realise where he was until a craft project starting loping around the kitchen like a drugged Loch Ness Monster. My husband's parents have rooms in their house that I've never seen and that Lego Man only has hazy recollections of visiting sometime in the 1990s. While I've – naturally – suspected some sort of dark Daphne du Maurier *Rebecca* scenario, or *The Secret Garden* style family mystery, I'm now wondering whether they might officially be hoarders.

And is there a, er, *genetic* link?

Simon gives me the answer I don't want to hear: 'Yes! Adoption studies have looked at identical twins raised in different families who share a genetic predisposition to hoarding. So people can be born with it. But there are also learned behaviours or "nurture-hoarders". Most people beneath the surface have some "stuff" going on.'

Simon isn't immune to the hoarding impulse himself. In a 2014 *Wall Street Journal* interview, he admitted 'saving' 600 disposable Allen keys that had come with IKEA furniture purchases over the years, 'just in case'.

Six hundred? That's a big 'just in case'. I ask how that's going for him and he assures me he's slimmed down his collection over the past couple of years.

'I still keep quite a few, as I have old pieces of furniture from college that I think I might need to take apart or fix one day and I don't know which one goes with which –' *Excuses, excuses, Simon* . . . '–but now I have around twenty of them.'

'Wow, okay. I'm glad you're down from 600 . . .'

'Thanks.'

So what can we do about the urge to accumulate?

'Well, some people get lucky and find a way to de-bulk over time. Others don't – and hoarding tends to worsen with age.'

'Oh.'

'The best treatment we have still isn't so great – in the UK, CBT is popular. Because cognitive behavioural therapy is all about awareness before change, it can help make us aware of the extent of the problem and then help us cope with it. But in modern life, there is a degree to which anxiety has to be tolerated. When we're irrational about this, that's when psychological disorders develop, so you have to learn to tolerate the anxiety of letting go – to become more resilient to those unpleasant feelings.' I remember my pilot's voice telling me: *'It's okay not to be okay'*.

Streamlining our 'stuff' before it becomes a problem is also helpful, Simon advises. If someone likes to accrue, there are two necessary steps that must be taken after the initial 'acquisition phase,' to avert hoarding: 'You have to have exposure to the extent of the problem,' says Simon, first off. This is the part where you lay out all your things and realise the true horror of everything you own. 'Then, you have to have a discarding phase. So creating a sorting zone – a place to work through things and see the scope of everything in front of you – can be a good starting point for taking action.'

This sounds a lot like one of the 'change theories' in one of Lego Man's books.

'Kurt Lewin!' I start, excitedly: 'Kurt Lewin's three-stage change model is like CBT for hoarding!'

'Kurt who?'

'Lewin?'

'?'

Simon obviously has better things to do with his time than monkey around with Lego Man's management tomes, but I feel bad for old Lewin (*'Oh hi, Kurt? It's history calling: we've forgotten you!'*).

Kurt Lewin was a Jewish German psychologist, physicist and social scientist who developed the 'unfreeze-change-freeze' theory for coping with upheavals – something he knew a lot about. Lewin served at the front during World War One but in 1933 recognised the danger for Jews in Germany and so moved to America to 'start over'. There, he developed his three-stage model, which bypassed inertia and opposition by shocking the mind into change. Once the status quo has been dismantled via 'unfreezing', as he called it, the second stage of 'change' – i.e. total confusion, chaos and transition – can occur. In the third stage, 'freezing', a new mindset or way of doing things is formed. Lewin's 'unfreeze-change-freeze' theory has been criticised for being a tad brutal in an HR environment at work, but for addressing stuffocation, it could be just the short, sharp shock we need.

I tell Simon that I'm planning to approach my home as though it's a giant ice tray and see what happens.

At the same time as I'm tackling a surfeit of stuff in the name of 'research', Table Flipper friend (you know, from Chapter One – who bested her Idiot Boss, then had the thing with Stuart from Sales on the stairs – keep up) is moving house. She currently rents a lovely room in London's Dollis Hill but the landlord is selling up, so she's having to move to a slightly smaller-but-still-lovely room in a shared house in Kilburn. Her monthly rent will be crippling but, she assures me, 'It'll be worth it because I'll be two stops closer to West Hampstead. Where there's a *Waitrose*.'

The 'Waitrose Effect' means that properties near the upmarket grocer's store locations are not only more desirable, they also sell for 12 per cent more than they would elsewhere, and so the corresponding rent is also hiked up. To make way for her new Duchy of Cornwall biscuit stash and raise funds to pay for them, Table Flipper is planning a purge and hopes to sell most of her worldly goods on eBay.

'I was going to KonMarie it,' says Table Flipper, referring to professional Japanese 'declutterer' Marie Kondo's manifesto, *The Life-Changing Magic of Tidying Up: The Japanese Art of Decluttering and Organizing*, 'but then she told me to thank my socks for their service, so, you know: *no*.'

Kondo recommends that everything we own has a designated place (kitchen surfaces don't count, sadly) to create tranquil homes free from clutter, and 2015 will be remembered as the year the world got Kondo-d. But some of her more avant-garde ideas include anthropomorphising underwear and the notion that cleaning the toilet brings us luck – and it was here that Table Flipper was forced to draw the line.

'History may judge me harshly for this, but I'm going to go ahead and say it: there is always something better to do in life than fold socks. And while I will clean my loo, I'm not about to make a wish while I'm doing it. It's not a well. So I need a plan that's less "woo".'

As she updates me on her adventures in tidy-land, I'm suddenly struck by an idea: perhaps there's a Danish Art of Decluttering, too?

I look around at Lego Man's Danish designer purchases interspersed with the life-silt of two Brits, a toddler and a dog and realise that there are several similarities between the Japanese and the Danish approach to homes. Both cultures boast design aesthetics infatuated with minimal simplicity, functionality and clean, pure lines. Neither do clutter. So could the Scandi approach to interiors be just what Table Flipper needs?

I get in touch with Danish interior designer Pernille Møller Folcarelli to test my theory and get the decor skinny.

'Danes tend to want fewer items of better quality in their homes,' says Pernille: 'We don't like too much "stuff" and we invest in a few items of high-quality design to make home a happy place where we can enjoy spending time.' Danes have been proven to be less materialistic than other cultures, according to studies from the Copenhagen-based Happiness Research Institute, and Pernille explains how her countrymen and women all grow up with a distinct aesthetic idea: 'We see the beauty in simple, functional design and have a big love for crafted everyday pieces – so you'll often see a hand-made ceramic cup, or a hand-woven cloth.' Just as Kondo asks converts to evaluate each of their belongings according to whether they 'spark joy', Danes put their possessions through 'the pleasure test', says Pernille.

'Everything should either have a specific function, or be beautiful, or give you a feeling of pleasure – each item needs to pass this test.' William Morris would have loved living Danishly. And my adopted countryfolk aren't sentimental about holding on to things they don't like or need, either.

Just as Kondo advises that the purpose of a present is to be received, every gift given in Denmark will have a returns sticker for the recipient to exchange it for something else. Hassle-free. Because in Denmark, it really is the thought that counts. As someone who regularly feels wretched with anxiety and horribly ungrateful when given any kind of off-grid gift, I'm drawn to this[27]. As well as returning unwanted presents,

---

27 Dear family and friends: I like books, cake, stationery and spa vouchers. Other than that, save your money. Many thanks.

Danes don't feel obliged to keep 'that lovely plate that little Tommy painted aged three' or family 'heirlooms' that no longer fit with their aesthetic. As Pernille says: 'Danes aren't afraid to change and move things around. Things that were useful years ago might not be any more – so we get rid of them! We look at our current lifestyle and adjust interiors accordingly.' The Danish approach is about curating homes and embracing minimalism. 'Which also makes it easier to clean . . .' adds Pernille. I tell her this is an excellent point.

Danes don't do cleaners, on the whole, because in a socially democratic society, you're expected to service your own loo (though not in the hope that an exemplary scrub will bring you luck). And with a short working week of just thirty-three hours on average, most Danes do. But Lego Man and I both work more than thirty-three hours a week. And we can't seem to keep a *Good Housekeeping*-ready home. I glance at the dog asleep in a patch of sunlight, snoring. Every exhalation sends a purple ball of fluff rolling across the floor, before the corresponding inhalation entices it back. Little Red used to point these out – often accompanied by a loud and judgy: 'Uh-oh!' So I told him they were 'dust bunnies' and that they could be his pets. He's been enchanted by them ever since, but we officially need to vacuum more. So having less 'stuff' will help, I hope.

Feeling clearer now on what we're setting out to achieve, I thank Pernille and summon up Table Flipper via FaceTime. I challenge her to execute Operation Ice Tray using the principles of The Danish Art of Decluttering and she accepts. So we set to work.

According to Lewin's first stage, 'unfreeze', the status quo needs to be dismantled and assessed. I decide that 'laying out every item of clothing I own and looking out for duplicates or things that no longer fit me' might be a good start and recommend that Table Flipper does the same.

'During the "unfreeze",' I warn, 'we may be dealing with strong emotions such as denial, impatience, and feeling "overwhelmed by uncertainty and doubt".'

Table Flipper tells me that our wardrobe winnowing should also include anything we haven't worn in the past year. I tell her I feel 'overwhelmed by uncertainty and doubt' and am not ready for that level of ruthlessness yet.

'Stop being a wuss. You know that statistic about how we wear twenty per cent of our clothes eighty per cent of the time?'

I murmur that I may have read something along those lines.

'Well you've worn *that* outfit pretty much every time I've seen you for the past year,' she tells me. I look down at my daily writing uniform of grey jeans and a bobbling black jumper and suspect she may be on to something. 'So either get rid of the things you never wear or start wearing them.'

I mumble an 'okay', then hang up and begin to upend drawers, pulling out long-forgotten dresses and crumpled jumpers. My fingers run over silks, wools and cool cotton, as well as some alarming man-made fibres that feel distinctly flammable.

These can definitely go, I think.

I arrange everything on the bed and then, when I run out of space, on the floor. Within ten minutes, the room resembles a jumble sale. Or TK Maxx. It feels chaotic and frenzied and my heart races as I take in just how many items of clothing I had entirely forgotten about. It feels obscene – to own so much and yet appreciate so little of it. I try to restore order with piles, but this only makes the problem worse: I realise I own *nineteen* black T-shirts.

No one needs that many black T-shirts. Not even roadies. Or stagehands. Or goths . . .

I sort through a tangle of pre-baby, maternity and post-baby clothes that I haven't worn in years and an amateur slingshot competition's worth of bras – of all sizes. Really. All. The. Sizes. Many of these I've kept because they had been expensive, but, really, what's the use? *It's a sunken cost,* I tell myself – *an outlay I made years ago.* Holding on to them makes no sense, so they're out.

There are dozens of dresses from my old life in London – dresses that don't fit with my lifestyle – or any 'style' in fact – any more. Then there are the 'party frocks'. A gold- and bronze-coloured puffball dress (looks better than it sounds) that an ex bought me as a present to wear for his sister's wedding before dumping me a fortnight before the event. I've worn it a few times since to try reclaiming its power for good, but I've never had a nice time in it. I also have an unfortunate knack of turning up to weddings in a near identical frock to the bridesmaids and have spent many a Saturday fending off enquiries about where the loos are from aged relatives. I have three 'wedding guest' dresses like this. Well, enough. These can go to a better home, too.

I pick up Little Red from daycare and he 'helps' by collecting balled-up socks and tights and throwing them at me, until I'm essentially decluttering while playing dodgeball. Lego Man comes home to find us still hard at it.

'I'm having a clear-out!' I tell him, out of breath from ducking hosiery bullets: 'A cluttered home equals a cluttered mind!'

I suggest, in a manner that I hope appears 'nonchalant', that he might like to join me. It's bad form to purge on somebody else's behalf, apparently[28], and I've already learned the hard way that you can't make someone change if they don't want to.

I *need to lead by example,* I think: *set off a chain-reaction of un-stuffing.*

'It'll be fun!' I promise.

He fixes me with a Paddington Bear stare, then goes away to make tea before shouting up the stairs: 'Tell me this: if a cluttered home equals a cluttered mind, what does an empty home mean? Hmm?'

I have no answer for this. But I know my husband: *he'll eventually get bored on his own downstairs and want to play. And if this is the only game we're playing*, I think, dodging a particularly well-aimed 60-denier bundle, *he'll join in . . .*

Ten minutes later, Lego Man appears in the doorway wearing a threadbare charcoal suit that might generously be termed 'snug'.

'D'you think it's too small?' he asks.

I pause as though considering. 'It does look *a little* as though you're dressed for a court appearance . . .'

There is a harrumph, then he says: 'Well, while we're at it, I never liked that hat –' he points at my 'millinery' pile – 'makes you look like a train driver.'

I asked for that, I think, as a sports sock is flung in my face.

---

28 Kondo tries it with her nearest and dearest, gets busted and vows never again, for fear of losing her family's trust. Chapter Two. Don't mention it . . .

The light fades, but we make progress. Table Flipper messages to tell me that she's on shoes and has unearthed seventy pairs 'so far'. I am a) agog and b) alarmed to realise I haven't even started on footwear. We break for supper and the parenting glide path of bath-book-bedtime begins, interrupted sporadically by partially freezing FaceTime calls from my mother, who reveals that she's also decluttering.

'I took my leather trousers to the charity shop yesterday,' she tells me. 'It's the end of an era!' She and Robert Wagner are having to appraise their belongings ahead of their move to (sodding) Devon and they're deciding what will make the grade. Experts agree that for cohabiting bliss, it's important that all parties have equal opportunity to inflict their aesthetics on a place and this takes compromise – something Lego Man and I found challenging when we first lived together. I moved into his flat and so inherited all his interiors decisions, including a carved wooden warrior mask above the bed that I begged him to move. He refused, until one day it fell and landed an inch from my head. So we 'compromised' and the terrifying assassin mask was relegated to the back of the wardrobe. In return, I continued to be his girlfriend.

At my mother's, a mild disagreement has erupted over a 'vintage' lamp that Robert Wagner isn't a fan of. In response, she has vetoed his 'vintage' painting of a boy in knickerbockers. The compromise?

'We'll see how we do for time, darling, but I'm tempted to let the charity shop have their pick of the lot,' is how my mother is approaching it.

Once Little Red is in bed, Lego Man and I move on to stage two of Lewin's process: change.

'It's crucial that this is implemented within a short time as the longer the process takes, the more inclined we are to relapse,' I read from my notes.

'Relapse?' He looks up. He is sporting an '*I Heart San Francisco*' T-shirt and a pair of bootcut jeans that he's giving a swansong wear.

'Before we change our minds and shove everything back in the wardrobe, I suppose . . .' *That is tempting*, I think as I take a black V-neck T-shirt off the 'discard' pile, put it back in the drawer, then get it out again. *What if I need it? What if my roadie-slash-stagehand career really takes off?* It would be easy to talk myself out of this – to leave everything just the way it was. But I look up to find Lego Man wearing a Christmas jumper and Bermuda shorts and the sight strengthens my resolve. I take up a roll of bin bags: 'Right then, let's get bagging'.

We work in silence after this. Or at least, it would be silence were it not for next door's cat taking part in what can only be described as a debauched feline orgy.

'Blimey, he's really going for it . . .' Lego Man mutters. 'Can't we take five until he's done?'

'No, we can't stop – I'll lose my nerve.'

'So we just have to stand here and listen to cat porn?' He pulls on a ski mask to shield his ears from the din.

'Is "cat porn" a thing?'

'Most things are nowadays. I'll Google—'

'No! Don't Google "cat porn" – that's something you can never un-see.'

He concedes and we continue to sort, more determined than ever now to get the job done. There is some aggressive humming to conceal the cat commotion until our feline neighbour is eventually sated. But by now the pile of bags destined for the charity shop is up to the door handle. I'm astounded that we've lived for so long with so much that we haven't needed.

' – And I'm done!' Lego Man announces, flinging a final bag at the door. I hurry along, cavalier now in my clothes clearance, eager to get to stage three.

'Okay, now: freeze.'

Lego Man stands stock-still.

'Not you: the next step. It's all about solidifying the change to stop ourselves reverting to old habits. So what can we do now to make sure things stay streamlined? What regular checks can we make to stop ourselves sliding back into clutter mode?'

'Other than you telling me to stop buying stuff?'

'Yes, other than that.'

'Ummm . . .' He thinks about this for a while, then comes up with: 'Let's get rid of the wardrobe!' My husband is nothing if not a maverick (or, in fact: Maverick). 'It's the perfect plan! We can't buy more stuff if we haven't got space!'

'No.'

'"No"?'

'No.'

'Is that a hard "no"?'

I remind him that a lack of wardrobe space hasn't been an impediment to his shopping habit to date and we have one of our very best 'whisper debates' so as not to wake up Little Red. Only Lego Man's designer mood lighting combined with my thrifty low-energy light bulbs mean we can't see very well after dusk, so we call a truce while he brings up a few candelabras (see 'Liberace') for extra illumination. Shadows leap up against the walls and Lego Man busts out his particularly impressive shadow-puppets.

'What if,' I suggest, joining in with an inexpert 'shadow-Bambi', 'we operated a "one in, one out" policy?'

'Yep, okay,' he agrees, using his hands to make a bird of prey (like I said: impressive). 'We could also keep the place tidier if you folded better.'

Bambi turns on him: 'What?'

'I'm just saying – everything would take up less space and look better. When I worked in fashion –' Lego Man had a Saturday job at Gap as a student – 'I was the store's *master* folder—'

'and don't we hear about it . . .'

'We learned that a folded T-shirt was a happy T-shirt.'

'You'll be thanking your socks, next . . .'

'What?'

'Nothing.'

'Anyway, it's a valuable life skill! I impressed a retail assistant only today by demonstrating my technique—' He stops, aware he's said too much. His face colours slightly and he drops his 'shadow-kestrel', reaching inside his work bag to retrieve a brand new grey jumper, still with its tags on. Then he sings like a canary: 'Before you say anything, it was heavily discounted and it's ten per cent cashmere . . .'

To atone for his heavily discounted goat's wool, Lego Man offers to load all the bags and boxes destined for the charity shop into the car to solidify stage three of Operation Ice Tray. We're both far too lazy to rifle through our things once they're packed up and ready to go – so the deed is done.

We move on to each room in the house by turn and find, counter-intuitively, that it gets easier the more tired we get. We become, finally, ruthless. Deciding whether to keep a box of old magazines when it's already 10 p.m. and you'd much prefer to be in a hot bath is easy. There's less agonising over chucking out the ugly blue and orange fruit bowl I've never liked when I can barely keep my eyes open. And of the 'stuff' that remains, I find that much of it can be 'tidied away' more effectively – either via Lego Man's origami-style folding skills or by some sneaky offloading. I don't need to keep all the receipts cluttering up my desk: I can take them to my lovely accountant, Lars, and let them clutter up his desk instead. The books I've kept for years but haven't read, or that I've read but didn't think much of, can all be passed on to others who might enjoy them. And by midnight, we've finished.

Before bed, I send Table Flipper a message to see how she's getting on and she sends a picture of her room – now almost completely bare.

'*Have you chucked away EVERYTHING?!*'

'*I got quite into it,*' is her response: '*Think I've gone too far?*'

'*Well, it's certainly minimalist . . .*' I avoid telling her it now looks as though she's living in a Travelodge. '*Don't worry,*' I type instead: '*tomorrow we can start on the next bit of The Danish Art of Decluttering: the beautiful touches. And I'll teach you about* hygge.'

I wait some minutes for a response but the next thing I know, she is bum-dialling me while brushing her teeth. At least, I hope that's what she's doing. So I leave her to it and collapse, spent but happy with what we've achieved.

In the morning, I drop Little Red off at daycare and am just walking the dog home when I bump into a New Age-y friend. The one who believes in fairies and turned me on to tapping, also loves a crystal – you know the sort. She tells me she's off to the woods (to hang out with some sprites, I suspect) so I tell her I'm off to complete my home makeover.

'Oh, you must smudge!' says Crystal Dangler.

'Sorry?'

'For a metaphysical cleansing!'

I tell her I haven't had a coffee yet this morning and she's going to have to clarify.

'Smudging! You know!'

I don't.

'It's only a two-thousand-year-old Indigenous American practice! Shamans burned sage plants as a ritual to call up ancestral spirits. Any conflict or evil is absorbed by the smoke to cleanse your energy field!'

I'm no wiser. *Did she not hear,* I think, *the bit about the coffee? I haven't got any energy . . . in a field or otherwise . . .*

'It's also good for aura polishing,' she goes on. For a New Age type she is surprisingly strident. 'You just need to get a handful of sage, bind it together with string and repeat: "Air, fire, water, earth. Cleanse, dismiss, dispel". Promise me you'll try? It'll change your life!'

The dog is now straining at the leash so I do some nodding, say 'bye' and near-gallop home.

Ping!

A text arrives as soon as I slot the key in the lock.

Remember: Air, fire, water, earth. Cleanse, dismiss, dispel. Enjoy!

I look at the potted shrubs on either side of our front door and decide that, in the spirit(s) of enquiry, I will give it a go. After coffee.

At 8.25 a.m., a smoking bowl of shrivelled ashen herbs in hand, I send a smudging SOS: *Feeling dizzy. Is this normal?*

Crystal Dangler: *That's the ancestral stirring within your blood!*

Me: *Should it smell funny?*

Crystal Dangler: *That's the smell of thousands of years of spiritual communion!*

Me, unconvinced: *Is it?*

I do some dry retching, then try a second coffee for fortification. Lego Man stops off at home on his way to a meeting. The dog hurtles through the air at the sound of the door, planting his paws on Lego Man as the two of them hover on the threshold, gasping for air.

'It stinks in here!' My husband wrinkles his nose. 'Have you been smoking weed?'

'Of course I haven't been smoking weed! I've been "smudging".' I tell him what Crystal Dangler told me: 'Ceremonial! Shamans! Sage!'

'But we haven't got any sage.'

'Yes we have!' I say, less sure now.

'No: we haven't.'

'What's *that* then?' I point at the plant to the right of the door.

'That's laurel.'

'Not sage?'

'No.'

'Oh.'

'And it's been raining for weeks – that'll be why it's so smoky . . .'

'Oh.'

I'm not great with horticulture (can you tell?) and gardening has always been on my list of 'Things to get into when I'm a proper grown-up'. I know 'nature etc' is good for us and that plants can even reduce stress, according to studies by the Norwegian University of Life Sciences and Uppsala University, Sweden. But I just can't keep them alive.

A child: yes. Basil: no.

Lego Man is fractionally more green-fingered than I am and has managed to sustain the mystery plants on our doorstep. So I vow to leave these to him for the foreseeable future and omit smudging from my home makeover advice for Table Flipper.

'Phase two of The Danish Art of Decluttering is about making Scandi minimalism cosy,' I tell her. 'You're basically turning a house into a home via the wonderful invention of *hygge*.' Just as there are links between kaizen and *hygge*, the Danish phenomenon really defines the way our friends in the Nord do things – and their famed interiors.

Candlelight is *hygge*, and Danes burn more candles per head than anywhere else in the EU, according to the European Candle Association (see 'fire hazard' in Chapter Five). Dinner with friends is *hygge*. And living Danishly has taught me the advantages of making my living space *hygge* with small touches that make a huge difference (hello kaizen!). Because although the concept may be about appreciating the little things in life, *hygge* is A Big Deal in Denmark.

'We're *hygge* fundamentalists,' Meik Wiking of the Happiness Research Institute told me recently for a UK newspaper article:

'You hear *hygge* being talked about all the time – by everyone, no matter who they are. It's like a form of Tourette's. We appreciate the simple things in life, like lighting some candles to create a cosy atmosphere.' And Danes do 'cosy' like no other nation. The average home looks like something out of a weekend living supplement, with lots of natural materials like wood and leather, as well as lamps artfully positioned to create pools of light or new areas of *hygge*.

'Danes take lighting and design very seriously,' I tell Table Flipper, 'so lights are used to make spaces feel warm, with lots of low-slung lamps—'

'Like a 1970s Barratt Home?' she asks.

'Yes, but more flattering.' I explain about Danish architect Poul Henningsen's iconic PH5 lamp that 50 per cent of Danes have *at least one of* in their homes: 'The idea is that the layered shades spread the light and conceal the bulb to create this diffused, soft lighting that makes everyone look hotter.' Because bathed in the warm peachy glow of *hygge* lamps, cheekbones are accentuated; greying roots are concealed; and under-eye bags are almost imperceptible. 'I'm pretty much Helena Christensen by dusk in Denmark,' I tell her. 'Then it's all about tactile textures – so a sheepskin rug, maybe, to line that wooden chair of yours in the corner –' I point to one of the few remaining sticks of furniture in her prison-cell room – 'then a few cushions, perhaps – Danes are obsessed with cushions.'

'So's my nan . . .'

I explain that Danes go mad for a perfectly plumped down pocket and even rotate them seasonally as an affordable way to refresh their living space. Table Flipper reminds me she won't have much square footage in her new flat ('because: nearer to Waitrose!') but I tell her this doesn't matter.

'We're not talking clutter – it's still about minimalism: less, but better. That goes for clothes, too. Now that you've eBayed everything, you can just keep a streamlined wardrobe like Danes do!' I tell her how Danish homes have small closet spaces because there's an emphasis on owning a few, beautifully made items of clothing that they wear a lot. 'Scandi style is mostly monochrome, which means everything goes with everything and getting dressed in the morning is easy!'

'Is that true?' She arches one eyebrow: 'Or are you just trying to justify your new "uniform" of black on grey?'

'Both? *Both*.'

Having been assured that she can make her new living space *hygge* for the cost of a cushion and a tealight, Table Flipper forgives me my fashion faux pas and tells me she's feeling better for her interiors overhaul.

'I feel lighter,' she says, '*thinner*, even – that's weird, isn't it? And there's so much space. I could totally do a cartwheel in my room now.' As a benchmark of decluttering, this feels like a good one. Although Table Flipper isn't stopping at mere conjecture: 'I'm going to try. Right now.' She does. And it's about as elegant as one might imagine a grown woman executing her first cartwheel in twenty-five years might look. But my friend is elated.

'Just watch out when you get candles on the go,' I warn. 'There's nothing like naked flames and singed hair to make a house feel like home.' *Or the stench of burnt laurel leaves*, I think but do not say.

Table Flipper promises to be match-safe and hangs up,

leaving me to my own decluttered home, a windy dog and my thoughts. Which, sadly, still appear to be utterly cluttered. And this is where the trouble starts . . .

Things I've learned from making changes to my home:

---

1. Lofts can be lovely places for reflection (and secret lives).

2. We're emotionally connected to what we own – and the things we choose to keep say a lot about us.

3. It's easy to slip from stuff-fan to psychologically diagnosed hoarder. If a room's not fit for purpose because of too many *things*, purge.

4. Operation Ice Tray – unfreeze-change-freeze – can help.

5. Ruthlessness is advisable (but it's okay not to feel okay about this *hello, pilot's voice*).

6. The Danish Art of Decluttering is a pretty good approach. You heard it here first . . .

7. No one needs nineteen black T-shirts. Not even roadies.

8. *Hygge* can make a house a home.

CHAPTER NINE

MIND

Send In The Hounds

In which I use neuroscience to reverse a 'Downward Spiral'; try meditation and mindfulness; go Facebook cold turkey; learn to unplug; practise 'Stimulus Control'; and give thanks for my own black dog

I am in Oslo, alone, for work, when my mind hits 'peak clutter'. This isn't ideal. It's snowing, it's minus three and I'm here to give a talk at an achingly cool rock music festival. Only I'm neither achingly cool nor into rock. And it's Oslo: where a sandwich costs the same as my monthly rent and even the ugly people are beautiful.

I haven't slept for a week as Little Red's had a fever and Lego Man's been away with work. He returned at 1 a.m. last night with a trundling suitcase that set the dog off barking. I lay awake after this, staring at the ceiling, until 4 a.m. when it was time to get up and catch my flight. On the plane, I read an article on the dangers of sleep deprivation and learned that getting less than six hours a night for just one week can alter the expression of 711 genes, including those involved in the metabolism and immunity, raising the risk of heart disease and obesity. Which was jolly.

My 'leap' year is nearly up, but although I've made lots of changes, my experiments in 'fixing' my approach to work, relationships, my body, friends, family, hobbies, money and my home still haven't safeguarded me against the biggest change-hurdle of all: what's going on in my head. Decluttering my mind feels like the final, fundamental piece of the puzzle.

If only I wasn't so flipping tired . . .

It's too early to check in to the hotel when I arrive in Oslo, so I wander the streets, aimlessly. Everyone is so tall and model-esque that I feel more like a Borrower than ever and, to make it worse, I realise that my shoulders are stooping slightly from carrying a laptop bag around with me for – I consult my watch – seven hours now. *This has gone beyond rucking,* I think: *we're into torture here . . .* I search for coffee, but it appears that the locals are so unconcerned with capitalism that nowhere opens until 11 a.m. By 11.05, I am attempting to pay for an 'espresso with milk' (Norwegians are too cool for lattes) but I'm not tall enough to read the display on the pin machine, so the barista has to disconnect it for me. The tables and chairs are all so high up that my legs dangle and I notice my arms hunching, elbows out to each side like a small child's, grasping my drink with both hands. I make a home-made booster seat out of my coat, which helps slightly, as I watch the coffee shop flood with hipsters. I'm surrounded by people with tattoo sleeves and realise that Oslo is the pinnacle of 'man-bun'. I had thought that last year's trip to Sweden was where it was at – we saw seventeen one morning in Gothenburg – but this is something else. *I am the squarest person in this entire city*, I think, wondering whether I've got time to get my septum pierced before the talk. Unsurprisingly, nowhere *that* cool is open yet[29] so I take in some cultural highlights instead, tramping through snow in my inappropriate footwear to the Munch Museum. *Because if you're feeling down, nothing lifts the mood like a little existential anguish . . .* a smarter woman than I might have realised.

An icy wind picks up, until my face is so cold it hurts and I have lost all sensation in my toes. I shuffle around the gallery with similarly weary-looking tourists and become transfixed by a painting called *Despair*. It's similar to old Edvard's most famous work but it features a man with more hair and two gents in top hats passing him in the opposite direction, as if to highlight his isolation. I'm just musing on this when the couple next to me start snogging enthusiastically, clearly 'moved' in another way. So I walk around the rest of the exhibition looking for *The Scream*, eventually giving up and asking a gallery attendant for help.

'Oh, we haven't got *that* one . . .'

What, the most famous 'one'? The only 'one' of Munch's I know? In the Munch Museum? *FFS* . . . I don't want to sound like a philistine but I can't help thinking this is something they might have mentioned earlier. I'm spat out into the gift shop and buy a spatula with the iconic howl of misery on it instead of seeing the real thing. That's post-modernism for you.

Back at the hotel, I'm finally permitted to check in. There are only a few minutes before my talk, so I have a wash (you're welcome, Oslo) and put on make-up, drawing a face that I hope appears 'approachable-and-just-about-keeping-my-shit-together'.

---

29 Plus I'm a massive, vanilla, fraidy-cat. Mostly this.

I needn't have bothered.

Understandably, most Norwegian heavy rock fans, given the choice between listening to someone with a pierced septum shout at them or a girl from the Home Counties chat about cake, opt for the former. As one lingerer told me by way of review: 'Books aren't really my bag . . .' Well, quite.

It isn't a roaring success and when it's over, I pick up emails telling me two interviews I'd also scheduled for my trip have fallen through and that the university friend I hoped might be in town has had to leave. There are no earlier flights home, so I'm on my own for a few days.

My *Pink Panther* eye twitch is back and my shoulders have seized up (thanks, rucking). I can't move my neck without grimacing and the hotel receptionist becomes convinced I'm giving her the glad eye. I am not.

A couple of speakers take pity on me and invite me out for a drink, but the bar is loud, I can't hear what the rest of our party are saying, and my tongue feels furry after two glasses of red. A middle-aged Canadian with facial hair that would put Poirot to shame proposes 'a crazy big one', 'hitting the clubs, hard,' at which point I bow out. 'Never trust a moustachioed man at a disco,' my mother always told me. I thank our eclectic group for their hospitality and opt for a 'crazy early one', 'hitting the duvet' instead.

But I don't sleep: I lie in bed and do some first-class fretting. I'm good at that. During the hours of daylight, I can usually talk myself down from the ledge and think rationally about the reality of any given situation – reminding myself that everything is fundamentally 'okay'. But in the dark, I'm anxious about all sorts of things – the babysitter I've booked for a talk I'm giving next week who Little Red doesn't know very well but Lego Man's away and all our non-child-breaking friends are booked up. Money. Lego Man's spending of it. Deadlines. Why my reproductive organs appear so lame and yet my thighs so substantial. Why this matters anyway. Inequality. Loss of control. Life, and where to spend the next few years of it. Ending up sad and poor. A dangerously charismatic ex who had a smile that would dominate the room. How Canada's prime minister Justin Trudeau balances babies on one hand[30] and how many he dropped before he mastered the technique. You know – the usual.

I try the cool side of the pillow but it makes no difference. So I play a 'sleep hypnotherapy' track I downloaded to my phone for just such occasions. It's filed under an unfortunately shouty-titled '*SLEEP*' playlist I made one frazzled 4 a.m. when I was too tired to realise the caps lock was on. It might have worked, had I not accidentally added 'Under Pressure' by David Bowie (RIP) to the end of the '*SLEEP*' playlist (instead of my '*Songs to sing loudly in the car*' playlist, just below in iTunes). As it is, the 2 a.m. audio assault goes something like this:

'And now, you drift deeply to sleep . . . safe in the knowledge that each and every day you are becoming an easy sleeper . . . rested and relaxed . . .'

'DUN DUN DUN DUN-DUN-DUN-DUN! DUN DUN DUN DUN-DUN-DUN-DUN. . . **PRESSURE!**'

By 2.05 a.m. I am Very Awake Indeed and the catastrophising continues. Now, I worry about the worrying. Studies show that night-time anxiety can impair our sleep so badly

---

30 Google 'justin trudeau balancing baby one hand' then let's talk. . .

that it leads to a weakened immune system and – ha! – more anxiety. I know that our bodies need sleep to carry out essential repairs. *So I'm sabotaging my own chances of feeling better tomorrow by staying awake and worrying about it!*

I have lots of work to do and now that I'm away from my family for no reason – interviews having been cancelled – I feel pressure to make it count. For me, time spent away from Little Red has to be worthwhile. I have to produce good work otherwise, well, bad things will happen . . . The last time I came back from a work trip, my son pointed at a picture of Danny Dyer's wife in *Hello!* magazine and said: 'Mama'. So my fears aren't totally unsubstantiated. But they are magnified in the small hours.

The mad apocalyptic thinking of night-time anxiety isn't unusual. According to an American Psychological Association survey, more millennials suffer from it than any other age group, thanks to pervasive technology and economic pressures. Psychologists at California State University have found that this bed-specific worrying happens because the anxiety we feel during the day is masked by all the other stimuli being processed in our brains. But because there's little else going on during our downtime, the stress hormone cortisol takes over. Our bodies react to a surge of this, keeping us awake – and worrying.

Instinctively, I reach for my phone and Google 'insomnia' for support. I read that baths can help, since we naturally experience a decrease in body temperature just before we fall asleep. A bath or shower artificially raises our body temperature so that when we get out, our temperature drops and sends a signal to our body that we're ready for sleep. But in the bath, scrolling through my phone, I read that 'scrolling through my phone' is the very worst thing I could be doing. A Harvard study proves that the blue light from electrical devices turns off a neural switch in the brain, decreasing production of melatonin – the sleep hormone. *Oh brilliant!* I make the display colours warmer, then set down the phone and pull the plug. As the water drains, the temporary sensation of weightlessness ebbs away and I feel heavy, lumbering and low. I crave daylight, with its promise of purpose and other people and an escape from the loneliness of night. But 'day' is still hours away. So I get back in bed and do some more eyelid-staring, eventually drifting off at around 4 a.m., only to wake with a start at 5.30 a.m. when, my body clock assures me, it's 'toddler-yelling and getting up to let the dog out for a wee' time. *Damn you, mind!*

Holding on to coffee and sugar to get me through, I attempt to work but reread the same paragraph in a scientific journal three times and then lose two hours looking at listicles online. By noon, I am a husk.

'It's pretty common to experience a "downward spiral",' says Alex Korb, adjunct assistant professor of neuroscience at UCLA, when I call and plead for help: 'The brain is a dynamic, complex system – like the weather or traffic – so small changes can have a huge downstream effect. And you can get stuck in patterns. These can become self-reinforcing, and we call that a "downward spiral". Take working from home: you might get less sunlight, less exercise, less social interaction. For many people that might be fine – especially one or two days a week. But two to three days is pushing it. And if you do this a lot, it can have small effects on the brain that can be magnified over time. You can become stuck, unfocused, down.'

It's like he's describing my week. Working from home as a freelancer presents some practical limitations and I sometimes feel as though I'm a child doing homework inside while everyone else is playing in the sunshine. Turns out I'm solar-powered – and I haven't seen enough of it since we got back from holiday. I've been working too much, and with Lego Man away, I've been focused on keeping the routine of 'parenting-work-parenting-housework-collapse-repeat' going – afraid that pressing 'pause' on the machine might make it stop completely.

Alex sympathises and shares his own experience: 'When I started my post-doctorate, there was no office space so my boss gave me a MacBook and said, "now you can work from home". So I did. From the couch. But in this position for several hours a day, I found I was less productive. I developed terrible posture and felt my body tighten. When I went into the office at UCLA, I had to pass the running track every day – so it was easy to exercise. But at home, I had to get in the car to drive to the gym. So I didn't. Our habit systems are triggered by our environment and our surroundings. And different people's brains are more or less sensitive to falling into depression.'

I've been depressed before and this isn't it. Yet. But that sense of unease – a dark energy riven by doubt and indecision – is something I'm well acquainted with, and something I know can get worse.

'We're often indecisive when we're feeling down because that brain region is too sensitive to losses or disappointment,' Alex confirms: 'We can't cope with making the "wrong" choice – so we protect ourselves.'

I remember this – being unable to see beauty because it

felt unattainable; days when I couldn't get out of the car to visit friends, unable to stop crying; that sense of hopelessness. For me, depression has always felt less like Winston Churchill's famous 'black dog' and more as though I'm stuck in a pit. A bit like a *Winnie the Pooh*-style heffalump trap – an analogy that probably came about as a result of first experiencing depression at a very young age. It feels insurmountable, the climb out. And I feel alone in the woods. Scared, cold and tired from the effort.

I haven't felt like this for a few years now, I'm relieved to report. Largely, I suspect, thanks to being aware of my triggers (overtiredness; stress), my symptoms (biting my hangnails until they bleed; depletion in patience) and how to turn the juggernaut round (sleep; QT with loved ones and my *actual* black dog – the great woolly, teddy bear of a mutt who doesn't allow for wallowing and is the only creature I've ever heard of to have been sedated for Happy Tail Syndrome[31]). But a couple of friends are in the pit at the moment. And I ache to see them like that.

One in four of us will suffer from mental health problems and depression is now the leading cause of disability worldwide, according to the World Health Organization. I look out of my hotel room window and speculate on the mental health of passers-by on the street below: *blue umbrella woman, not you; man-bun skateboarder, not you; portly*

---

31 When a dog wags its tail so much that it bashes against doors/walls/your legs until it bleeds. Yes, my black dog is THAT happy. When we moved house to somewhere with a garden, the entire ground floor looked like a Tarantino film by day two. He's fine now, don't worry.

shopping man, not you; Nordic goddess-alike . . . bad luck
– it's you . . .

So what can we do to stop a downward spiral in its tracks?
I ask Alex.

'Well, the tuning of your brain is down to three forces:
firstly, genetics, which shape our propensity to certain brain
circuits.' A recent study published in the journal *Neuron*
found that our genes even shape the way we deal with uncertainty (lucky old Lego Man/Maverick/Beyoncé: nailing the
'good with change' gene). 'Secondly,' Alex goes on, 'it's early
childhood experiences – including *in utero*, caretaking,
attachment and any traumatic experiences that happened to
you as a child. This shapes how our brain circuits start to
develop.' *Bugger* . . . A house swarming with medical professionals and black starlings of sorrow when I was two years
old probably ticks the box for this one. 'But the third is about
our current circumstances, including our coping habits, our
relationship, our job and our lifestyle. So the first two we
can't control – but the third, we can.'

Hoorah! How?

'Practising gratitude, mindfulness and meditation can
help.'

'Oh.' My heart sinks: 'I was worried you might say that . . .'

Mindfulness, I *get*: it's about being aware, and attentive
to what's going on around us. I've been a *hygge* advocate
for years now and having a child, for whom everything is
new, has made me more sensitive to my surroundings than
ever.

But meditation is defined as 'intentionally setting aside
time to *practise a tool* that cultivates mindfulness'. And this
feels trickier. I know that meditation is 'good' for me, but I

can't keep my mind from wandering. And I find it a bit (a lot) dull. We're used to 'doing' rather than just 'being', and psychologists from Harvard and the University of Virginia recently discovered that the impulse to avoid being alone with our thoughts is so strong, we'd prefer to give ourselves electric shocks. So becoming a meditation-bore does not appeal.

'I already floss!' I wail to Alex: 'Isn't that enough?'

I tried, really tried, to get to grips with meditation during fertility treatment on the advice of various medical professionals, but to no avail. I went on a meditation course once for a feature, and am pretty sure we had a session on it at school. Despite having been *made* to meditate during three separate periods of my life, I've never found it helpful. But this, Alex says, is where I may have been going wrong.

'Studies show that *actively choosing* something changes how we feel about it and releases dopamine – so just deciding to do something, voluntarily, gives us a pleasure hit. We don't just choose the things we like; we also like the things we choose.'

This reminds me of biscuit-fan Benjamin's advice that successful change happens when we really want to do it, for ourselves. The challenge may be getting to a point where I actually want to mediate. But after Alex has impressed me further with his frankly enormous brain, I am galvanised to do something, anything, to avoid another sleepless night alone in an anonymous hotel room.

'*Random question: have you ever tried mindfulness or meditated?*' I send a WhatsApp message to my inner circle. There is an instant '. . .' to indicate that Head Girl is composing a reply and then a message flashes up:

'*I'd rather be flayed alive.*'

Right. Helpful. Thanks.

Table Flipper tells me she has a mindfulness colouring book. I tell her that doesn't count ('Even my mother has a mindfulness colouring book . . .') but I'm intrigued that the tail of this particular trend keeps on lashing. Multiple tomes are still hovering around the Amazon top ten and Table Flipper assures me, from her newly Zen room nearer Waitrose, that the activity makes her calm. This seems perverse: most of us sit at desks all day 'colouring between the lines' at work, following someone else's instructions. So why would we want to do the same thing in our leisure time?

'Why colouring-in rather than drawing?' I write back.

'Because I'm crap at art,' is Table Flipper's response: *'Colouring-in slows down my brain after a long day. I don't knit or anything, so this feels like "accessible craft".'*

I can understand this – we all need an art-related outlet of some kind and sales of origami paper are apparently on the up as well. Most of the psychological claims for colouring-in et al have been debunked, but perhaps it's another case of 'If it makes you feel better and it's not hurting anyone else, go for it.' Table Flipper sends a picture of some beautifully sharpened Faber-Castell pencils, adding: *'Plus, I really like the excuse to buy stationery.'* I'm with her on this one.

Divorcee Friend has a more nuanced response.

'I've meditated daily for the past year. Wish I'd done it earlier. Would have made a big difference to my marriage.'

'God, I had no idea, I'm sorry . . .' I start typing, not knowing quite what to say, then think better of it and call.

'Don't worry,' she assures me: 'it's fine: meditation just really helps crystallise things for me.'

'Huh . . .'

'Yeah – if I'd done it while I was married, I wouldn't have stayed with him so long.'

'Oh!'

She tells me about another friend of ours who's suffered from chronic pain for years.

'She's been doing a body scanning meditation for the past month and by day two she only needed half her usual dose of co-codamol. After a week, the pain was virtually gone and now she doesn't have to take that special cushion with her everywhere. She just meditates – even driving on the M1.'

I'm not convinced that this is advised, but the revelation is significant: neither Chronic Pain Friend nor the divorcee are easily swayed and the latter tells me, 'The best thing is, the science shows that you don't have to believe in it for it to work.'

This seems amazing. *A bit like religion should be . . .* So I do some digging.

According to research from Carnegie Mellon University in Pennsylvania, just twenty-five minutes of meditation a day for three days in a row has the power to alleviate physiological stress symptoms. I come across numerous clinical trials showing that meditation can improve memory and concentration as well as helping to treat clinical-level depression. A study published in *Clinical Psychology & Psychotherapy* (the *Grazia* of medical journals, possibly . . .) showed that meditation could make self-critical people feel better after three months. Researchers also found that practising a special 'loving-kindness meditation' (this term makes me want to vom slightly but I'm trying to keep an open mind) may increase positive emotions and make us more compassionate – to ourselves as well as to others. It can even slow down ageing, according to a study published in everyone's favourite US beach read, *Brain, Behavior,*[32]*and Immunity*. Research from the University of California found that meditators experienced an increase in telomerase activity – the enzyme that maintains and builds telomeres (the youth-boosting felt tip pen caps from Chapter Three) – after only three months.

Stuff the kale, I think: *I can BREATHE myself younger!*

But precisely because it's so powerful, meditation comes with some caveats. Dr Florian Ruths, consultant psychiatrist at the Maudsley Hospital in south London, launched an investigation into unusual or even adverse reactions to secular Mindfulness Based Interventions (MBI) – the umbrella term for structured practices designed to encourage mindfulness. These unfavourable effects include rare cases of 'depersonalisation', where meditators feel as though they're watching themselves in a film. Florian's inquiry coincides with Brown University's 'Varieties of Contemplative Experience' project (recently renamed from the alarmingly sinister 'Dark Night Project' – a PR disaster) documenting how meditation can bring to the surface repressed emotional trauma. Another study at the University of California found that 63 per cent of participants had suffered at least one negative effect from meditation retreats, while 7 per cent reported serious adverse effects including depression, pain and anxiety. It seems that meditation can unpack some pretty intense stuff – and things can feel worse before they feel better. Despite all this, Florian believes that, for most people, the benefits far outweigh the risks. 'It's a lot like fitness training,' he tells me when I call

---

32 Americans: what did the letter 'u' ever do to you? Or, rather, 'yo'?

to quiz him on this. 'There are lots of known health benefits and building up your fitness under supervision is less likely to do you any harm. But if you've had health issues in the past – from a bad back in the physical realm to severe anxiety in the psychological – it's worth being mindful of your vulner-abilities and getting some guidance from an experienced teacher. A qualified practitioner will be able to guide you through any unexpected or unusual side-effects.'

And so, after another sleepless night, I resolve to proceed at risk and hope – really hope – I don't become disassociated and have an existential crisis. On my own. In a two-metre-by-two-metre hotel room in Oslo.

To reduce the likelihood of this, I consult a professional.

Dr Danny Penman is a journalist turned meditation teacher who came to the practice following a paragliding accident in the Cotswolds ten years ago. Danny was cruising along, taking in the view, when his canopy collapsed and he fell headlong into a hillside.

'I was in unimaginable pain, my leg was broken in twelve places and the only pain relief I had until the ambulance arrived was a meditation I'd learned at school. I didn't hold out huge hope, but I started meditating and found it effective. I was still aware of the pain but it felt separate from me somehow,' he tells me. 'After that, I was in hospital for a month, which is pretty boring, so I had a lot of time on my hands. I started looking into meditation more seriously and working with Professor Mark Williams from Oxford University.' Impressed by the research, he became a devotee and has now written four books on the topic.

I speak to Danny over Skype and find he doesn't look anything like the image of a hippy meditation guru that I've been harbouring all these years. He looks nice and normal with short, tousled hair, and he yawns a lot before explaining that he's very, very tired: 'Three-month-old baby . . .' he adds by way of explanation.

Danny tells me he's keen to promote meditation as a 'vaccine' against stress: 'So you're not waiting until you get stressed to try it. I'm not of the full-on Matthieu Ricard school of thought,' Danny adds, referring to the French writer and Buddhist monk oft labelled the 'happiest man in the world'. 'For me,' Danny says, 'meditation is still about experiencing the ups and downs of life. Happiness is great and all, but it gets a bit boring after a while, doesn't it?' There speaks a true Brit. 'Blissful happiness isn't the goal: the aim is a more meaningful existence. Otherwise you could just take loads of drugs – that would be quicker.'

Fair point. So how do I start? Meditation, not drugs . . .

'Well, I recommend sitting in a straight-backed chair, rather than lying down or sitting cross-legged – this will encourage alertness. Your feet should be flat on the floor about hip-width apart; then you could start with a simple breathing meditation. Close your eyes, tune in to the world around you – any noises you can hear – and then, starting with your feet and working upwards, focus on a different part of the body in turn and how it feels. Once you've checked in with your whole body, focus on the breath. The rise and fall of your chest or stomach. Whenever your mind wanders, bring it back to the breath. Do this for about ten minutes and then gently become aware of your surroundings again – the noises you can hear, how your body is feeling etc. Then, gradually start to move – and get on with your day.'

I had been expecting some cosmic conjuring, or at the very

least, *bells*. Possibly whistles. But this seems relatively straightforward.

'That's it?'

'To start with, yes.'

'And I only have to do it for ten minutes?'

'Twice a day, yes. That's what we recommend for beginners.'

Danny tells me that he meditates for half an hour a day ('babies take up lots of time . . .'): 'You do have to *make time* to meditate, but it tends to free up more time than it consumes because it helps to streamline life. So you may find you get more done.'

Part of me is still reluctant to develop the necessary solipsism to buy into this wholesale. When I try to express this to Danny, he essentially advises me to woman up: 'Many people invest time in their physical health and wouldn't think twice about exercising for three hours a week – so you can always think of meditation as a fitness programme for the mind. Something you learn to make time for.'

I remember the two hours lost on listicles this morning and the twenty minutes I've just spent looking at pictures of friends' holidays on Facebook. *Maybe*, I think, *if I meditated I wouldn't need to look at online sunshine-porn to lift my mood . . .*

'Whatever you can manage at the start will be a positive,' Danny assures me: 'and you can't "fail" at meditation. The great thing is that everyone can do it and it's absolutely free.' Whereas stress management has become a multibillion-dollar industry, the principles of Buddhism dictate that meditation should be accessible to all, and so guided meditations, like the one Danny has just run me through, are all available online at no cost[33]. Once newbies have got to grips with the basics, Danny recommends various prescriptions to help us through life's challenges – the breathing space technique is apparently excellent for acute stress; the insight meditation is great for creativity; the resilience meditation works well for anxiety or unhappiness; and when we're feeling overwhelmed and need some mental peace, the sounds and thoughts meditation can be useful. I want all of these things, so I'll start at the beginning and work my way through. Danny wishes me luck and I wish him an infant who sleeps through the night, then hang up. Alone once more in my hotel room, I'm determined to crack this. And so once I'm sitting comfortably, I begin.

Listening to Danny's dulcet tones in a guided meditation, I'm encouraged to think about how my feet feel, 'pressing down on the floor'. But I realise that they aren't – they're dangling. Again. *Stupid giant Vikings with their giant chairs!* I scan the rest of my body for tension and find I have unconsciously interlaced my fingers in a prayer position. Despite my Catholic education coming to an end in 1994, a deep-rooted part of me still equates quiet contemplation with religious apology and/or gratitude. I have to wrench my hands apart and plant them, palms down, on my lap to break the spell. Sitting still is also a challenge. I fidget, constantly, moving my shoulders; twisting and turning my torso; clenching and unclenching each butt cheek in turn (TMI?) – dancing, almost, in my seat. *Dr Dance might be proud,* I think: *Dr Danny, less so . . .* Stasis isn't my forte. When I'm

---

33 Danny's website franticworld.com has dozens of meditations available.

stationary, I feel heavy. And some archaic conditioning in me equates 'heavy' with 'lady failure'. *Must keep moving, must burn calories,* my overstimulated brain seems to tell me.

Every time my mind wanders, Danny's voice reminds me that 'thoughts aren't facts' – and returns my focus to the breath: 'in and out, in and out.'

I get into a rhythm until I feel a cool, tingly sensation and become aware of the whirring of air conditioning. It's set too low and my feet are cold. Being aware that I'm cold makes me think that perhaps I need a wee. *And possibly a lick of something . . . I can't possibly meditate with cold feet, a full bladder and an empty stomach . . .* I convince myself that I should postpone my debut meditation session until I'm less hungry. *Because you can't concentrate when you're peckish. Everyone knows that. The mind is a powerful thing.* This is true: studies show that the chances of prisoners being granted parole are far higher after a judge has eaten than if they're hungry.[34] *Who knows what ill-advised life decisions I might make if I don't refuel?*

A strawberry yoghurt, two squares of dark chocolate, a pear and a handful of cashews later, I try again. I manage to sit still, and listen, for ten whole minutes. It is the longest ten minutes of my life. But I do it – and I work well that afternoon. And then I struggle to drop off at bedtime and wake just after 2 a.m.

Argh!

The next day I try again. I still think about food a lot and

---

34 A remarkable 65 per cent versus almost zero, according to a study carried out by the Columbia Business School in the US. Life lesson #142: pack snacks.

my mind refuses to empty. But I find that, actually, I quite enjoy the thoughts racing through my head. I'm not sure this is exactly the point, but Danny describes in his book, *Mindfulness for Creativity*, how inspiration can strike in the spaces, the small gaps between our 'normal' train of thought that meditation allows us to access. I don't have any *Aha!* moments but I do get to sleep more easily that night and don't wake until the luxurious hour of SIX A.M! As a result, by breakfast I am a new woman.

In addition to being my favourite meal of the day ('*break*' +'*fast*' = legitimised eatathon), I get very excited about a hotel buffet (Melon? Pain au chocolat? And sardines? In the same bowl? With a Sugar Puffs chaser? Yes please . . .). I'm in good spirits and even feeling buoyed-up enough to try an extra, supplementary meditation that I hope I'll be better at incorporating into everyday life.

Traditionally known as the 'raisin meditation', the idea is that by paying attention and appreciating the tastes, textures and sensations that arise while consuming something we usually take for granted, we can become more mindful. But there are foodstuffs we typically take for granted and then there are *raisins*. Unless you're Liz Hurley or Little Red, raisins are not exciting. No matter how mindful we choose to be. So Danny (clever Danny) has updated this for the twenty-first century to coffee. Settling into a cosy corner of the breakfast room, I ignore the skiers[35] clomping around burning toast (it's hard to move swiftly in ski boots, even when your bread's on fire) and focus on the steaming mug

---

35 I know: get Oslo! Man-buns, snow AND mountains! It's too much . . .

in front of me. The aroma is warm and rich and I feel a lot like the woman from the Kenco ads in the mid-1990s as I inhale through my nose, eyes closed in bliss. Lifting the cup to my lips, I pay full attention and sip, tentatively, in case it's too hot, savouring the first tang. I've used lots of delicious cow juice to 'fake' a latte, so there's a sweetness that lifts the slightly bitter notes of the hotel coffee.

I can't remember when I last drank anything with such focus. I'm used to slurping while scrolling through emails or Facebook or Twitter; or hammering out copy; or talking; or tussling with a toddler/dog. But now, with all my intention focused on the cup in front of me, I'm reminded again of *hygge* – 'taking pleasure from the presence of gentle, soothing things'. And it feels good.

But to reap the full mental decluttering benefits and even anti-ageing powers of meditation, I'm going to have to stick with the more formal practice, too. Even if it's dull. Danny recommends that beginners persevere for at least six weeks, so I warn Lego Man to clear the fridge ('Honestly, I'll eat anything that isn't nailed down to avoid meditating . . .') and pack my bags – because, finally, there's a flight available. I'm going home.

On the train to the airport, however, I scroll through Facebook to kill time and feel my mood, previously upbeat, deteriorate with each new update about friends' new babies or swanky holidays or career milestones. My Zen is eroded and by the time I check my bags in, I feel poor, underachieving and angry with the world. *This is daft,* I think: *these people are my friends/aquaintances/people-I-met-once-and-felt-obliged-to-accept-a-Facebook-friend-invitation-from! Why aren't I happy for them? Them and their fancy holidays and*

their proper jobs and their von Trapp-style family albums?
Am I that much of a horrible human being?

Fortunately, as well as being 'friends' with people who go on holiday to Barbados ~~too much~~ a lot [36], a few appear to have as conflicted a relationship with social media as I'm currently experiencing. One former colleague has written:

'I appreciate the irony of posting this on Facebook, but this piece on the dangers of . . . er . . . Facebook . . . is well worth a read : l'

He links to an article on 'Facebook depression', with research from the University of Pittsburgh School of Medicine showing that the more time young adults spend on social media, the more likely they are to be depressed.

Just like Head Girl told us! I think.

Depressed people tend to return to social media for support because they're feeling isolated from the 'real world', but this exacerbates their depression – and so the cycle continues. I click through to another study from Meik Wiking's Happiness Research Institute, where sociologists made 500 regular Facebook users go on a sabbatical from the social media site, while another 500 regular users continued as normal. After a week, the group 'on a break' were 55 per cent less stressed; reported higher levels of life satisfaction; experienced better concentration; felt less lonely and more sociable. In SEVEN DAYS. On the one hand I'm flabbergasted, but on the other hand – the one currently five years deep into someone else's Facebook photos – I'm not surprised at all.

---

36 I've never been. I'm sure it's lovely. But really, on a writer's income and with Little Red's complexion, we won't be holidaying anywhere more exotic than Wales, in winter, for the next decade . . .

I call Meik to ask why Facebook is making so many of us *sad-face-weeping-cat-emoji* and he tells me: 'We look at a lot of data on happiness and one of the things that often comes up is that comparing ourselves to our peers can increase dissatisfaction. Facebook is a constant bombardment of everyone else's great news, but many of us look out of the window and see grey skies and rain. This makes the "Facebook world", where everyone's showing their "best side", seem even more distortedly bright by contrast.'

So Facebook is akin to one vast, sprawling dating site, only where our 'friends' spend a lot of time telling us – consciously or otherwise – that they're better than us? Or on holiday in Bar-bloody-bados?

'Pretty much.'

Oh brilliant . . .

Being alive is arduous enough without unnecessarily exposing ourselves to incessant one-upmanship from the people who are supposed to be our friends – for *fun*. Meik reveals that he's trying the Facebook ban himself ('it's going okay . . . so far') so, in solidarity, I tell him I'll do the same.

It's easy to start with: I delete the app from my phone and log out of the site on my computer. My mind is (still) too cluttered to remember passwords so once I'm out, I'm out. But even though Facebook isn't there any more, I still catch myself 'checking' for updates. Before my conscious brain kicks in and I realise what I'm doing, I've unlocked the screen and am pressing the space where the app used to be. A few minutes later, I'm scrolling through Twitter without knowing how I got there, then checking my email, when the handy clock at the top of the screen reminds me that I last checked it . . . three minutes ago. It's as though my phone is an extension of my arm. Or, as it turns out, all of our arms.

A study published in *Computers in Human Behavior* journal found that many of us spend so much time on our smartphones that they become 'part of our body' – with 90 per cent of phone users suffering from 'phantom vibration syndrome', where we mistakenly think our phone is vibrating when it isn't.

I can do all the meditations in the world, but if I'm still addicted to my smartphone, can I ever be truly mindful? Will I have to go offline completely and communicate only by semaphore or carrier pigeon . . .?

'No,' Rohan Gunatillake assures me: 'Technology isn't the enemy of mindfulness – it's just about learning to be less reactive and more intentional about where we put our attention.' Rohan is the director of Mindfulness Everywhere, an organisation that sets out to combine mindfulness and technology and the founder of the 'buddhify' mindfulness app. It's not much of a surprise then that he's a fan of a smartphone, but he's also been a trustee of the British Council and in 2012, *Wired* named him in their 'Smart List' of people who will change the *actual* world. So, you know, worth listening to.

I telephone as I wait for my flight, and Rohan confesses that he too is a subconscious-smartphone-scroller: 'I'm trying to be more aware and notice the impulse now – the moment my arm wants to reach out for my phone. I want to catch the process before my fingers move. And be aware of the emotion that normally precedes this – whether it's boredom or loneliness or social awkwardness. I want to try to seek comfort in other ways.' I tell him I feel the same, only with the postscript '. . . other ways *that aren't Kettle Chips*'.

Rohan is a realist, so when I explain how I'm finding traditional meditation challenging he sympathises: 'It shouldn't be a chore. You should do what works for you – and it's not heretical to adapt meditation and mindfulness practices to your own needs.' Because mindfulness, he assures me, is all about change. 'It may have been brought to the West by people on the hippy trail who weren't into technology but it's always adapted and innovated. Zen Buddhism was more of a clean, monochrome, disciplined idea – but Tibetan Buddhism is colourful, with bells and whistles.'

I KNEW there'd be bells somewhere!

'In the US and in Europe, Buddhism met science and psychology and corporate culture – so it changed again,' says Rohan. He believes we can make most things into a 'mindfulness meditation' if we try hard enough: 'You can download a favourite podcast and then just listen to the content as closely as you can for the duration of the podcast. Don't try doing anything else at the same time: just listen. Taking the podcast as the meditation object in this way requires us to stay with the audio and its meaning. You'll notice that your mind gets distracted from the content but when that happens, just call it back.'

Interesting . . . I thank Rohan, hang up, and consider this.

I love a podcast, but usually listen to them while attempting to clean/cook/tidy/walk the dog/do a bench-press[37]. I am a classic multitasker – something that, until now, I'd considered an asset. But then I read research from Stanford University showing that multitaskers are markedly less productive than

_____

37 I still don't know what this is but it sounds like something I *should* be doing.

monotaskers and typically experience difficulties concentrating, recalling information and switching from one job to another. A study from the University of London found that multitaskers experienced declines in IQ similar to people who had smoked pot or stayed up all night. Some fully functioning adults found that their IQ scores dropped to those of an eight-year-old child while multitasking. Which, unless we're talking an eight-year-old Stephen Hawking or chess prodigy, is alarming.

As a journalist, news junkie and fan of multi-screen viewing (i.e. Tweeting during *Bake Off* about soggy bottoms and 'good forkings') this hits a nerve. There is plenty of multitasking in my life that is unavoidable: I regularly have to do my job while being cried at by a toddler and bounced at by a dog. But reading *all* the news and listening to *all* the podcasts, *all* the time, as well as working and being cried at and bounced at, could, possibly, be a bit much. As my mother recently pointed out: 'Life's not one long rehearsal for an appearance on *Question Time*, darling!'

It's good to care; but we don't get extra points for reading everything. In fact, we get compassion fatigue. I habitually check news sites as well as Twitter and email before bed and first thing in the morning, and a fifth of the UK workforce admit to checking their emails before they get out of bed in the mornings. But even if there's good news, there's always bad news, too. If something I've posted on social media has been 'liked', I'll wonder why it hasn't been 'liked' twice. An email about a new commission will regularly nestle alongside a tax bill or an offer to enlarge my penis. For every news story on Trudeau, there are a hundred on Donald Trump.

And this is how I start and end my days? With a news/ email/Twitter triangle of disappointment?

Well, no more.

I'm going to try single tasking and logging off, occasionally!
I will check Twitter twice a day and email, er, three times.
And I'll only use my phone as a PHONE at weekends!
As well as meditating (Urgh . . .).

I decide all of this as I board my flight home, then fall promptly asleep until touchdown.

'Mama!' Arms are flung round me and I experience a rush of gratitude at being back with my family. Little Red appears to have grown an inch and he can now say 'giraffe', 'come' and 'bun' in Danish. Lego Man has made some changes, too – moving around pictures and furniture to stave off his urge to shop and introducing some novel parenting techniques.

'If anyone's feeling down –' he inclines his head pointedly to Little Red – 'say, if they're *missing* someone –' here he nods at me – '. . . we do *this*.' He opens the door to the living room and sings 'Send in the Hounds' to the tune of Stephen Sondheim's 'Send in the Clowns'. A tail whips past as the dog does a lap of honour before bouncing at me, repeatedly, then allowing himself to be mauled by Little Red. 'It's hug-bombing! See? You can't stay cross or feel sad when you're getting hug-bombed by a twenty-six-kilo bear-dog. Unless you're holding coffee. Or liquids of any kind in fact. Because then, well, you know . . .' I notice a brown stain up his sleeve and a wet patch down his trousers. 'Other than that, it's worked well!' It's an offbeat approach but it seems to be effective, with the dog's tail lashing and the toddler now giggling hysterically.

Hugging animals is almost as good for us as hugging

humans, according to neuroscientist Alex Korb, and 'therapy dogs' have proven so effective that some hospitals are now employing their services for patients and staff[38]. Although not traditionally a dog person (the hound was Lego Man's idea), I find that with a woolly creature curled up on my lap, chest rising and falling, it's impossible not to feel soothed.

'Ahhh, I missed you, too!' I tell him, stroking his fur. 'And did you know that as well as reducing stress, when dogs are with their owners they synchronise heartbeats!'

Lego Man looks at me.

'What? I read it online . . .'

'Watch out, you'll turn into one of those women with a bum bag full of dog treats and a tatty sofa . . .' Lego Man starts singing Lionel Ritchie's 'Endless Love' as I cast around for something to throw at him. As it happens, there's nothing handy and I'm pinned down by 26kg of dog, so I let this one slide and vow to continue my mindfulness plan despite the cynics.

My brand new gratitude-n-meditation-n-stuff diary reads as follows:

> *End of week one: Breathing meditation isn't any easier but focusing on 'mindfulness' means I'm noticing more: the sensation of water on my fingertips in the shower; the insanely hot new helper at Little Red's daycare; how annoyingly delicious the coffee from Lego Man's upgraded*

---

38 The University of Pennsylvania's hospital and Rush University Medical Center in Chicago both run 'pet a pooch' programmes for staff.

machine is etc. Keeping off Facebook surprisingly bear-
able. Only things I've missed = another Tupperware party
(shame . . .) and the news that D&B are having another
baby. But instead of feeling jealous – Bar-bloody-bados
style – find I'm happy for them. Unusual . . .

Week two: Try 'sounds and thoughts' meditation,
paying attention to . . . er, sounds. And thoughts.
Realise I've pretty much had headphones in since first
bought iPod in 2006. Taking them out, I start to hear
again. And listen. Turns out we have wood pigeons!
Who knew?[39] Still waking most nights, but instead of
reaching for social media 'reward pellet', doing body
scan meditation instead. Fallen back asleep 5/7 times
and slightly less catatonic come 3 p.m. Still eating
like it's a contest and on intimate terms with 'relapse'
part of Jim's Transtheoretical Model of Behaviour
Change. The wagon = now a mere speck on the
horizon . . .

Week three: Loving-kindness meditation – also known
as 'resilience' or 'metta' meditation – all about extending
the love you feel for child/parent/partner to yourself, the
people around you, then strangers. Smile at the postman
so much that he asks if I'm okay, but find I'm more
patient with bouncy males in household. Walked dog
this evening and chased sun to the top of the hill before
it disappeared. Nice times ☺

---

39 Yes, I'm excited: I've got ten years of birdsong to catch up on.

Week four: Insight meditation (urgh). Supposed to find gaps between thoughts then make these longer. Apparently, learning to notice when our mind has wandered is the secret to calming it. Cannot. Still find it dull, so trying it lying down, because: lying down. On the plus side, still haven't missed anything on Facebook and using phone less, so wrists have stopped aching [the RSI that I normally accept as par for the course of my job being largely absent]. *Sleep: nothing to report because: asleep. Result!*

Week five: Meditation medi-schmation. Supposed to know enough to 'freestyle' now, with whatever meditation I think I need. But can't quite be bothered. Mindfulness has been helpful but formal practice = not so much. Experience overwhelming urge to raid fridge whenever attempt to meditate. Currently up 2kg and counting. Danny says this is normal ('meh' feeling, not snack-induced-weight-gain). Apparently 'restless and despondent' is classic week five, though nobody knows why. Great . . .

So I go off-piste.

I find a quick and dirty fix that I hope will put any remaining worries to rest – rather than distracting myself from them. At least, for twenty-three and a half hours a day.

In between dreaming of hoverboards and listening to Huey Lewis and the News, scientists at Pennsylvania State University in the 1980s discovered that by scheduling specific 'Worry Time', we can fend off anxiety during the rest of our day. Numerous studies have since confirmed that 'stimulus control', as it's known, reduces stress and all we need to do is set aside fifteen to thirty minutes, preferably at the same time each day, to wallow in our woes. Experts agree that it's best not to do this before bed (hello night-time anxiety!) and that we shouldn't feel obliged to 'fix' our problems. Because 'it's okay not to be okay'. If we feel ourselves veering towards worry outside of our allotted times, we can tell them to 'bog off' until later. Writing down our thoughts can help us identify patterns and our most common areas of concern – like a worry top ten.

I decide that 3.30 p.m. will be my designated Worry Time – half an hour before I have to pick Little Red up from daycare. I'll be guaranteed a gear change afterwards with a walk to the nursery and it will be useful to mark the shift from 'work mode' to 'parent mode'.

To get in the zone, I download the baggy-trousered bard MC Hammer's 1990 (only?) hit, substituting 'Worry Time' for his famous refrain. Then I start, writing down all my 'what if' thoughts as they occur to me:

1. *What if moving back to the UK is a terrible idea?*

2. *What if I don't have enough work as a freelancer?*

3. *What if the commute drives Lego Man mad?*

4. *What if we can't afford to pay for childcare?*

5. *What if I get pregnant?*

6. *What if I don't?*

7. *What if we don't end up living near anyone we know and I sink into a Netflix-n-online-shopping loneliness funk?*

8. *What if we can't find anywhere nice to live?*

9. *What if we stay put?*

10. *What if all this meditation sends me into existential angst and makes me pull the ripcord until I end up subsisting entirely on potato products?*

After fifteen minutes, I am spent. So I stop for the day and go outside to fill my lungs with fresh, worry-free air. When I pick up Little Red, I notice I'm more relaxed than usual because my mind isn't on other things.

'Other people are our best metric of progress,' Rohan tells me when I share this revelation: 'I always emphasise the social aspects of mindfulness – I have a better relationship with others since I'm really *with* them when I'm with them. And mindfulness doesn't have to be a solitary activity – the reason that meditators spend time up on mountaintops isn't for the isolation, it's for the views. It literally puts things in perspective. But time with friends and family is also a domain of practice – and a great way to notice any changes.'

So I try another session of Worry Time the next day. And my list looks largely the same.

At least I'm consistent, I think.

By the end of the week I'm starting to think about answers, despite being nowhere near 'fixing' anything. Friday's list goes like this:

1. *We don't have to move. Maybe that's why we've been struggling with the decision – because it isn't right for us.*

2. *If I don't have enough work, I'll work less (I won't: it'll be fine).*

3. *Commuting could be rough, see point #1.*

4. *We'll find a way to make childcare work, wherever we are. People do . . . *'Hello Granny! Fancy babysitting . . .?'**

5. *If I get pregnant, my body will be taken hostage, again; we'll get to reuse a loft-full of baby gear; and my heart will triple in size. Again.*

6. *If Little Red is an only child, he'll be fine – like I am (mostly). Also, my lady garden will swerve another oak tree of varicose veins . . .*

7. *I'll try very hard to avoid hermit-esque isolation, wherever I am (but House of Cards IS excellent #TeamClaire).*

8. *We can keep renting until we find the right place for us.*

9. *If we stay, we'll keep trying to learn Danish and pay our taxes graciously.*

10. *Put down the Kettle Chips and step away from the crisp aisle . . .*

And that's it. There's nothing I'm routinely worrying about in my own life that can't be addressed.

If there's something I can do about a worry, I'll do it, it occurs to me in something approaching an Archimedes moment: *But if there isn't, I needn't worry anyway . . .*

I share this thought with Lego Man, who says: 'Isn't that a meme?' He learned this word recently and now uses it A Lot.

'*Is it?*'

'Isn't it?'

'I don't know.'

'If it isn't, we should make it one!' His eyes widen. 'Our very own meme!'

He checks on Facebook, muttering as he scrolls: 'Meme or no meme, that is the question . . .', then he reports back: 'Oh bad luck, the Dalai Lama got there first!'

'Doesn't he always . . .?'

Lego Man ignores this and slings an arm round my shoulder: 'Keep trying, eh?' I try to explain that it has never been my ambition to create a 'meme', but he just hugs me – as though keen to soften the blow of 'no-meme'.

By the end of week six, I don't feel vastly different but I am having fewer anxiety dreams and I'm less worried about waking at 2 a.m. I'm picking and choosing the aspects of meditation and mindfulness that work for me – the ones that don't feel too wanky. I regularly perform a body scan for a couple of minutes before bed; I pay attention when I drink my coffee; and I unplug when I walk the dog. This means that although I'm horribly behind on *The Archers* omnibus[40], I have started to notice the explosion of green on my street

---

40 What's happening with Rex and Pip ('Rip'?) Has Miranda cottoned on? Updates gratefully received @MsHelenRussell.

and that the countryside has turned butter-coloured with rapeseed flowers. Worry Time means that I'm more efficient with my fretting and I feel present and more patient with the people around me.

What is this curious new sensation? I wonder. *Am I in mind-clutter recovery? Have I successfully made a change to the biggest area of self-sabotage in my life?* This feels huge. *Send a blimp! And trumpets! Someone get Céline Dion on the phone to sing a stirring ballad as I raise my arms in slow motion to optimum power pose and ticker-tape rains down from the heavens!* I wait, but nothing happens. So I flick on the kettle instead.

After a conflict-free weekend with my family where we have all got along, played nicely, eaten well and indulged in our various hobbies (orca-cycling, stick-chasing, sand-flinging and genitalia pottery respectively), I sleep deeply and barely move my exhausted body until my eyes ping open, awake and refreshed at 5.55 a.m. Yes, it's still objectively early, but compared to 2 a.m. this is a lie-in.

I listen to the birds for a few minutes before swinging my legs out of bed and stumbling downstairs to let the dog out. Then I hear the Valhalla roar of a just-roused Little Red: 'Gaaaaaaaaaaaaaah!'

And a new day begins.

Things I've learned about
changing my mind:

---

1. There's a lot of Actual Science saying meditation is a good idea, so it's worth a go . . .

2. . . . but we shouldn't beat ourselves up if formal practice feels hard (humans have been found to be 84 per cent more relaxed after watching fish, if meditation isn't your thing).

3. Mindfulness is eminently achievable and enhances the pleasure in everyday life . . .

4. . . . a lot like *hygge*.

5. Unplugging – headphones, smartphones, electronic devices in general – is A Good Idea.

6. Still stuck? Schedule 'Worry Time' (theme tune and dance routine recommended).

EPILOGUE: FOUR
MONTHS LATER

Few of us in life could have envisaged where we are today. But having spoken to some of the best minds on the planet about change and how to handle it, I'm inclined to think that this is just as it should be. Yes, it's useful to have a plan, but there's no point cleaving to it like a barnacle on a sinking ship. Adaptability and resilience – either via natural flair or nurtured techniques – are what keep us happy and healthy, as well as the ability to see things with fresh eyes. Zen Buddhists call this 'beginner's mind', or 'Shoshin'. 'In the beginner's mind there are many possibilities, in the expert's mind there are few,' is how the late Sōtō Zen monk Shunryu Suzuki described the attitude of openness and eagerness, free from preconceptions, that we should all aspire to in our daily lives. Living far from home is a useful exercise in this. Spending time somewhere different makes us notice things, from the sights and smells we encounter, to working out how to post a letter, to deciphering the strange markings on tinned goods in Danish supermarkets and what on earth *'Makrel Guf'* entails. (I don't recommend . . .)

I've had my eyes opened over the past few years, but I want to carry on reaping the benefits of 'beginner's mind', wherever I am. Over the course of my experiments, I've come to see that a new beginning for us isn't about emigrating: it's about changing the way we think about life, in all of its facets. Because we can't run from our problems or our fears, or ourselves. This is a sentiment that would have filled me with dread, historically, but now . . . well . . . I'm okay with that. We don't need an excuse to change and we can do it at any time – as long as *we* want to.

The last missive I received from the family friend I haven't seen as much of as I'd have liked over the past few years included a catalogue of regrets. Things he'd never got around to, or experiences he wished he'd savoured more at the time. But the thrust of his distress was that he hadn't done what he'd truly wanted to do. If we want something, we just need to go for it. There are different methods and techniques to help us, but in the end it's down to us. We need, he reminded me, to stop postponing 'life'.

My year of experiments in change and becoming more resilient was the spur I needed to start doing this – I've learned that it's okay to be frightened as long as we do the thing anyway. Failure is always an option – for all of us – and the real strength is in being honest about it.

Now, I'm more confident at work and have a much greater belief both in what I do, and that the things I'm good at have 'value'. So much so that when the opportunity to have a 'big, scary meeting' that I'd ordinarily avoid came along a couple of months ago, I seized it with both sweaty-palmed hands. Power Posing beforehand, I went in, confident. A commissioning editor said she liked my work and asked whether I'd thought about writing a novel next. I hadn't. But I liked the idea. I went away to look at my Interrelational Diagram and saw that, actually, writing a novel would meet a lot of my criteria for a fulfilling work life. Instead of getting

The Fear and procrastinating on the actual 'doing' part (*because if you don't try, you can't fail* – as 'Old Me' would have said) I danced my way around the kitchen, twice, then sat down to start. I researched, then wrote, then researched some more and wrote some more until I was happy with this new creation. And now my debut novel is out next year.

I don't work at the weekend any more and Lego Man and I are getting on better as a result. By letting go of the non-relationship-defining (daily) irritants, I'm able to be nicer and more forgiving of sock-missing-the-laundry-bin-gate. Lego Man is solely responsible for tick medicine and the dog's dental hygiene and I have vowed to share my superpower of 'finding stuff' that he's lost.

I start each morning with a nourishing breakfast, as instructed in chapter three[41], because no matter what else happens that day, starting it with an egg means that I know I've put something good into my body. I'll never enjoy hanging out with BO-scented, balloon-stretched, veiny muscle men in the weights section of my local gym, but I like getting stronger, in all respects. It's empowering to see exercise as a way to be more, rather than something to be endured or making myself smaller as a '21st century lady woman'. I'm tougher than I thought, too. And although there are still things that I could change, I'm *OK*, just as I am. I could be healthier and fitter and more toned, but I don't need to be – and I don't want to be enough to deprive myself unduly. I like broccoli AND buns. And that's fine.

I'm doing Nia every week – otherwise known as 'grinning solidly for an hour' – and getting out of my comfort zone

---

41 The Sugar Puffs were a blip.

in the 'free dance' section has been mind-expanding. Just as Dr Dance advised me that improvised shimmying was great for divergent thinking and the psychologist Scott Barry Kaufman proved that openness to new experiences boosted creativity, I now find that I come up with some of my best ideas while dancing on the cusp of chaos. My fellow class-mates and I have become friends, and The Brit even dispatched some incalculably useful advice last Wednesday, saying: 'Don't curve your spine so much when you're doing the "sexy weed picker" move and you won't look like you're crimping one out.' This has already transformed my approach to dance – if not life – and I shall be forever in her debt.

I'm more empathetic with old friends and trying to remember that 'no news' isn't necessarily 'good news'. 'No need to reply' is a phrase I've started using whenever I want to check in with anyone in my gang who I suspect may be having a tough time – with work, relationships or a bumpy patch of mental health. Because sometimes, all that's required is an 'I'm here for you.' That, or a gif of a micro pig.

I'm less scared about discussing money and I'm gradually overcoming my martyr-like tendencies, so that recently I was able to admit to the world: 'I need a holiday and I am allowed one.' (Portugal, five days, thanks for asking . . .)

Lego Man still likes to accumulate, and the flotsam and jetsam of toddlerhood mean that our living room regularly looks as though burglars have had a Duplo fight. But my wardrobe is at least streamlined and Table Flipper has chal-lenged me to wear all my remaining clothes over the next few months. This has resulted in some bold choices for the daycare run. But since one of the dads is in the Danish air force and occasionally rocks up in full *Top Gun* jumpsuit (cue a dozen mothers and several fathers sucking in stomachs, flicking hair and giggling like teenagers), my 'fancy dress' of a polka dot ra-ra skirt barely warrants a second glance.

But it's been the change principles around family that have made the biggest impact. Enmeshment theory has been a monumental learning curve for me. We are all a product of our genes and where we come from – but we're also *just us*. Which means I get to choose. I have agency for the first time and I'm not just doing what other people expect of me. I don't have to move back for my mother: she doesn't need me. She likes me and wants me nearby, but she doesn't need me. She's married now – and she's moved house. She and Robert Wagner have become *heavily* involved in the local hanging basket association and are regulars at 'pensioners' swimming'. My mother has her own life and I have mine. This realisation means that choosing is all of my own doing. I may get it wrong, but I have to take responsibility.

One of the slices of the 'moving back to the UK' pie that was about me, rather than external pressures, was about wanting a home. With clearer heads, we realised that we wouldn't be able to live near my mum and Robert Wagner in (sodding) Devon, whatever happens next – and Denmark is a great place for kids. So we decided we'd try to buy a house in Denmark and keep living Danishly until we need to start thinking about schools. And after doing a lot of sniffing of friends' newborns, I opted to have one last crack at fertility treatment, too.

IVF isn't cheap. And it isn't fun. But we saved up and booked an appointment. I felt sick for a month thanks to all the drugs and injections needed to kick-start my ovaries. Once my eggs were ready they were 'harvested'. *shudders*

Lego Man spent some quality time with a sample cup, then his sample cup took my test-tube out for dinner, before the results were 'implanted' back inside me. I had a week on the sofa recovering/whimpering and even had to stop writing for a while. But despite a lot of medical professionals shaking their heads, looking sceptical, and predicting an '80 per cent chance of failure' (Danes are optimistic types . . .) it worked.

IT WORKED!

There was whooping, shimmying and even some air guitar to celebrate.

'Do you think perhaps a new book, a new house, and a new baby all at the same time might be pushing it a bit?' Lego Man asked as we looked around the garden of prospective house number twelve and I tried not to barf up my breakfast in the begonias.

'Maybe,' I admitted, wiping my mouth with the back of my sleeve just in case. 'But no-one can say I don't take my research seriously . . .'

'It's been *quite* the year of taking leaps . . .' he muttered, before feigning interest in an ornamental sundial and asking the estate agent something sensible about loft lagging (Lego Man: still loves a loft).

I can see that, on paper, my change trilogy might appear stressful. But I'm beginning to understand that some degree of turbulence in all our lives is normal – proof we're alive, in fact. The bumps are what make the road interesting.

The Austrian-born endocrinologist Hans Selye coined the term 'stress' in 1936, defining it as a 'non-specific response of the body to any demand for change'. But since life is a state of flux, it means that some degree of anxiety at adapting to circumstances and the accruing years is inevitable. We can't stop things from happening – that's life. Change is all there is.

The experience of researching into starting over and facing my own change demons has been like a software upgrade, and I'm different now. I recognise that perfect is an illusion and that to be able to withstand the storms that buffet us, we need to face our problems and work on fixing them until they're good enough. Not perfect, but good enough. And these days, I can accept that sometimes I'll get this wrong.

I'm trying to live a life with #nofantasyfilter – in relationships, work, home, family, friends, finances, everything in fact. A new friend came over yesterday and her daughter defecated on my floor. That's okay. That's life, in its messy, absurd entirety. No one's existence is a steady stream of green smoothies and selfies in infinity pools. So now, when Lego Man points out that I have muesli in the folds of my scarf, I *own* it, telling him: 'I'm saving it for later.'

After the house viewing, we drive to the clinic for our first scan, along familiar roads, and taking our usual detour via our favourite bakery en route for what Lego Man likes to call 'essential supplies'. I'm nervous. We both are. There's still so much that can go wrong, I know. *It's early days,* I tell myself. Either way, buns are probably a good idea. We've been warned that the weeing on a stick bit is only the beginning, so I try to stay calm and collected as we trot up the steps of the clinic. Because the treatment requires constant monitoring, we're being treated to a scan far earlier than normal.

Ice-cold jelly is smeared across my stomach and the doctor dims the lights to get a better look at her monitor as I hold Lego Man's hand, tightly.

'Let's see,' she murmurs, pressing the scanner into my belly and rubbing it around a bit. 'Ah yes, there is the egg.' She points at a small but clearly visible blob on her monitor and we exhale with relief.

This is happening! We're having another baby! Little Red will get a brother or sister and we'll be able to use all our baby stuff from the loft and I'll get a lattice of varicose veins on my lady garden again! But the doctor isn't finished.

'– and here's the other one.'

Lego Man's hand is suddenly clammy in mine.

'What?' I stammer.

Without looking away from the screen, the doctor tilts her scanning wand slightly to scout around another area of my innards and repeats: 'Here's one,' she shifts her ultrasound probe again, 'and here's the other one.'

'One and an "other one"? *Two?*' Lego Man manages in disbelief.

Well done, Carol Vorderman . . .

'Yes,' the doctor says, matter of factly: 'it's twins.'

In films, these moments are met by tears of joy, soft-focus close-ups of the parents-to-be, and, often, a Westlife soundtrack.

In real life (IRL) the news is met by a white-as-a-sheet Lego Man struggling not to lose control of his bowels and a soon-to-be mother of three muttering something along the lines of: '*Holy crap . . .*'

We drive home in silence.

Finally, passing the bungalow we'd been planning to put in an offer for, Lego Man whispers: 'We're going to need a bigger house.'

This is true. *And we definitely can't afford South East*

England house prices or childcare for three children in the UK now . . . Living Danishly = wins again.

I flick on the indicator and check behind me in the rear view mirror before turning into our street. 'We're going to need a bigger car, too,' I realise, clocking the just-big-enough-for-two-baby-chairs back seat.

Because neither of us can imagine going back to our normal life straight away with this momentous news ringing in our ears, I double back and we drive around for a while. Deciding 'buns' might be a good idea, I pull in to a side street by a river and we sit, mute, munching.

'Are you going to finish that?' Lego Man asks eventually, eyeing up the pastry hovering halfway between my mouth and the napkin on my lap.

'Uh-huh: I'm eating for three now,' I tell him stoically, stuffing it into my mouth. But something has caught my eye. There's a sign, in red, outside a pretty white house with blue windows. It's for sale. And it's *our house*. I can just feel it. In a moment of unprecedented decisiveness, I call the number on the sign and ask if we can look around. We're told 'yes', and that the estate agent is already on the road showing another house to a young couple. Inside, it's not perfect – nothing is – but it's what we need, right now. So we make an offer. And it's accepted.

We move next month – all five of us, the three on the outside and the two mini Vikings marauding on the inside. I'm ready. Finally. For all that's in store. Another journey is about to begin. But we can handle it.

TEN WAYS TO WIN AT NEW BEGINNINGS

1. Feel small

Get some perspective by looking at something bigger than you. Hills will do. Or the sky. Even a really tall tree. Just look up; look out; and marvel at the world and how huge it is. Take comfort from the fact that we are tiny in comparison and that nothing we do is likely to cause it to end.

2. Employ a #nofantasyfilter

Forget *Love Actually* – this is *Life, Honestly.* In all its imperfect splendour. If you're going to Barbados soon, just enjoy it. No need to curate a conceit to share with people back home, uploading eight thousand Facetuned pictures that conveniently exclude mosquito bites/dysentery/existential angst (delete as appropriate). Life isn't a Pinterest board; we don't need to be performing all the time and no one has all their shit together.

3. Get out more

Everything is better with fresh air in our lungs and the clarity that comes with getting our trudge on is not to be underestimated. Move; see people; take in 'nature 'n' stuff' and de-fug. There is beauty, all around. And there are some really cool diggers. Just waiting, for all of us.

4. Log off
Social media, email and the sidebar of shame are not our friends. They can be entertaining, diverting, challenging, even, but they are no substitute for 'life'. Feel your arm reaching for a phantom scroll? Take action. My friend with the chronic back pain now has my Facebook password – and I've never felt freer.

5. Look after yourself
I don't work so well when I've only had Sugar Puffs for break-fast. Or kale juice. But wang an egg in there and everything's sunnier. Self-care keeps us sane. Same with our homes – have a clear-out and make it *hygge*. Things that seem trivial have a big impact downstream.

6. Value your values
Donald Trump used to be a Democrat. This is what happens when we don't value our values. You get an orange face and become one of the most hated people on the planet. Work out what you stand for and do something about it. Say 'no' to the things that aren't right for you and don't worry if everyone else's journey doesn't look like yours.

7. Be nicer, now
To friends, family members, partners – everyone, even. Being more considerate isn't always easy, but it's always worth it. I've

taken to pretending my kinsfolk are people I've just met and got drunk with in a skip. It's mixing things up a treat and I'm far more thoughtful (and less snippy . . .)

8. Do something scary for the heck of it
If feeling silly and getting sweaty palms is the worst that can happen when we get out of our comfort zone, we need to get out of our comfort zone. More. Mild bowel rumblings are a price worth paying for the benefits of doing something new – and dancing like a sexy wheel is something everyone should try at least once.

9. Think 'baby steps'
Unless we're Beyoncé/Maverick/Lego Man, changes work best when we start small. Do something, anything, for a minute, and then do it again tomorrow. Until the minutes build up. And you've written a book. Or got a PENSION! Just keep putting one foot in front of the other.

10. Remember: it's okay not to be okay
A completely stress-free life isn't the goal. That's a *Mr Men* book. Making friends with some level of discomfort and building up tolerance and resilience is the key to a half-decent stab at this thing called 'life'. Something I'm still working at . . .

WHERE ARE THEY NOW?

Cue closing titles accompanied by Don LaFontaine voiceover and lilting panpipe music – or anything by Journey (Spoiler alert: nobody dies in Vietnam)

Newly Unemployed Friend – still giving cheese a chance and hoping to graduate to a food truck in future, if only he can stop eating all the stock . . .

Table Flipper – colouring and cartwheeling in her Zen-flat near Waitrose; kicking ass in the office and *newsflash* 'seeing' Stuart from Sales.

Recent Dumpee – honing her 'cockwomble' radar skills on Match.com and working on her inner confidence-coach.

PT Friend – looking amazing six months on (because: self-control) and offering regular suggestions for people I might like to send near-naked selfies to next. How we laugh.

Swim Buddy – more confident and exuding an inner glow. You can't move in her house for goggles balanced on radiators and, when not swimming, she thoughtfully sends me numerous recipes for sugar-free baking. I read these while eating Snickers bars and everyone's happy.

The American – recently ran a Prince (RIP)-themed Nia class that I couldn't attend. Something that may well turn out to be one of the greatest disappointments of my adult life. She's roped me into 5Rythmns next (Google it – and wish me luck).

Head Girl – working on her MBA; plotting to take over the planet (Who Runs The World? Head Girl); overhauling the local dog walking scheme (tatty sofa and bum bag = imminent); and suffering from trampoline mentionitis.

Pans Solo – joined a choir, attempting to jog, and has stopped buying kitchenware. For now. Getting hug-bombed whenever possible and has put a collar on Adele ('Possession is nine-tenths of the law . . .').

The Twin – getting on better with her extended family since she started unleashing ADKAR at the first signs of strife. Now in charge of bulk confectionary purchases for all family members (and answering my 'twin-questions' several times a day).

Crystal Dangler – recently tried to persuade me that I needed a dreamcatcher. I told her I already had one to fob her off and can thus never invite her round for tea again.

My mother – is married; retired and regularly to be found elbow-deep in hanging baskets. She is also – I am forced to admit – fine without me, and doesn't appear to need pestering via Facetime/Skype/email/text/WhatsApp half as much as I'd thought. Which is freeing up a lot more time to enmesh my own children, instead . . .

Lego Man – has been working away for the past week . . . and no parcels have come for him! Texted this morning to tell me he's already procured me five pillow-chocolates from his travels. This is love.

Little Red – learned to say 'old man' last week and now does so, often, while pointing at ladies, which is awkward. Can also ride a balance bike, scale a climbing wall and beat Usain Bolt in a 50-metre sprint, but still refuses to sleep beyond 5 a.m. #Viking

The Dog – less windy since I started running with him (trumping in the open air = better for everyone). Currently excited about the next 'camping and shouting' excursion but tail, so far, intact.

THE LEAP YEAR PLAYLIST

This book has mostly been
written to the strains of:

---

1. 'Pompeii' by Bastille

2. 'When Smokey Sings' by ABC

3. 'You Were Always on My Mind' by the Pet Shop Boys

4. 'Changes' by David Bowie

5. 'What a Fool Believes' by the Doobie Brothers

6. 'Crazy in Love' by Beyoncé

7. 'Foundations' by Kate Nash

8. 'Proud Mary' by Tina Turner

9. 'Little Red Corvette' by Prince

10. 'I'm Gonna Be (500 Miles)' by The Proclaimers

Guest experts were also asked to share their favourite songs for inspiring change – and they delivered[42]. Feat (in order of appearance):

11. 'Can't Stop Now' by Keane – Ellen Bard ('Reminds me that sometimes I can get stuck, but that if it's not right, I can change my mind')

12. 'Givin Up Food for Funk' by The JBs – Benjamin Gardner ('A high-tempo track about making a sacrifice.' – i.e. biscuits)

13. 'I Will Survive' by Cake – Ilona Jerabek

14. 'The Impossible Dream' by Matt Monroe – Stephen Powell

15. 'I Am What I Am' by George Hearn from *La Cage Aux Folles* – Peter 'Dr Dance' Lovatt ('Affirming and says to me, "make your own path, be prepared to override resistance". I can't hear it without welling up and feeling invincible . . .' = one to beat. Your move, reader . . .)

16. 'Holy Grail' by Jay Z ft Justin Timberlake – Natascha Nielsen ('Gives me energy and makes me train harder')

17. 'You Make My Dreams (Come True)' by Hall & Oates – Leo Pemberton ('Makes you want to jump up and run dancing in

---

42 Mostly. Some were so overwhelmed by the challenge of choosing just one track that they politely declined/exploded into a million tiny change-expert pieces. Should *Desert Island Discs* ever come calling, I'd suggest having paramedics on hand . . .

the streets . . .' Also, my mother and I once saw them at the Hammersmith Apollo. Great times.)

18. 'Get Ur Freak On' by Missy Elliot – Veronica Walsh ('When I want to lift myself – dancing and moving your body is added brain gravy.' Steady on . . .)

19. 'Cantata 208: Sheep May Safely Graze' by Johann Sebastian Bach – William Phillips ('The most beautiful piece of music I have ever heard')

20. 'Chariots of Fire' by Vangelis – Scott Symington (It's like Scott spied us running for the departure gate after Lego Man got caught flirting with the anti-sisterhood A-Lister . . .)

21. 'Gimme Shelter' by the Rolling Stones – Phil Parker

22. 'Old Friends' by Simon and Garfunkle – Irene S. Levine

23. 'Us and Them' by Pink Floyd – Robin Dunbar

24. 'Take Five' by Dave Brubeck – Chuck Dymer (Yes, Chuck is *this* smooth)

25. 'Symphony No. 9' by Ludwig van Beethoven – Will Napier ('For nobility of solidarity with humanity.' That's what I like about Will: keeps it real)

26. 'My Way' by Frank Sinatra – Gary Noesner ('I like the line about regrets. It's a song about life's challenges.')

27. 'Theme from Rocky' by Bill Conti – Robert 'Bob' Maurer (I LOVE Bob.)

28. 'Imagine' by John Lennon – Lori Leyden

29. 'Car Wash' by Rose Royce – Pernille Folcarelli ('Perfect for getting something done.')

30. 'Back in Black' by AC/DC – Meik Wiking ('Also brilliant to walk through airports to – even strut.')

31. 'Some Nights' by Fun – Alex Korb ('Reminds me that regardless of how you feel, the most important task of the prefrontal cortex is to decide on your values.' Quite right, Alex: you let your hair down . . .)

32. 'Here Comes The Sun' by the Beatles – Florian Ruths

33. 'Lebanese Blonde' by Thievery Corporation – Danny Penman ('Always good for a pick-me-up')

34. 'Try a Little Tenderness' by Otis Redding – Rohan Gunatillake

---

To listen to the playlist, download the free Spotify software or app and go to http://tinyurl.com/jqrtk7r

ACKNOWLEDGEMENTS

Thank you to Anna Power, who has agented me beautifully since I had considerably fewer of the wrinkles that so repulsed Dr Franken-mean. And to my excellent editor Kate Hewson, with whom I have now developed a shorthand and whose support has been a constant source of enlightenment, encouragement and smiles.

To my change guinea pigs and all the experts who generously shared their time and knowledge – in particular, Stephen Powell, Will Napier and Bob Maurer, whose insights continue to blow my actual mind.

To Tara, Frauke, Katie, Fen and Jackie for camaraderie, cake, coffee and a fair amount of gin. And Chrissy, Emily, Alfie, Gaye, Simon, Joss, Sally, Tony, Caroline, Sarah and Joe, who contributed to the writing of this book via deliveries of chocolate, reading material from the motherland, inspiration, moral support and a stuffed fox.

To Lego Man, my teammate, who has foregone expeditions and solo-parented on bank holidays to allow me to write this, keeping me in Bendicks Bittermints throughout. And Little Red, because: Little Red. I will try very hard not to enmesh you (but you are the best one!)

Huge congratulations to my marvellous mother and lovely Robert Wagner: may you be wonderfully happy, healthy and high on John Lewis outings for many years to come.

And to Justin Marsh, who won't get to read this but who I hope appreciated how much he meant to the world and how it's a less funny and brilliant place without him in it.

ABOUT HELEN RUSSELL

Helen Russell is a journalist and the bestselling author of *The Year of Living Danishly*.

Formerly editor of MarieClaire.co.uk, she now lives in Denmark and works as a Scandinavia correspondent for the *Guardian*, as well as writing a column on Denmark for the *Telegraph* and features for *The Times*, the *Observer*, *Grazia*, *Stylist* and the *Independent*.

@MsHelenRussell

facebook.com/MsHelenRussell

TWO
ROADS

Stories . . . voices . . . places . . . lives

We hope you enjoyed *Leap Year*. If you'd like to know more about this book or any other title on our list, please go to www.tworoadsbooks.com

For news on forthcoming Two Roads titles, please sign up for our newsletter.

enquiries@tworoadsbooks.com

TwoRoadsBooks